Charles Washington Eves

The West Indies

Charles Washington Eves

The West Indies

ISBN/EAN: 9783337317478

Printed in Europe, USA, Canada, Australia, Japan

Cover: Foto ©ninafisch / pixelio.de

More available books at **www.hansebooks.com**

THE
WEST INDIES

BY

C. WASHINGTON EVES, C.M.G., F.R.G.S.

MEMBER OF THE COUNCIL OF THE ROYAL COLONIAL INSTITUTE

PUBLISHED UNDER THE AUSPICES OF
THE ROYAL COLONIAL INSTITUTE

FOURTH EDITION

LONDON
SAMPSON LOW, MARSTON, & COMPANY
LIMITED
St. Dunstan's House
FETTER LANE, FLEET STREET, E.C.
1897

all rights reserved

CONTENTS.

	PAGE
INTRODUCTION	xi
NOTE ON SOME OF THE EARLIER VOYAGERS	xxix

CHAPTER I.
The Voyage, old Style—Monk Lewis's Visit to Jamaica . . 1

CHAPTER II.
The Voyage, new Style—Waterloo Station—Southampton Water—The Needles—The Azores—Sir Richard Grenville—Life on Board 5

CHAPTER III.
Arrival at Barbados—Bridgetown—Government House—Codrington College—Farley Hill—Geographical Particulars—History—Population—Sugar Cultivation—Trade and Commerce—Constitution—Education 13

CHAPTER IV.
Hayti 33

CHAPTER V.
Jamaica—Port Royal—Kingston—Tom Cringle—Mico Institute—Jamaica Institute—Clubs and Institutions—Parish Church—King's House—Spanish Town—Geographical Details—Climate—Parishes—Elevations—Rivers—Ports—Springs—Description of Parishes—Internal Communication—Newcastle—Excursions through Island—Caribs—History—Maroons—Slave Insurrections—Rodney and De Grasse—Constitution and Government—Trade—Industries—West India Regiment 39

CHAPTER VI.

Panama 110

CHAPTER VII.

British Guiana — Georgetown — Schomburgk's Explorations — Victoria Regia — Roraima — Kaieteur Fall — Rivers — Sugar Estates — Gold Industry — Climate — Caribs — Brett's Legends — Coolies — Creoles — Produce and Trade — History — Constitution — Sugar Making — Sugar Cane from Seed — Diffusion and other Processes 113

CHAPTER VIII.

Surinam — Nikerie — Paramaribo — History — Trade . . . 164

CHAPTER IX.

Cayenne 174

CHAPTER X.

Trinidad — The Bocas — The Gulf of Paria — Port of Spain — Physical Features — San Fernando — Prince's Town and Mud Volcanoes — Pitch Lake — High Woods — Falls — Natural Scenery — Production — Trade — Government — History — Education — Religion 176

CHAPTER XI.

Tobago 208

CHAPTER XII.

Grenada — St. George's — History — Constitution — Parishes — Trade — Education — Carriacou — Grenadines . . . 214

CHAPTER XIII.

St. Vincent — Kingstown — Soufrière — Caribs — Production — Trade 225

CHAPTER XIV.

St. Lucia — Pitons — Castries — Soufrière — Roads — Caribs — History — Imperial Wars — Morne Fortuné — Pigeon Island — Government — Trade — Report of Colonial Defence Committee 238

CONTENTS.

CHAPTER XV.
Martinique—Fort de France—St. Pierre—Production—H.M.S. 'Diamond Rock' 254

CHAPTER XVI.
Dominica—Roseau—Natural Features—History—Population—Trade 259

CHAPTER XVII.
Guadeloupe — Basseterre—Grande-Terre — Mountains—Usines—Marie Galante and Dependencies 268

CHAPTER XVIII.
Montserrat—Plymouth—Limes—Sugar—Trade 272

CHAPTER XIX.
Nevis—St. Kitts—Anguilla—Physical Aspects—Cultivation—Grainger's 'Sugar Cane'—Population—Trade . . . 277

CHAPTER XX.
Antigua—St. John's—English Harbour—Leeward Islands Federation—Production—Trade—Barbuda—Redonda . . . 289

CHAPTER XXI.
Virgin Islands—Tortola—Virgin Gorda—Drake's Channel—St. Thomas—Santa Cruz—Saba—Sombrero—St. Eustatius . 300

CHAPTER XXII.
Porto Rico—Trade—Population, &c. 308

CHAPTER XXIII.
Cuba—Havana—City Life and Country Life—Moro—Productions—Tobacco—Sugar—Trade 310

CHAPTER XXIV.
Bahamas—New Providence—Nassau—Trade—Fibre Cultivation 329

CHAPTER XXV.

British Honduras—Belize—History—Trade 339
Statistical View of West Indies and British Guiana, 1895-96 . 347

CHAPTER XXVI.

Banks and Money 348

CHAPTER XXVII.

The Royal Colonial Institute 354

CHAPTER XXVIII.

Steam Communication 356

MAPS.

JAMAICA	*Facing page* 55
BRITISH GUIANA	,, 151
TRINIDAD AND TOBAGO	,, 177
THE WINDWARD ISLANDS AND BARBADOS . .	,, 219
THE LEEWARD ISLANDS	,, 289
THE VIRGIN ISLANDS AND SANTA CRUZ . .	,, 300
BRITISH HONDURAS	,, 339

LIST OF ILLUSTRATIONS.

CHRISTOPHER COLUMBUS	*To face Introduction*
TRAFALGAR SQUARE, BARBADOS	*To face page* 15
BRIDGETOWN, BARBADOS	,, 17
BATHSHEBA, BARBADOS, LOOKING NORTH	,, 19
A BIT OF KINGSTON HARBOUR, JAMAICA	,, 39
PORT ROYAL, JAMAICA	,, 41
KING'S STREET, KINGSTON, JAMAICA	,, 45
JETTY AT KINGSTON, JAMAICA	,, 47
RODNEY STATUE, SPANISH TOWN, JAMAICA	,, 51
MONTEGO BAY, JAMAICA	,, 67
LINSTEAD, JAMAICA	,, 71
THE CAMP, NEWCASTLE, JAMAICA	,, 75
OX CART WITH LOAD OF BANANAS	,, 105
BRITISH GUIANA, WHARF AT GEORGETOWN	,, 113
,, SEA WALL, GEORGETOWN	,, 115
,, STREET IN GEORGETOWN	,, 117
,, KAIETEUR FALL	,, 121
,, TRAVELLING ON THE DEMERARA RIVER	,, 123
,, ESSEQUEBO EXTENSION RAILWAY	,, 125
,, MAZARUNI RIVER	,, 131
,, ESSEQUEBO RIVER	,, 137

DUTCH GUIANA, GRAVENSTRAAT, SURINAM	*to face page* 169
GOVERNMENT HOUSE, TRINIDAD	,, 179
WHARF AT TRINIDAD	,, 183
PITCH LAKE, TRINIDAD	,, 191
GRAND ETANG, GRENADA	,, 215
ST. GEORGE'S, GRENADA	,, 217
GOVERNMENT HOUSE, GRENADA	,, 223
LANDING-PLACE AT KINGSTOWN, ST. VINCENT	,, 225
VIEW OF KINGSTOWN, ST. VINCENT	,, 227
MARKET SCENE AT KINGSTOWN, ST. VINCENT	,, 237
THE PITONS, ST. LUCIA	,, 239
MARTINIQUE	,, 255
GOVERNMENT HOUSE, DOMINICA	,, 261
SEA WALL AND JETTY AT ROSEAU, DOMINICA	,, 265
LABOURER'S HUT, DOMINICA	,, 267
ST. JOHN'S, ANTIGUA	,, 291
THE CATHEDRAL, ST. JOHN'S, ANTIGUA	,, 299
HARBOUR OF ST. THOMAS	,, 303
GOVERNMENT HOUSE, NASSAU, BAHAMAS	,, 333
NEGRO HUT, EAST NASSAU, BAHAMAS	,, 335
A SISAL PLANTATION	,, 337
WESLEYAN MISSION HOUSE, BRITISH HONDURAS	,, 343
MAIL STEAMER CALLING FOR FRUIT AT STANN CREEK, BRITISH HONDURAS	,, 345

CHRISTOPHER COLUMBUS.

INTRODUCTION.

(REVISED FOR THE FOURTH EDITION.)

THE sixtieth anniversary of Her Majesty's accession to the throne, an event unparalleled in British history, finds the nation united in loyalty to the Crown, which is the symbol of true union. No event in the history of the British people, both of Great and Greater Britain, has caused so much enthusiasm and national pride amongst all classes, or has evoked such universal rejoicing amongst the vast and varied populations of every part of the Empire. Among the most remarkable features of Her Majesty's reign is the marvellous expansion of the Colonies, and the development of their trade and resources. In 1837 the Colonies were, comparatively speaking, undeveloped, and to a great extent ignored and regarded as incumbrances by the home authorities. In both hemispheres there were isolated territories with sparse populations owing allegiance to the Crown, but of small commercial value. The expense of their civil and military establishments was shared by the United

Kingdom, and communication was both difficult and costly. Responsible government was unknown, the Colonies being chiefly governed from Downing Street, whereas at the present time the Empire comprises vast territories peopled by the British race, possessing every attribute which makes a nation, and united to the Mother Country by that slender thread of sentiment which is the wonder and envy of the world. The gathering in the heart of the Empire of representatives of all parts of Great and Greater Britain to celebrate Her Majesty's Diamond Jubilee, is an event of much importance, and forms a demonstration such as no other country can make—a demonstration which has been described by the Secretary of State for the Colonies (the Right Hon. Joseph Chamberlain, M.P.) as one of power, of influence, and of beneficent work, which will be a fitting tribute to the best and most revered of British Sovereigns.

Like the great Colonial and Indian Exhibition of 1886, which was presided over by his Royal Highness the Prince of Wales with so much energy and success, the prominent part taken by the Colonies in the celebration of Her Majesty's Diamond Jubilee has stimulated inquiry into their history, resources, present condition, and general attractions for visitors and settlers. During recent years many people from the United Kingdom have visited our West Indian and South American possessions, and have returned gratified and benefited by their experience. To exchange the hard English winter for genial warmth, and the bare trees of an English landscape for all the richness of tropical nature, is not only pleasant in itself, but must be conducive to the maintenance or restoration of mental and bodily health. A voyage of eleven days and fourteen hours to Barbados, covering 3,635 miles, a run through some of the islands, perhaps including a visit to that portion of the South American continent where British Guiana is situated, then a return either by Barbados or by way of Jamaica and New York, would make up an enjoyable three months' trip, although of course it need not take quite so long a time. The numerous requests for information I have received since the Colonial and Indian Exhibition, as to the West Indies, the best method of proceeding to those countries, and what there is to be seen on arrival there, have led me to the conclusion that a book giving, in a clear and concise form, various details that might be useful and even necessary to the traveller, would be acceptable. It is true that many publications have been issued dealing with particular places or discussing special questions, but a visitor cannot take a whole library about with him, and the literature connected with the West Indies is remarkably extensive and varied. For several of the larger Colonies there are some books which are very useful. The 'Handbook of Jamaica,' for instance, published under the authority of the Colonial Government, is probably to be ranked among the best and most complete of all similar publications in the Colonies throughout the Empire ; the 'British Guiana Directory,' Collens' 'Guide to Trinidad,' the 'Trinidad Almanac,' the 'Grenada Handbook,' and the 'Handbook of British Honduras,' may also be mentioned for the useful information they contain, and there are important publications in substantial pamphlet form containing discussions of special subjects, matters of history, ethnology, and other departments of inquiry incident to the respective countries, and descriptions of contemporary adventure and research—such as the Journal of the Institute of Jamaica, and 'Timehri,' the Journal of the Royal Agricultural and Commercial Society of British Guiana. But with regard to the West Indies generally there is room for a compendium of information which might suggest to the most casual reader a fairly accurate picture of an important group of Colonies.

Information of a merely local character may often suggest general principles and large questions of Imperial policy. These Colonies, with all their varied characteristics, may be treated separately or may be regarded as an historic whole, notwithstanding the varied dates at which they were respectively acquired. The contemplation of the energy of the men who planted these settlements, and who fought for them against many attacks, might strengthen the nerves of modern Englishmen—it might lead to the enlargement of political vision so as to allow the admission of the idea that the Colonies—even the smallest and most struggling of them—are worthy not merely of the cold attention, but of the sympathetic affection of the Mother Country. They should be regarded as communities of kindred people, and not simply as coaling stations. The effect of this incomplete and chequered narrative ought to be that these Colonies should be looked upon as a real part of the British Empire, the mere separation by an expanse of sea making no difference in kindred, and weakening no political and social tie. And the carrying out of this idea ought to be regarded as much for the benefit of the Mother Country as of the Colonies.

This appeal to readers for their interest and attention is justified on various grounds. First, by the romantic history of these Colonies. Upon nearly all of them the shadow of one great figure rests—Columbus. This name has come to mean, not a mere individual with weaknesses and defects, such as might be apparent to his contemporaries, but an embodiment of all the most energetic and stirring influences of his time. In this sense he is like Shakespeare, whose personality has faded away and become lost in the largeness and permanence of his creations. Possibly there is no grander figure than Columbus, apart from the inner world of books, but rather in the outer world of things, to stand at the historical entrance of modern life and enterprise, and to enlarge the boundaries of European thought and work. Henry VII. of England, although the patron of Cabot, made a royal mistake in rejecting the ideas of Columbus, and causing him to offer his services to Spain. The main idea of Columbus as to a short route to India might have been geographically incomplete—although it was in accordance with the best information of his time—his ships might have been rude in construction and slow of speed, but they made their appearance in unknown waters, and anchored off shores untrodden by European foot. His sailors might have been ignorant and often mutinous, they were, nevertheless, carried along by his resistless energy and subdued by his personal influence. Possibly his ideas were crude, his intentions only vaguely known to himself, and it may be that he was animated largely by a desire for gold; but the ideas in course of time have taken tangible form, the intentions have resulted in a completion he never dreamt of, and the ambition which left him in his lifetime poor in purse and broken-hearted beneath the ingratitude of monarchs, has been abundantly justified by the willing admiration of the succeeding centuries. The fact of his name having been coupled with scenes of apparent cruelty to native races arose rather from the conduct of his followers and successors than from himself, and his own existence may have often depended upon the immediate conquest of savage tribes. Where he conquered, he desired to colonise. He took with him all the civilisation that he knew, and with a rare magnanimity of spirit, far in advance of his age, he endeavoured to carry out its precepts. No misfortunes bore him down, no wrongs tempted him to an ignoble revenge. He had the power to govern himself as well as he controlled others. He may have been bigoted and superstitious, but deep in his heart and apparent in his conduct was the religion that tempered and ennobled his enthusiasm. He had the faults of his time combined with the excellences of one more advanced. His ideas of slavery were not those of the nineteenth century, although had he been living in this period he would have been among the first in adventurous exploration of the dark places of the earth. Mere sentiments of nationality would have made little difference. No trouble was too great for him, no difficulty insuperable. He was above all things cosmopolitan, and he was a man of such a temperament that in whatever time his lot might have been cast he must always have taken a prominent part in the most adventurous of the world's work. He was a visionary with a definite object. If he had not been a visionary, he would not have gone through what he did. He heard 'voices,' like other enthusiasts, and went on his way strong in the faith of ultimate success. And yet the accomplishment was not for him, but for others. In petitioning Isabella in the last days of his life, he did not fully understand the grandeur of the discoveries he had made, or their effect upon the human race. His mind was still haunted with dreams of the ancient East when he was discovering the countries of the West, and he would have recognised without much surprise the Garden of Eden in the suburbs of a West Indian or South American town. When he skirted Trinidad and sailed through the Gulf of Paria, such thoughts were probably in his mind. However, what he did is known : what he thought is speculative, and one statement or impression may be traversed or destroyed by another. Some things are certain : strong in his individuality, perseverance, and enthusiasm, steadfast in his faith and determined in his courage, he stands before us, not as an often-baffled mariner, but as a man with all those elements of greatness which are capable of being recognised and appreciated more and more as the Old and the New World progress in their material development and their moral power.

Whatever views may be entertained of the character and plans of Columbus, he practically discovered the West Indies, and his name is directly connected with many of the islands. Some of the points of their subsequent history are mentioned in the following pages. The story of the treatment of the Caribs need not be told again in detail ; the fluctuations of possession caused by the fortunes of the European wars are part of history and embodied in many treaties. Imperial quarrels were fought out in West Indian seas. After fighting, the Colonies were exchanged like counters over a board. To capture a Colony was a great triumph for an enterprising admiral or general. It is somewhat appalling, and yet in one sense exhilarating, to an Englishman to think of the sea and land fights which have taken place. There was Benbow in 1702, who after fighting Du Casse was buried in Kingston parish church. We may think of the capture of Jamaica under Penn and Venables, of Rodney's great naval battle with De Grasse, of Abercromby taking over Trinidad from Chacon and Apodaca, of the terrible fights on the hillsides of Morne Fortuné in St. Lucia, and remember also the resistance to the French revolutionary ideas which British troops and seamen had to make in the West Indies, while Burke was supporting and inspiring that resistance by his spoken and written appeals at home. Truly the thunder of the cannon in West Indian seas was full of political significance for Europe, and affected the relative strength of nations. Otherwise, why were the Colonies so prominently brought forward in every European treaty of peace for two centuries?

As the result of all this turmoil and bargaining, Great Britain now finds herself possessed of a portion of South America, a slice of Central America, and the largest number of islands in the West Indian archipelago. Several of these islands we have held for a much longer period than a century; but assuming our possession from the beginning of this century, what have we done with them? Emancipation of the African slave was a great work, and the pioneer measure of freedom in all parts of the world : the United States were rent, a comparatively short time ago, with civil war upon the question, and it is only quite recently that the black populations of Cuba and Brazil have become nominally or actually free. It was thought at one time, and perhaps naturally so, that when the English duties were equalised on free and slave grown sugar, the free British Colonies would be placed at a disadvantage. So, indeed, they were, for Cuba imported her hundreds of thousands of slaves from Africa, and the horrors of the middle passage were in full activity. What did it matter? Lord John Russell argued that the world's market was but one, and prices would find their level. The moral distinction was swamped in the mercantile and political argument, and the practical result was that plantations went down to 'prairie' value, and sank to a 'ruinate' condition.

What, however, is the use of treading with uncertain feet upon the still warm cinders of this quiet but not quite extinct volcano? In British Guiana and Trinidad, by means of coolie immigration, progress has been made. Jamaica has stood still, so far as sugar is concerned. Barbados, with its superabundant population, has barely held its own, the other islands have decreased in sugar production, and in some, such as St. Vincent, Grenada, and Dominica, it has almost disappeared. It is not desirable in these pages to explain the reason, or alleged reason, of this. Such might be considered controversial; still the fact may be noted that in all the countries not regularly employing exotic labour the cultivation of the staple has stood still or become nearly non-existent (as in several of the islands mentioned above). Of course there are other industries growing up. The fruit industry in Jamaica, for instance, owes very much to the late Botanic Superintendent in the Colony, Dr. D. Morris, C.M.G., M.A., now the Assistant Director of the Royal Gardens at Kew, and he is gratefully remembered for the general services he rendered while he held the chief position at the Botanical Gardens in Jamaica. In the absence of sugar, fruit is all-important, and if by geographical conveniences, the advantage of which a few days' steaming can secure, fruit can be profitably exported, the better for all classes of the community and the greater relief to the Government, which is responsible for revenue and taxation. Grenada might also be mentioned as having substituted for sugar the growth of cocoa and spices, and, in connection with other islands, schemes are being put forward for the utilisation of their vegetable and other resources.

Some general particulars might now be given regarding these Colonies in the West Indies and British Guiana. Great Britain has in this region about 130,000 square miles, 109,000 being ascribed to that portion of the interior of Guiana claimed as British territory, and which is becoming famous as a gold-bearing region. There is a population of 1,670,000, principally belonging to a race in which the English people have always taken a great interest. There is a future for the African race in the West Indies, however slow the progress may be. These Colonies, including British Guiana and British Honduras, raise a yearly revenue of 2,463,000*l.*; they spend about the same amount in the administration of their affairs, and in roads and bridges and other public works. They have a public debt (for railways and other works of utility) of 4,852,000*l.*, and their total trade is: imports 8,140,000*l.* and exports 7,400,000*l.*, or a total of over 15,000,000*l.*, a very respectable amount, but not more than they have achieved in past years, and about a fourth of what they are really capable of doing in the exchange of their productions with Europe and America. The tendency of trade to the United States is a fact which cannot be overlooked. Vicinity, of course, has a great deal to do with this. Perishable goods, such as fruit, must always go to the nearest market; but the remarkable fact is that nearly the whole of the British West Indian sugar production now goes to the United States. The effect of the McKinley tariff has clearly strengthened and rendered more attractive the market of the United States for the reception of West Indian sugar. The United States is the great consuming country, and all the West India sugar must go, as Lord Derby once said, to its natural market. It is not, however, mere vicinity that brings about this result, but often a better price in New York, Baltimore, and other distributing ports. This price may be raised by speculations and sugar trusts, by artificial depletion of stocks, and by devices intended for temporary inflation and immediate gains; but as things go, speculation can only be possible upon demand increasing faster than supply. This is the most hopeful feature of the American market. The fact remains: the British West Indies join in contributing a raw material, upon the reception and manipulation of which the existence of a great American industry depends, and the demand for that raw material, increasing year by year, must become more than ever the mainstay of the Colonies. And with regard to the return trade—apart from any recent tariff changes—the West Indian market is not only not despised, but eagerly sought after by American manufacturers and shippers. Manchester goods will hold their own for a time in the West Indies, Sheffield hardware is keeping up, but care will have to be taken lest the United States should compete in these things and take command of the West Indian market (as it now does in the matter of provisions and everything eatable), and lest the Germans (as they are now in many parts successfully doing) substitute their own goods for those of British manufacturers. The German traders are always energetic and successful, but the English ought to be able to maintain their position.

No one interested in these Colonies can be blind to the importance of the present trade relations between them and the United States. These relations may be only temporary, so far as their extent and closeness (in a commercial and not a political sense) are concerned. But they are not of mushroom growth, and they must always exist, if only from the sheer force of propinquity. We have fought for these Colonies, we have expended much blood and treasure upon them, we secured the monopoly of their trade, and now, with every sentiment of loyalty and with the deepest devotion to the Queen, as shown by the Jubilee rejoicings, with face presented straight to the Mother Country and eyes expectant of encouragement and of hope, trade seems to be diverted from the flag. It is not our duty to discuss the economical or any other bearings of this question. We have simply to note the fact. Of the 8,140,000*l.* of imports less than half (or 3,728,000*l.*) are from the United Kingdom. Of the 7,400,000*l.* of exports only 2,832,253*l.* are sent to the United Kingdom.

Bearing in mind the fact that formerly the whole of the West Indian sugar came to the United Kingdom, and that now a very large proportion of it goes to the United States, the reason of this diversion of trade might be asked. Some answer may be found in the enormous increase of the beet-root production under the bounty system. Beet sugar has been substituted largely for cane in Europe, and it has supplied to a very great extent the increased consumption of the world. Formerly the imports of beet sugar into the United Kingdom were only five per cent. of the total supply—they formed upwards of sixty per cent. of that supply in 1889, and the percentage is still higher now.

The British West India possessions comprise Jamaica (with the Turks and Caicos Islands and the Caymans), the Bahama Islands, Trinidad and Tobago (now one colony), Barbados, and the Windward and Leeward Islands. The possessions on the mainland, or continental Colonies, are British Guiana and British Honduras. The name Indies arose from Columbus endeavouring to find a western route to the East Indies. The name Antilles appears to have been found on an early map. The larger islands, such as Cuba, Jamaica, Hayti, and Porto Rico, are now classed as the Greater, and the smaller islands to the east as the Lesser Antilles. Whether Trinidad should be included under the title of the 'Lesser' is not quite clear from the geographical authorities. The Windward Islands are naturally those which are exposed to the north-east trade-wind, the Leeward those which are less subject to that wind.

The North American Colonies may be said to be generally of a continental character, whilst the West

Indian, with the exception of British Honduras, are insular. The different character of the two sets of dependencies have not prevented ideas of political and commercial union between them. It was thought some years ago that if Jamaica entered the Dominion as a province, she would, with her tropical produce, give to Canada what could not be grown in her colder regions. In such a case Jamaica would have shared in the political arrangements of the Dominion, with any tariff advantage belonging to a Canadian province with representation in Parliament at Ottawa, and a share of the trade which must always exist between Canada and the United States.

To the political economist interested in the conditions of trade; to the agriculturist, who wishes to make two blades of grass grow instead of one; to the English manufacturer, anxious to keep open his markets and find new ones, the West India Colonies afford extensive material for observation. To those who have made forms of government their study, the disappearance of old representative institutions and the steady and regular establishment of Crown government, is a problem demanding consideration; and the results of Crown government, as compared, say, with the freer constitution of Barbados, might be capable of explanation. To the ethnological student, the various races, from the oldest Carib to the newest coolie, give plenty of opportunity for thought. To the philanthropist, whose main idea is to benefit the negro, the results of his efforts are apparent. To those who direct their minds to the contemplation of the forces of nature, the volcanic ridges, the smoking craters, the boiling springs, the old lava, the bituminous deposits, give plenty of scope for investigation and discussion. To the lover of scenery, ranging from the most terrible jagged forms to the most exquisite and delicate beauty, an unfailing series of pictures is unfolded. To the man who wishes to make money, a field is open to energy and enterprise.

It is to interest all these classes of readers that this book has been written and compiled. It has been desirable to supplement one's own knowledge with the results of the observation of other people. In all cases the authority has been mentioned. The attention which has been given to the West Indies of late years by well-known and influential visitors from England, has been very gratifying to any one whose fortunes are to a considerable extent dependent upon good crops and prosperous times in these Colonies. The narratives of some of the more distinguished of these travellers, including, of course, the Princes in the 'Bacchante,' Charles Kingsley, the late Lady Brassey, and Mr. Froude, have necessarily been mentioned in the following pages. For history, Bryan Edwards, Schomburgk, and Montgomery Martin have been taken; for statistics, the blue-books of the different Colonies, the Colonial Office List, and the Colonial Abstracts presented annually to Parliament, have been used, besides the Colonial publications previously mentioned. I am also indebted to the Hon. N. Darnell Davis, C.M.G., of British Guiana, for a number of facts connected with the early history of Barbados, as well as to the proprietors of 'Commerce' for permission to use many of the illustrations. In dealing with so many countries, no doubt errors have crept in and incomplete information been given, and any corrections and further facts will be welcomed for future editions. Critics have been lenient, and full of good advice which has been utilised in the present edition. In dealing separately with Colonies, often subject to the same historical events and conditions, many repetitions have unavoidably been made. It is still my earnest hope that all shortcomings will be charitably dealt with, and that the result will be a larger amount of interest in these Colonies on the part of the English people, a warmer sympathy in their condition and progress, and an exemplification of a real desire to make them truly feel that they belong to Great Britain, that they share her great traditions, and have a right to participate in her glorious future.

C. WASHINGTON EVES.

1 Fen Court,
    London.
July 1897.

NOTE ON SOME OF THE EARLIER VOYAGERS

THE literature which describes the exploits of the discoverers of the New World would require a volume for a mere summary. A few leading names, however, at once suggest themselves, and recall the dangers, the hardships, and the heroism of the great explorers. The voyage of Sebastian Cabot, during which he first saw the mainland of America in 1497, the discoveries of the West Indies by Columbus in his four voyages, the visit of Amerigo Vespucci, the Florentine, in 1499, which, according to many authorities, gave the continent its name—such are the incidents that spring first to the mind. Richard Hakluyt, who was born in 1553, who went to Paris in 1584 as chaplain to the English ambassador, and was made Prebendary of Bristol, took much interest in distant countries and tales of adventure by sea. In 1582 his first publication appeared, 'Divers Voyages touching the Discoverie of America, and the lands adjacent unto the same, made first of all by our Englishmen, and afterward by the Frenchmen and Bretons ; and certain notes of advertisements for observations, necessarie for such as shall hereafter make the like attempt.' He also translated Spanish books, but his principal work was the folio of 1589, 'The Principal Navigations, Voyages, and Discoveries made by the English Nation.' Hakluyt's work was continued by Samuel Purchas, who resigned his vicarage of Eastwood to devote himself exclusively to the manuscripts of the earlier writer. His first volume appeared in folio in 1613, and there were four other volumes in 1625, 'Hakluytus Posthumus; or, Purchas his Pilgrimes.' The 16th and 17th centuries were indeed rich in publications of this nature. Among these may be mentioned 'The Generall Historie of Virginia, New England, and the Summer Isles, by Captain John Smith, sometimes Governour in those countryes and Admirall of New England' (1632 edition), containing a story plainly told of the risks on sea and land incidental to the settlement of the Virginia plantations. 'The Historie of the West Indies, contayning the acts and adventures of the Spanyardes, written by Peter Martyr, a Milanoise of Angleria, Chief Secretary to the Emperour Charles the "fift," and of his Privie Councell,' translated into English by R. Eden and M. Lok, is also a notable book. The best known early edition of this book is probably that of 1612. The treatise of Sir Humphrey Gilbert, printed in 1576, respecting a passage by the north-west to Cathay and the East Indies, excited much interest at the time, as is shown by the records of Frobisher's voyages and the formation of the 'Company of Cathay.' The visits of Raleigh to the

West Indies and Guiana are of course known to every student of Elizabethan adventure, and indeed to everyone who takes an interest in a life full of energy in its prime, and of dignity and pathos in its close. Amongst these few of the leading books the splendid volumes (1728 edition) of Antonio de Herrera, 'Historia General de las Indias Ocidentales,' with their portraits of Spanish captains and pictures of stirring scenes of conquest, should not be left unmentioned.

One of the most interesting of the early books is that of Richard Ligon, gent. It sets forth 'A true and exact History of the Island of Barbados' (edition 1657). Ligon addresses his friend, Dr. Brian Duppa, Lord Bishop of Salisbury, from the Upper Bench Prison in July 1653. He was deprived of light and loneliness, and therefore could only express his artistic designs in black and white. The Bishop replies to Ligon, telling him of the pleasure he had felt in reading his book, and denouncing the iniquity of the times. Finding himself a stranger in his own country, stript of all he had by a 'barbarous riot,' Ligon embarked on June 16, 1647, on the good ship *Achilles*, 350 tons. The voyage was a long one, and he must be left to tell his own tale, to any one who likes to consult him, of what he saw while he was on board ship, the way in which he enjoyed himself on shore, the natural features and social condition of Barbados, and his experience as a planter and sugar-maker.

THE WEST INDIES.

CHAPTER I.

THE VOYAGE—OLD STYLE.

WITHOUT going back to the days of the early adventurers, and discussing their perils upon the sea, it will be sufficient, in order to produce a sharp contrast, to refer to the graphic descriptions of a voyage to Jamaica, when the present century was still in its teens, written by Matthew Gregory Lewis, Esq., M.P., better known in English literature as 'Monk' Lewis, from the title of the most popular of his romances. He was the man of whom Byron wrote, 'I would give many a sugar cane, Matt Lewis were alive again!' His voyage, or rather voyages, to the West Indies were prosaic and painful enough, but they were lit up with his own literary fancies and the expressions of his poetical imagination. He thus enjoyed himself in a different way from that adopted by many visitors, and fortunately so, else a considerable amount of bad poetry, the result of sea-sickness and dreams, might have been thrown by careless hands upon the world. Lewis died on the voyage homewards from the West Indies in the year 1818, leaving in his Journal the story of his ocean experiences. He reached Gravesend from London, on his first outward trip, on November 8, 1815, and embarked on board the 'Sir Godfrey Webster,' an old East India ship of 600 tons, on November 10, amid the squeaking of the pigs, the quacking of the ducks, and the screaming of the fowls who were being hoisted on board. The ship proceeded three miles and then anchored for the night. One of the cabin passengers passed the time by discussing the backwardness of education in the West Indies, and said that in 'his umble opinion heddication was hall in hall.' The Downs were reached in the afternoon of November 12, and the ship anchored about four miles off Deal. A westerly gale made the situation dangerous, and it was not until November 15 that the ship could proceed. However, on the 16th she was off the Isle of Wight. On the 17th the author of the story was sick to death, and his mind 'all disgust.' On the 18th, or more than a week from starting, the Lizard was passed. Then came more bad weather. The ship rolled from side to side, and the passengers rolled with it until they were stopped by the cabin furniture. The captain snuffed out one of the candles, and both being tied to the table, he could not relight it with the other; so the steward came to do it, when a sudden heel of the ship made him extinguish the second candle, and sent him rolling. Then the intolerable noise! the cracking of bulkheads, the sawing of ropes, the screeching of the tiller, the trampling of the sailors, the clattering of the crockery. Everything above deck and below deck all in motion at once. Chairs, writing-desks, books, boxes, bundles, fire-irons and fenders flying to one end of the room, and the next moment (as if they had made a mistake) flying back again. Up to November 21 the weather continued intolerable, dead calms by day, violent storms by night. But the soul of the poet rose superior to all this distress, and in the intervals of sickness he could write in a quaintly humorous fashion of Pandora's box. On November 25 letters were sent to England by a small vessel bound for Plymouth, and laden with oranges from St. Michael's, one of the Azores. The 'Sir Godfrey Webster' laboured on her way with rent sails and water coming into the cabins, but Lewis calmly read his 'Don Quixote.' On December 7 matters improved. Assisted by the Trade wind, rapid and steady progress was made, and the deep blue of the sea was noted. The dolphin and the flying-fish awakened the interest and amusement of the passengers. Upon December 10 the new aspect of things produces a burst from the poet :

> What triumph moves on the billows so blue?
> In his car of pellucid pearl I view,
> With glorious pomp, on the dancing tide,
> The tropic Genius proudly ride.

In another verse, which may be quoted for the expression 'harvest of sweets' in the first line as describing a sugar plantation, he prays the above-mentioned 'Genius :'

> From thy locks on my harvest of sweets diffuse,
> To swell my canes, refreshing dews;
> And kindly breathe, with cooling powers,
> Through my coffee walks and shaddock bowers.

On December 14 we read of magical effects of sunset, of a 'rose-coloured' moon produced by the setting rays of the sun, of a perfect clearness of atmosphere, and a smooth ocean. The year was waning rapidly and still the voyage was incomplete. Both Shakespeare and Milton are called in to describe the stars, the last-named author's 'firmament of living sapphires' being considered appropriate. The floating lights around the ship, poetised into 'a kind of sea-meteors' were also much admired. On Christmas Eve the ship crawled into the Caribbean Sea, and at sunset Antigua was in sight. The Christmas sun rose upon Montserrat and Nevis. Then came St. Christopher's and St. Eustatius; Santa Cruz was duly passed, an island then called the Garden of the West Indies on account of its perfect cultivation. Porto Rico was left behind, and as St. Domingo was sighted the guns were loaded and the muskets put in repair to give a greeting to the pirates with which this part of the sea was infested. On December 30 Jamaica was in sight, and the West India proprietor from Europe thought the rain and wind which accompanied the prospect might proceed from the eyes and lungs of his agents and overseers, who for the last twenty years had been reigning in his dominions with despotic authority, and who would have to resign the deputed sceptre on his arrival. On New Year's Day the ship anchored in Black River Bay, the nearest harbour to that part of the island where Lewis's estates were situated, after a voyage, which could hardly be described as a run, of fifty-two days from Gravesend. Probably a fairly representative trip for the times and the class of boat. The return voyage commenced on April 1, and terminated on June 5 at Gravesend.

CHAPTER II.

THE VOYAGE—NEW STYLE.

THE Royal Mail Steam Packet Company may be particularly referred to because it has the Government contract for carrying the mails, and without suggesting anything to the disadvantage of the other admirable lines of steamers supported entirely by private enterprise. On board the mail steamers discomfort is at a minimum, and after the preliminary attack of sea-sickness, which is alleviated as much as possible by every thoughtful device and attention, the voyage is one of unalloyed enjoyment. The steamers start from Southampton on the afternoon of every alternate Wednesday, and it may suit the convenience of some travellers, who may or may not be going direct from London, to arrive in Southampton on the Tuesday, and pass the night at the South-Western or Radley's or other convenient hotel. The boat train from London on Wednesday morning is that which leaves Waterloo station at 9.45. There is a later train at 10.30, but the passenger with all his *impedimenta* to look after would find himself a little hurried, and perhaps a little flurried, if he waited for this. The earlier one is the train by which the bulk of the passengers go down from London. After nine o'clock the long main outward platform of the South-Western Railway is studded with little groups of people in earnest conversation. Here the Governor of an important Colony may be seen in a travelling suit of fine blue serge, with cap to match. His Excellency is accompanied by his wife and daughters, and each is surrounded by groups of particular friends who have come to say 'good bye,' or to go in the train to Southampton and wish the final *bon voyage* on the deck of the steamer itself. On the platform, too, may be seen husbands parting from their wives, and lovers from their sweethearts; grave proprietors and merchants, well known in Mincing Lane, are going on a visit to see after the interests in which they are so deeply concerned and the moneys locked up in their estates; young men are going out as overseers, and anxious attorneys and managers are returning to their duties from a spell of rest among their friends in this country; youths and maidens fresh from school are returning to the distant home, where their parents are expecting them, after it may be long years of separation. Indeed, hardly any variety of human life, or any expression (pathetic or hopeful) of emotion, called up by parting from relatives and friends, is absent from the platform on the morning when the mail train leaves. The visitors who are simply going for a few months' pleasant trip among new scenes, fresh faces, other minds, are easily to be distinguished by their bustling movements and their spick-and-span costumes. Occasionally literary men, whose visits have produced works which all the world may wish to read, may be noted. Anthony Trollope stood here on November 17, 1858. On December 2, 1869, the spare form and intellectual face of Charles Kingsley might have formed the centre of one of these groups, losing for a time his conversational stammer in his emotional leave-taking, and his face lighting up with the prospect of seeing 'At Last' the West Indies and the

Spanish Main, which he had dreamed about for forty years, and whose natural history, charts, romances, and tragedies he had studied from childhood. And again, on the mail morning of the last week in December 1886, Mr. James Anthony Froude, with his grave, intellectual, and really genial manner, stepped into the train on his way to explore these western Colonies, to discuss their politics in connection with the Irish question, to enjoy their natural beauties and their no less comforting hospitality, and generally to tighten the unstrung bow of Ulysses.

A pleasant run of about two hours, and the train draws up at the edge of Southampton Water. If the tide serves, the great steamer is alongside, and the passengers go up the gangways at once; if the tide will not suit, the ship lies in the middle of the stream, and the passengers reach her in a tender. Then begins rather a confused scene. People are searching for their cabins (and often locate themselves in the wrong ones); all the stewards, and even the officers of the ship, are brought into requisition to answer questions and indicate berths. The captain is evidently well known, and shakes hands heartily with old friends. After an hour or two some kind of order comes out of all this bustle, the passengers and their friends dropping into the saloon for luncheon, whilst the heavy baggage is lowered into the hold, the hundreds of sacks of mails are put on board, the latest telegrams and letters for passengers are delivered, the last words are said to friends, and about four o'clock in the afternoon the big ship moves slowly through Southampton Water, past Netley Abbey, Hurst Castle, and the Needles, and so on until the open sea is reached, and the vessel puts forth her greatest strength and fastness to overcome the waves, and carry the many human lives entrusted to her to their respective destinations in the West Indies and South America.

Passengers proof against sickness (for which complaint many remedies have been tried) soon settle regularly to their meals, even if the fiddles are fastened to the tables. A cup of tea and bread and butter at six o'clock A.M. in the cabin; a promenade on deck, if the weather is fine and the morning light; a sea-water bath and general morning toilet; then a hearty breakfast at nine o'clock. Smoking, talking, reading until twelve o'clock, when the run of the steamer during the preceding twenty-four hours is posted, and the pool is handed over to the fortunate individual who has secured the number nearest to the actual result as published. Luncheon follows, and the afternoon wears away until dinner time is reached. Again smoke and talk for the men, and conversation (which is a longer and more genteel word than talk) for the ladies. Light refreshments later in the evening, and then to bed to sleep the sleep of the just.

The Lizard is the last point of the English mainland seen. The outline of the coast of Brittany may be noticed. After passing Ushant, the Bay of Biscay is fairly entered upon, 'where the stormy winds do blow.' Coming safely through the Bay, the Azores or Western Islands are reached, lying about 800 miles from the coast of Portugal. Pico, the highest of them, 7,600 feet high, may be seen from a considerable distance. There are three distinct groups: the south-eastern containing St. Michael's, famous for its oranges, and Sta. Maria; the central and largest group, comprising Fayal, Pico, São Jorge, Terceira, and Graciosa; and the north-western with Flores and Corvo. These islands derive much of their interest from the fact that they were in the olden time the rendezvous for the fleets on their way home from the Indies, and they have witnessed many striking and historic scenes. But perhaps the most interesting of these islands to an Englishman is Flores, one of the north-westerly group, where the great fight occurred between the 'Revenge,' commanded by Sir Richard Grenville, and the Spanish ships of war, on August 30, 1591. 'Wounded again and again, and shot through body and through head, Sir Richard Grenville was taken on board the Spanish Admiral's ship to die, and gave up his gallant ghost with these once famous words: " Here die I, Richard Grenville, with a joyful and quiet mind, for that I have ended my life as a true soldier ought, fighting for his Country, Queen, Religion, and Honour, my soul willingly departing from this body, leaving behind the lasting fame of having behaved as every valiant soldier is in his duty bound to do."' So Kingsley quotes from Sir Walter Raleigh's account of the fight, and the voyager nearing this historic spot might also turn to Tennyson's spirited ballad on this same subject, where the fight and the death of the old hero are vividly described. The few lines here quoted may induce the passenger to borrow a Tennyson from the ship's library and read the whole of the ballad, which is full of energy.

> Sir Richard spoke and he laugh'd, and we roar'd a hurrah, and so
> The little 'Revenge' ran on sheer into the heart of the foe,
> With her hundred fighters on deck, and her ninety sick below;
> For half of their fleet to the right and half to the left were seen,
> And the little 'Revenge' ran on thro' the long sea-lane between.
> . . . . .
> And the sun went down, and the stars came out far over the summer sea,
> But never a moment ceased the fight of the one and the fifty-three.
> Ship after ship, the whole night long, their high-built galleons came,
> Ship after ship, the whole night long, with her battle-thunder and flame;
> Ship after ship, the whole night long, drew back with her dead and her shame.

For some were sunk and many were shatter'd, and so could fight us
   no more—
God of battles, was ever a battle like this in the world before?

For he said 'Fight on! fight on!'
Tho' his vessel was all but a wreck;
And it chanced that, when half of the summer night was gone,
With a grisly wound to be drest he had left the deck,
But a bullet struck him that was dressing it suddenly dead,
And himself he was wounded again in the side and the head,
And he said 'Fight on! fight on!'

  . . . . .

And the stately Spanish men to their flagship bore him then,
Where they laid him by the mast, old Sir Richard caught at last,
And they praised him to his face with their courtly foreign grace;
But he rose upon their decks, and he cried:
'I have fought for Queen and Faith like a valiant man and true;
I have only done my duty as a man is bound to do:
With a joyful spirit I Sir Richard Grenville die!'
And he fell upon their decks, and he died.

Kingsley's 'Westward Ho!' and Henry Nelson Coleridge's delightful 'Six Months in the West Indies' might also be consulted with interest.

From heroic fights to Gulf weed is an easy transition to the observing mind, and one which tends to the amusement of the passenger. Kingsley says that this remarkable weed, or 'ocean meadow,' has nothing to do with the Gulf Stream, but is bounded on the north by it. It lies in a vast eddy, or central pool of the Atlantic, between the Gulf Stream and the equatorial current, unmoved save by floating drifts of weed. It lost long ago the habit of growing on rock or sea-bottom, and now propagates itself for ever floating, feeding among its branches a whole family of fish, crabs, &c., the like of which are found nowhere else in the world. 'Day after day we passed more and more of it, often in long processions ranged in the direction of the wind;

while a few feet below the surface, here and there, floated large fronds of a lettuce-like weed, seemingly an ulva, the bright green of which, as well as the rich orange hue of the sargasso, brought out by contrast the intense blue of the water.' Another source of amusement is to watch the flying fish. They go such a distance out of the water that they seem actually to fly, and not simply depend upon an original impetus for a jump, and they can also see their course when flying. The sunsets, after getting into tropic seas, become more and more beautiful, but fade away more quickly. There is no twilight, for 'The sun's rim dips, the stars rush out; at one stride comes the dark.'

Lighter clothing becomes necessary on board. The Princes on board the 'Bacchante,' after passing Teneriffe, and being yet 2,000 miles from Barbados, record that at this stage of the voyage they got into white jackets for dinner for the first time. When 217 miles from Barbados, they first saw the Southern Cross at four o'clock on Christmas morning. It appeared to them more to resemble a lily bent than a cross.

Reverting to life on board, it may be remarked that, thrown into familiar intercourse day by day, the idiosyncrasies of the passengers soon appear, and indeed are exaggerated by the enforced companionship. The quiet man becomes quieter, the jovial soul still more noisy, the loud-voiced man more peremptory, the scolding wife more shrill, the mischievous person increasingly unbearable, and the gambler more passionately engrossed in his play. But with tact and temper and mutual forbearance all difficulties are smoothed away, and by the time the softer temperature sets in, when the seas become more blue every day and the skies more brilliant every night, a general harmony reigns on board, notwithstanding the diversity of habits of the various nationalities represented. English, French, Americans, and Spaniards, a sprinkling of Germans (who are generally chemists or engineers going to large sugar usines in Trinidad or to set up diffusion sugar processes in Demerara), and some Dutch going to Surinam. To this motley school the genial captain (and there are surely none otherwise) is at once a master and a friend.

It is not necessary to enter into minute details of the life on board. It is impossible to feel much interest in the games so gravely pursued on deck, which games are of the mildest character : such as pitching leather quoits on to wooden pegs, and shoving a round weight on to squares chalked on the deck. There may of course be more dangerous games played. Flirtation is not unknown ; even earnest love-making may begin as the tropics are neared, and many a marriage has been arranged on board a Royal Mail steamer. Matrimony by Royal Mail steamer is probably as successful as it is by other means.

CHAPTER III

BARBADOS.

THE arrival at Barbados is an interesting event. The pleasant party in the saloon breaks up. A long, low, grey-looking shore is seen, with a lighthouse at the southern end.

The steamer anchors in the roadstead, and passengers are taken on shore in boats. The noise and confusion made by the boatmen in their exciting competition for passengers and luggage has been often described. It is rather an ordeal to go through, and perhaps a little more order might be preserved. Passengers who have not gone through it before are bewildered by the scene. The boatmen are very clamorous, and the traveller must keep a cool head. The aspect of things is indeed lively. England may have been left in cold and fog, whilst here a warm summer day is experienced. There is nothing very striking about the first appearance of Barbados. But the soft risings of the ground, the green of the cane fields, the white houses relieved by their attendant trees, the cultivation down to the water's edge, the evident activity of the people who crowd the island—all these make up a fresh and entertaining picture, the remembrance of which will always cling to the mind. The people are industrious because there are no waste lands on which to squat, and work is essential to procure the means of living. Barbados stands alone among the West India Islands in having a superabundant population, to which a moderate emigration is almost a necessity, and certainly a relief. But the Barbadians (or Bims, as they are colloquially called) are proud of their country and their homes, and it is difficult to induce them to leave the island; or if they do leave it for spells of work in the neighbouring Colonies, they, with few exceptions, come back again. This is not the place to discuss social conditions. Let the eye dwell upon the harbour, full of shipping of all sizes and shapes, from Her Majesty's war ships to the smart schooners waiting to take the sugar to Baltimore or New York. The scene is a thoroughly English one in its animation and signs of trade. Carlisle Bay (so called after James Hay, Earl of Carlisle, an early lord proprietor of Barbados and the Caribbee Islands) is an open roadstead, exposed to the wind from the south and south-west. There is an inner harbour or careenage protected by a construction called the mole head. On landing the busy activity of Bridgetown presents itself. Here is the railway terminus, with trucks loaded with sugar casks brought to the port for shipment. This railway is laid for a distance of twenty-four miles to the parish of St. Andrew, its route lying close to the coast. Where the railway is not available, wagons drawn by mules or bullocks are employed to bring the produce down. The streets are full of a somewhat noisy crowd. Negresses with their bright bits of coloured finery, and mostly with trays of fruit or other things upon their heads, are chattering and laughing. Men, women, and children all seem to be light-hearted and jolly, and actuated by the idea of making as much money out of the innocent visitor as possible. In Trafalgar Square stands a bronze

TRAFALGAR SQUARE, BARBADOS.

statue of Lord Nelson, who in the year 1805 lay in Carlisle Bay for about sixteen hours before searching the neighbouring Colonies for the French and Spanish fleet, which hastily returned to Europe on his approach.

The visitor at first has a confused notion of trade, trees, warehouses, and cocktail : the latter a delicate and aromatic mixture of rum, sugar, lime juice, Angostura bitters, all stirred into a lively froth by a swizzle stick, which is a rod of empire throughout the West Indies, and of no small importance as an indication of their hospitality. It is a concoction, as served at the Ice House in the principal street of Bridgetown, under the influence of which the severest literary men of the age, on a visit to these countries, have unbent. On a memorable occasion it gave strength to the bow of Ulysses. The public buildings of Bridgetown may be first noticed. There is Government House, the residence of the Governor, which is a large airy building, with trees in front and a lovely garden at the back, which was described by Mr. Froude in the following language : 'There were great cabbage palms, cannon-ball trees, mahogany trees, almond trees, and many more which were wholly new acquaintances. There was a grotto made by climbing plants and creepers, with a fountain playing in the middle of it, where orchids hanging on wires threw out their clusters of flowers for the moths to fertilise ; ferns waved their long fronds in the dripping showers ; humming-birds cooled their wings in the spray, and flashed in and out like rubies and emeralds.'

Bridgetown contains about 21,000 inhabitants. It takes its name from an old Indian piece of history. The Indians had built a bridge over a creek or outlet, through which the water from the higher lands descended to the sea. This was known for a long time as the Indian Bridge, and it finally gave its name to the town which was built around it. Great damage was caused by fire in 1666, and also in 1766 and 1845. The buildings in Bridgetown are now principally of stone, and the town is handsomely laid out. The garrison buildings are at the southern extremity. The Council Chamber in the Government Buildings contains a full-length picture of Field-Marshal Viscount Combermere, a former Governor of the Colony, and portraits of two Earls of Harewood, landowners in Barbados.

In attending a picnic at Codrington College, the Princes Albert Victor and George drove across the island, stopping first at St. John's, and noticing on their way the small one-storied houses of the negroes. The houses have their gardens with bananas and maize, their swarms of children, and, apparently, happy and prosperous men and women. Pigs, sheep, and goats may be seen tethered to these huts. Then come the cane fields, the chimneys of the sugar houses, the numerous windmills, and other outward and visible signs of the principal industry of the island. St. John's Church impresses the visitor with its English appearance. It stands on the eastern cliff, which commands a splendid sea view. The church contains two monuments in white marble, by Flaxman, and old tombs of 1666 and 1789. The visitor would drive along the top of the cliff to Society Chapel, and then walk to Codrington College, which is on the level ground below. It is a large collegiate-looking building of white stone, and has been described as a finishing school, where boys go through an advanced course of study. In one corner of the grounds is a delightful fresh-water bath, about ten yards wide and twenty long, where the visitor can splash about and enjoy himself. The garden at the back of the College looks upon the sea. The institution, which

BRIDGETOWN, BARBADOS.

is now affiliated to Durham University, was founded by General Christopher Codrington, who bequeathed two estates (Consett's and Codrington's) to the Society for the Propagation of the Gospel. They consisted of 763 acres, 3 windmills, sugar buildings, 315 negroes, and 100 head of cattle. The Society took possession in 1712. The will provided for the continuance of the plantations, with 300 negro labourers on them; professors and scholars were to be maintained; physic, chirurgery, and divinity were to be taught. The latter appears to have been the most popular study, many candidates for Holy Orders having been prepared. Several 30*l.* scholarships are given, and four of 40*l.* per annum are granted by the Colonial Treasury, the latter being confined to natives or sons of natives. The late Bishop Rawle of Trinidad was for many years a successful and esteemed Principal of Codrington College, which possesses a very good library.

Another visit of interest is to Farley Hill, at the northern end of the island, the palatial residence of the late Sir Graham Briggs, who was made a baronet by Mr. Gladstone for his support of the Federation scheme in the Leeward Islands, and for his general services to Barbados. This house was by far the finest in the island, and was full of many quaint and curious things, but these have been dispersed since the death of the owner. The road from Bridgetown by which the Princes went was along the western shore to Speight's (pronounced Spikes) Town, or Little Bristol, where there are some fairly good houses and stores, and two jetties for the convenience of ships loading sugar. From Speight's Town the visitors turned off. At the summer-house at the top of Farley Hill a good view of the hilly northern part of the island, called Scotland, is obtained. The fernery is in a valley shaded by evergreen and tamarind trees, and contains many beautiful specimens. Part of the road from Speight's Town to Farley Hill runs through a cutting of coral rock some fifty feet high, covered with vegetation.

There are other interesting spots to visit. One of these is Coles' Cave, situated in the central part of the island, in the parish of St. Thomas. The entrance is at the bottom of a steep gully, clothed with ferns, plants, and trees. The visitor first enters a large cavern, and descends from this into the cave proper with a lighted candle in his hand. A stream of running water comes out of the wall and flows away until it is said it finds an exit into the sea. The roof is crowded with stalactites, though not of a large size. The only explorers who have gone the length of the stream are said to be some ducks, who afterwards came back to light and civilisation again on the eastern coast. There are many of these mysterious streams in the coral formation of Barbados. Harrison's Cavern, some little distance from Coles' Cave, is another natural curiosity. The following description of some characteristic features of Barbados scenery is quoted from an interesting book, 'Under a Tropical Sky,' by Mr. John Amphlett. 'After leaving Waterford the country gradually changed its character, and instead of gently undulating ground, clothed with bright green fields of waving sugar cane, jagged and abrupt rocks rose here and there, and long rows of grey cliffs. These rocks all bear evidence on the face of them that they are of coralline formation, and that at some time or other they have been worn and wasted by the sea. In places too the road would cross a deep gully or ravine leading up from the sea, in the bottom of which would grow wild palms and other trees. And here let me say that no

BARBADOS: BATHSHEBA, LOOKING NORTH

one who has not walked along and explored one of these gullies can have any idea of a great beauty of Barbados, which does not lie on the surface. Between upright walls of coral rock, reminding one strongly of Cheddar Cliffs, hollowed out into a thousand fantastic shapes, covered with green plants where the slightest clinging hold is afforded, the ravine winds along, here adorned with a stately silk-cotton tree, there fringed with clumps of Spanish needle or wild palms, and everywhere the home of countless shrubs.' Turner's Hall Wood, a piece of virgin forest, was visited by Mr. Amphlett, also a boiling spring, gas coming through the water; a light being applied the gas will burn. The animal-flower cave, at the northern end of the island, containing many beautiful sea anemones, can only be visited under favourable conditions of wind and sea. The 'Spout' is another curiosity, a column of spray coming out of a hole and rising to a considerable height. The Crane, a watering place in the south-east, where the Barbados aloes are grown, affords a pleasant visit.

Barbados, on the map, takes the shape of a leg of mutton, although perhaps a shoulder of mutton might be the more appropriate description. It is the most easterly of the Caribbean Islands, being situated in latitude $13°\ 4'$ N. and longitude $59°\ 37'$ W., and lies about 100 miles east of St. Vincent, the island nearest to it in the Caribbean Chain. Its position makes it a centre of trade for the archipelago. It is about the size of the Isle of Wight, 21 miles long, and $14\frac{1}{2}$ miles in its broadest part. The superficial area is 106,470 acres, equivalent to 166 square miles. Coral reefs encircle the island, which is formed largely of coral. There are two lighthouses, one on the south point, and the other on the south-east coast. Needham's

Point, with its harbour light, is seen by the steamers going into Carlisle Bay. Barbados is very varied in scenery, including table land and rocky elevations. The limestone and coral terraces will be noticed, the undulations being gradual, and yet distinctly marked. Mount Hillaby, the highest point in the island, is 1,104 feet above the level of the sea. There are many gullies or ravines, the result, no doubt, of volcanic agency. They radiate from the high semicircular ridge of the coralline formation in a regular manner to the west, north, and south, but not to the east, where the coral rocks end abruptly. The chalky soil of the district called Scotland, the most rugged part of the island, contains *infusoria*. Little water is found except by digging into the coral. With an equable and moderate temperature Barbados presents many attractions.

For a large part of the year the sea breezes keep the air cool and pleasant. The winds, principally the Trades from the north-east, laden with moisture, keep the island in a satisfactory condition as regards cultivation. The average rainfall of the four years 1753–6 was 55·89 inches ; of the twenty-five years 1847–71, 57·74 inches, and of the single year 1895, 73·32 inches. There is no miasma, owing to the extent of the cultivation and the porous character of the soil. There is a close connection between the rainfall and the sugar produced. Indeed the rainfall is all-important, and good reaping weather means that winds are blowing to turn the windmills. Dry weather is experienced in March, and the wet season is prevalent in the autumn. The theory of the Trade winds, and their influence in producing the wet and dry seasons, is explained in Schomburgk's 'History of Barbados,' and it would be interesting to notice, if space permitted, the fuller information of recent years, which has a bearing upon the undoubted changes of seasons to be noticed in several of the West India Colonies.

We now come to the history of the island, and the meaning and derivation of its name. The origin of the latter is probably Spanish, and comes from a word signifying a 'bearded vine,' that is, a peculiar kind of vine which has long branches: these branches grow downwards, and strike root in the earth. A beautiful specimen was seen in the Barbados Court at the Colonial and Indian Exhibition. The island was not always known by its present name of Barbados. In the sixteenth century it was canonised under the title of St. Bernardo, and it also appears in the different maps and charts of that period designated as Bernardos, Barnodos, Barnado, or Barbudoso. The earliest inhabitants were Indians, of whom traces are to be found here as in any other of the Caribbean Islands. It was not until the beginning of the reign of James I. that we hear of any visits paid by Englishmen; in 1605 there is mention made of a party of English, the crew of the ship 'Olive Blossome,' who descried the island, and landed there. Finding no one to dispute possession with them, the patriotic sailors forthwith claimed the fertile little isle in the name of their country and their King. So they raised a cross in honour of the occasion, and on the bark of a tree inscribed the following legend: 'James, K. of E. and of this island.' Then they sailed away in search of further adventures, and since that time Barbados has been an English colony, with a history and a character of its own. The colonists enjoy the same rights and privileges as their brethren in the mother country, and have similar laws and institutions. They are, and always have been, good Englishmen and loyal subjects. Barbados, from its position, which renders it easy of access, is necessarily an important island. It was used as a military station during the wars with the French and Dutch ; and from the time of Cromwell's Navigation Laws down to 1874, when the English sugar duties were repealed, we may trace in the various vicissitudes and changes of the island the direct effects of English commercial legislation. It is noteworthy that Barbados was the first English settlement where the sugar cane was planted and cultivated. Bermuda is an older Colony than Barbados, and a similar claim has been put forward by Newfoundland. St. Kitts is one of the oldest British possessions in the West Indies, and is the Mother Colony of a group of islands.

In February 1627 thirty settlers arrived in the vessel called the 'William and John,' the captain of which was one John Powell. These emigrants founded a town which they named the Hole. This was many years afterwards called St. James's Town, as Bridgetown was called St. Michael's Town, each after its own parish. The Governor of the Colony was Captain John Powell the younger, two names appearing before his, however, in the Colonial Official List, viz. William Deane in 1625, and Charles Wolferstone in 1628, Powell's name coming next in 1629. For the next twenty years the island was in a very unsettled state, owing to a difficulty that arose in deciding who had the best right to a proprietary interest in it. For, in 1627, the year that Sir William Courteen's men had visited the island, the Earl of Carlisle had obtained from Charles a grant of all the Caribbees, which numbered twenty-two and included Barbados. As the Earl of Marlborough had previously a promise of a patent, the Earl of Carlisle engaged to pay 300*l.* a year from the revenues of Barbados for ever to the Earl of Marlborough and his heirs in consideration of that nobleman foregoing his claim to a part of Barbados. This offer was made and accepted in 1627, and on July 2 the transfer passed the Great Seal. But Sir William Courteen was not willing to give up his interest in the Colony, and so through the agency of the Earl of Montgomery, afterwards Earl of Pembroke, the Lord Chamberlain, a grant of Barbados, together with several other islands, was made in trust for Courteen. When Lord Carlisle returned from a diplomatic mission in which he had been engaged, and found what had been done, he proceeded to obtain a confirmation of his own rights and a revocation of those obtained by Lord Pembroke, and soon showed that he understood himself to be proprietor of the island by offering to sell portions of land, and demanding in return a yearly payment of forty pounds of cotton. This offer was taken advantage of by several London merchants who had lent money to Lord Carlisle, and who purchased from him a grant of 10,000 acres, and they appointed as governor of this settlement the above-mentioned Charles Wolferstone, a native of Bermuda. Wolferstone was to hold the commission of the Earl of Carlisle, and, with the co-operation of 64 settlers from St. Christopher's, to take care of and govern the island. It was in honour of the Earl that Wolferstone and his followers christened the bay on the south-west of the island, where they arrived in July 1628, Carlisle Bay. And now a small guerilla warfare broke out between Carlisle's people and the earlier settlers who had emigrated under the direction of Courteen. Some fighting having taken place, Lord Carlisle, seeing that his right was still disputed, further strengthened its validity by obtaining a confirmation of it from the King in April 1629.

'Having thus accomplished his covetous desire, the Earl of Carlisle appointed Sir William Tufton, a kinsman of the Earl of Thanet, to be Governor of Barbados for four years upon good behaviour. Sir William arrived in the Colony in September 1629, but appears not to have given satisfaction to the Lord Proprietor, for on the 15th March 1630 his Lordship commissioned the fire-eating Captain Henry Hawley as Governor, with power to establish a council and to depose Sir William Tufton by force if need be. With some intervals, during which he visited England, Captain Hawley governed Barbados from 1630 to 1640, by which time he had come to set at defiance the authority of the second Earl of Carlisle, who in consequence of his father's death in 1636 had become proprietor of the Colony. The first high-handed act which Hawley perpetrated was to cause Sir William Tufton and two others to be arraigned for mutiny before Sir Walter Calverley, Master Reynold Alleyne, and other councillors, who to their undying disgrace sentenced the accused to death, and these were accordingly executed in August 1630.' (It should be stated here that the above quotations are made and other particulars obtained from a book written by the Hon. N. Darnell Davis, C.M.G., now a high official in British Guiana, entitled 'Cavaliers and Roundheads in Barbados.' This book contains the result of much original research among the early records of Barbados.)

The real prosperity of the island began in 1645, when Philip Bell was Governor. The council, which had been formed in the time of Wolferstone, was then elaborated into a general assembly, which comprised two representatives from each of the eleven parishes into which the island was divided. And generally the foundations of law and order and good government were laid. Then followed the establishment of the sugar industry, the subsequent importation of slaves from Africa, the increase in the value of property, the administration of Lord Willoughby of Parham, the recognition of King Charles II., and Sir George Ayscue's expedition in 1651 to reduce the island to the authority of the Parliament, with the treaty which was made as the result of that expedition, declaring the authority of Parliament, but preserving to the inhabitants their privileges. During the Civil War, Cromwell sent prisoners to the island, and many gentlemen emigrated there to escape the persecutions at home. Lord Willoughby returned to Barbados at the Restoration in his official capacity. The proprietary interest became again the subject of discussion, especially with regard to the title possessed by the individual owners of property. In 1663, in consequence of this unsettled state as to ownership, the general proprietary interest was extinguished, and the Crown assumed sovereign rights, which were fully completed nine years afterwards by the Crown appointing the council, a legislative body formed in addition to the assembly. The duty of $4\frac{1}{2}$ per cent. on the produce of the island was first imposed to satisfy the claims of the grantees. All laws were made subject to confirmation by the King.

Lord Willoughby lost his life in 1666 on an expedition against Guadeloupe. The Colony underwent a misfortune in 1675 through a serious hurricane, and difficulties arose with regard to the supply of labour owing to the operations of the Royal African Company, at the head of which was the Duke of York. In 1684, under Sir Richard Dutton, a census was made, showing the population to consist of 20,000 whites and 46,000 slaves. The influence of European politics and wars was felt now for many years, and the

Peace of Ryswick, as well as the subsequent declaration of war against France and Spain, necessarily affected the West India Colonies, which constituted an important centre of Imperial military and naval operations. In the eighteenth century some of the $4\frac{1}{2}$ per cent. duty went towards the Governor's salary. The war between England and France which began in 1756 was fought out to some extent in West Indian waters. In 1761 the conflict for the West Indian Colonies became more intense. Barbados has always been to the front in loyally supporting the British power in the archipelago. The effort to retain the American Colonies about 1770-1780 also had its share in the fortunes of Barbados, especially in restricting the importation of provisions from those Colonies. In 1778 the island was so distressed for provisions that the Imperial Government forwarded relief. In 1782, a hurricane having occurred, the British Parliament voted 80,000*l*. Towards the close of the eighteenth century the efforts for the retention of the West India possessions became even more acute, and the victory of Admiral Rodney over De Grasse off Dominica (1782) prevented Barbados, with other islands, from falling into the hands of the enemy. The Peace at Amiens in 1802 gave a breathing time to all engaged in this warfare; but in 1805, when Napoleon was extending his conquests, great disquietude was experienced in the West Indies; Barbados was, however, saved by the timely arrival of Admiral Cochrane, and, since that time, notwithstanding the subsequent fortunes of war in the archipelago, nothing of any consequence has threatened the British possession of Barbados. It might be mentioned, however, that the rupture between Great Britain and the United States in 1812, by allowing the revival of privateering, had a most disastrous influence for a time upon the trade of the island. The 4½ per cent. duty was still exacted, and a large portion of it was employed to pay home pensions to persons entirely unconnected with the Colony, and to aid in defraying the expenses of the Royal household. Frequent efforts were made to induce Parliament to repeal these duties, but until the year 1838 such efforts were unsuccessful. The hurricane of 1831 must also be mentioned as a serious event in the history of the island.

The slave trade was stopped in 1806, but slavery itself was not abolished in the West India Islands until the Act of Emancipation came into force on the 1st of August, 1834. Barbados received out of the parliamentary grant of 20,000,000*l.* 1,720,345*l.*, being 20*l.* 14*s.* each on 83,176 slaves. There being a very large population in the island, the interference with industry was not so great as in other Colonies. The number of people has since been rapidly increasing, and subject to the commercial legislation of the Mother Country, often of a restrictive character, the production of the island has been gradually augmented.

The population of Barbados, according to the census of 1891, was returned at 182,306, or about 1,098 to the square mile. A more rapid increase of population has, to some extent, been checked by emigration to other Colonies. But the above figures represent a very large average per square mile in a place no bigger than the Isle of Wight. The principal production is sugar, which has during the past two or three years been largely increased. In one of Addison's essays in the 'Spectator,' he says that 'the fruits of Portugal are corrected by the products of Barbados, and the infusion of a China plant is sweetened by the pith of an Indian cane.' New machinery is being introduced, and cultivation is constantly being improved, so that from much the same area a larger quantity of sugar is obtained. Instead of 30,000, 40,000, or 50,000 tons (which latter used to be considered a very good crop), an average of 60,000 tons is produced, but during 1895, owing to the long drought and the ravages of the fungus disease, the exported crop fell to 36,451 tons, or about 29,600 tons short of the average for the last five years. Production, of course, fluctuates according to the seasons. Windmills are still largely used in grinding the canes, and as the wind cannot now be calculated upon with the same certainty as in past years, delay and loss in working up the crop are often caused. The use of steam mills becomes more and more imperative. If the system of central factories, by which is meant a factory with the latest improvements, and very best machinery to work up the canes from a number of contiguous estates, could be established, the quantity of sugar would be still more largely increased, the quality improved, and the cost of manufacture reduced. This is the system which has been carried out with great success in the French colonies, and has also been fairly started in Trinidad and St. Lucia. Two or three sites in Barbados are particularly adapted for central factories. It is obvious that a single estate—and in this island the estates do not as a rule run to a very large extent—could not afford costly buildings and plant all to itself. Such a system could only be a success when carried out upon a large scale, with a constant and full supply of canes to keep the factories going. In some such scheme as this, indeed, lies the future prosperity of the sugar islands. Experts say that Barbados ought to turn out good sugar at a cost of 8*l.* to 10*l.* per ton, which at moderate prices (and prices will rarely be very high again) ought to leave margin for sufficient profit. The value of exports from Barbados in 1894 was 984,512*l.* and the imports 1,279,335*l.*, making a total trade of 2,263,847*l.*, whereas the value of exports in 1895 was only 587,298*l.* and imports 956,921*l.*, making a total trade of 1,544,219*l.* Most of the provisions and food consumed in the island are brought from the United States, and to the same country is sent a very large proportion of the sugar crop. Great Britain supplies hardware, dry goods, cottons, calicoes, and wearing apparel. The central position of Barbados has made it a kind of emporium for other islands. The distribution of trade may be gathered from the following figures: The exports in 1895 were—To the United Kingdom, 69,760*l.*; to Colonies, 262,991*l.*; to Foreign Countries (United States, &c.), 254,547*l.* The imports for 1895 were— From United Kingdom, 391,434*l.*; Colonies, 184,154*l.*; Foreign Countries (United States), 381,333*l.* The shipping entered and cleared averages considerably over 1,000,000 tons a year, a large proportion being British tonnage. The public revenue—raised principally, as all Colonial revenues are and must be, from a somewhat lengthy scale of import duties—amounted in 1895 to 146,315*l.* and the expenditure to 152,039*l.*

The Constitution of Barbados is of peculiar interest. It has passed through many storms, only to become the more deeply rooted. Interference by the Imperial Parliament with island taxation has several times been the cause of a struggle. In 1832 an Act of Parliament was passed altering the operation of some tonnage dues imposed by a local Act of 1773. The Assembly protested on the ground that Parliament had no right to tax Colonies possessing representative institutions. This contention was put forward with much ability and force, but Lord Stanley in 1833 remained firm to his declaration that the right of taxing such Colonies existed, whatever might be the expediency of doing so in particular cases.

The island has always had for two and a half centuries its elected House of Assembly. It thus possesses representative institutions, but not responsible Government in the strict sense of that term. The Crown has only a veto on legislation, and does not initiate it as in Crown Colonies. The Queen, under the advice of the Secretary of State for the Colonies, may approve or disapprove of any island Act, and the Home Government possess the appointment and control of public officers, including of course the most important personage of all, viz. the Governor. Formerly, Barbados was the seat of the Governor-in-Chief of the Windward Islands; but under the present arrangement, settled only in 1885, this connection was severed, and Barbados has now a Governor all to itself at a salary of 3,000*l.* a year, with 600*l.* per annum table allowance, paid, as all such salaries now are, out of the Colonial revenue. Its Chief Justice, a gentleman of great attainments and possessing the full confidence of the people, is one of the most conspicuous examples of the success attained or attainable by members of the African race in the West Indies. Besides the Assembly, there is the Legislative Council, which might be called the House of Lords of the island, consisting of nine members, appointed by the Queen. The House of Assembly comprises twenty-four members, elected annually upon a moderate franchise, the exercise of which is open to a considerable number of industrious black people, although many of these take no part in politics, the register containing between two and three thousand names. The business of the Legislature is conducted according to English parliamentary forms; a Speaker is elected to preside, and all money bills must be introduced into the Lower House. An Executive Committee carries on the practical work of Government, and the management of Government business in the House of Assembly, such as the introduction of money votes, estimates, &c. This Executive Committee may be said to be the pivot of public business. It consists of the Governor, the Officer commanding the troops, the Colonial Secretary, the Attorney-General, and such other persons as may be nominated by the Queen, together with one member of the Legislative Council, and four members of the House of Assembly nominated by the Governor. This system works smoothly and well, and when officials are introduced into the island who have no wish to distinguish themselves by upsetting long-established institutions, all classes work together contentedly for the common good, and in this peaceful atmosphere race prejudices are fast becoming extinct.

The Church of England in Barbados claims the main body of the population as within her fold. Each of the eleven parishes has a rector, and there are also a number of curates in the island, all paid by the Colonial revenue. The other denominations are entitled to grants. It is stated that in the early days of the Colony, before currency and values had become adjusted, the clergy were paid by one pound of sugar for every acre of land in their respective parishes. The first bishop of the diocese (which then included other colonies) was the Right Rev. W. Hart Coleridge, who remained from 1825 to 1842. Dr. Bree is now bishop, having succeeded Dr. Mitchinson, and receives a salary of 1,000*l.* a year. The salary of a rector is 320*l.* a year, with house and glebe. A Government system of elementary education has been established since 1878, managed by a Central Board nominated by the Governor at a cost to the public revenue of about 16,000*l.* annually. There are 201 schools, with an average attendance of 14,442, out of 27,000 on the rolls. Besides Codrington College, and Harrison College in Bridgetown, there are several schools for higher education. The Education Board gives four scholarships out of the public funds, of the annual value of 175*l.* each, to be held at Oxford or Cambridge, for four years. The Queen's College for the higher education of girls was established in 1883, and the Alexandra Girls' School in Speight's Town was established in 1894, and is progressing very satisfactorily.

CHAPTER IV.

HAYTI.

ABOUT nine hours having been allowed for the landing of passengers and cargo, or their transference to the inter-colonial steamers, the big ocean steamer takes her departure for Jacmel, the Haytian port, a distance of 812 miles from Barbados, and occupying two days sixteen hours. Hispaniola (Little Spain) was the name given to this beautiful and fertile island by Columbus. It was the first Spanish settlement in the West Indies. There is indeed no place in the West Indies more intimately connected with Columbus than the City of St. Domingo. The cathedral is described as 'a grand old church with pillars and arches, crypts and altars innumerable.' It contains the first mausoleum of Columbus in the New World. The accounts of the splendours of the cathedral in the older days may be readily believed. It stands facing the public square, and is built of solid stone, Gothic in architecture, and has a nave and two wings. It was begun in 1512 and finished in 1540. The city, with its broad streets and stone buildings, must have formerly presented an imposing appearance. At the present time there is little business doing in the City of St. Domingo. It is an old Spanish town, with substantially-built houses having porticoes and balconies, but apparently steeped in the lethargy of a Spanish South American town where it is always afternoon. The commerce of the place has departed to other parts of the island. The interior town of Santiago, more in the centre of the island, may in time become of greater importance. It is situated in the midst of a fertile agricultural country, with water communication to every part, and with additional railroad communication might become the real capital of the island. The limited trade of St. Domingo City is confined to the export of mahogany, dye and cabinet woods, and a small quantity of cattle hides. But its importance has departed, and its sleepy streets and heavy buildings, bathed in a tropical sunlight, are only interesting as the remnants of Spanish conquest, and the illustration of the adventurous and colonising spirit of Old Spain.

The island lies in 18° 20′ N. latitude, and longitude 68° 40′ west of Greenwich. It is 70 miles S.E. of Cuba and 130 miles N.E. of Jamaica, and 60 miles W.N.W. of Porto Rico. Within its boundary is found almost every kind of climate, and the character of its soils and vegetation is equally varied. There are two chains of mountains stretching from east to west. Upon these a number of subsidiary ranges and valleys depend. The waters from the mountains would be a fertile source of production, if the time should come again for the hand of man to be brought to bear upon agricultural industries. The desire of the United States to acquire this island is one that might be easily understood. It is certainly doing no good for itself. In 1869 and in subsequent years there was a movement in favour of annexation to that country. With the consent of the Dominican Republic, a Commission was appointed in 1871 respecting the acquisition of Samana Bay by the United States, but nothing has come of these negotiations, to which at the time there was some hostile feeling (whether well founded or not) in England. It is stated by an American writer (Hazard, 1873) that the territorial extent of the whole island from its extreme eastern point to its most western cape (Tiburon) is about 400 English miles, and its extreme breadth (that is, in its widest part) nearly 180 miles; the area within its boundaries, exclusive of the adjacent isles, being about 25,000 square miles, or some 7,000 miles less than Ireland. Of this territory, the Negro Republic of Hayti occupies at the western end less than one third of the whole extent, the remainder being nominally under the control of the Dominican Republic.

The island has a most eventful history. Its natural resources and latent wealth might have made it the centre of empire in these seas. The conflicts with the Indians, the rivalries of Spaniards at home, the cruelties in the mines, the weakness of Diego Columbus, the introduction of African slaves, the restrictions imposed by Spain, the fluctuations in the prosperity of the place, the contests which took place for its possession,—all these things might be noted.

Originally peopled by Arawaks, the island was taken by the Spaniards, the aboriginal population being in course of time gradually exterminated, and negroes from Africa were introduced. It has been said that little is known of the Spanish occupation of this island and of Jamaica. The starting point may perhaps be indicated as follows: Upon his return to Spain from his first voyage to the New World, Columbus naturally took advantage of the great interest shown in his discoveries. On September 25, 1493, encouraged by a great crowd of spectators, his second expedition set sail from the Bay of Cadiz. After a prosperous voyage, touching at various points and islands, the fleet came to anchor in the Bay of Samana on November 22. Columbus laid out the settlement in the form of a regular town, and began to prospect for gold. After expeditions into the interior, after being worried by mutinies among his men and by attacks from the Indians, he endeavoured to establish his power, and to form a council. 'Isabella' may claim to be the first Christian settlement in the West Indies. The spot he selected for this settlement is said to be now unknown, or only to exist as a heap of ruins. The Spanish invasions of the Indian strongholds need not be described. The desire to find gold led to many energetic expeditions. Columbus returned to Spain amid every sign of honour, and in August, 1496, St. Domingo was recognised as the great Spanish Colony, and indeed a Colony was founded, or a possession obtained, that with proper management might have been a lasting source of profit and honour to the Mother Country.

A passing reference may be made to Sir Francis Drake's connection with the island, to the unsuccessful expedition of Penn and Venables in 1654–55, and to the doings of the Buccaneers. In 1665, the French took possession of the western part, and the eastern portion, renamed St. Domingo, continued as a Spanish Colony. For many years the former territory remained a very valuable possession of the French, and the sugar there produced formed for a very long period the principal part of the European supplies. Previous to its devastation in 1790 no less a quantity than 65,000 tons of sugar a year had been exported from this French portion of the island. But towards the end of the eighteenth century, in the French revolutionary times, it became the scene of much disturbance and bloodshed, and the French population was massacred by the freed slaves. Napoleon tried to recover the Colony, and Toussaint l'Ouverture, the apostle of freedom—or perhaps license might be a better word—was taken prisoner to France, where he died. The French troops which were left in the island died so rapidly that the recovered possession by the French was not long maintained. The vagaries of the Emperor Soulouque, between thirty and forty years ago, will be remembered. Columbus was originally buried in the cathedral at St. Domingo, but the body was removed in quite recent times to Havana. Sir Spenser St. John, the English Consul-General at Port-au-Prince, the principal town of Hayti, reported a few years ago that a horrible system of cannibalism prevailed. It is only fair to say that these statements provoked much controversy. In the present state of things it is not desirable for English passengers to go ashore at Jacmel, as it is generally in a very backward state.

The Republic of Hayti has a Constitution dating from June 14, 1867. There are two Chambers, a National Assembly and a Senate, the former elected by manhood suffrage. The term of the President is usually seven years, unless prematurely terminated by revolution. It is indeed in a chronic state of disturbance. The Republic trades with Great Britain and the United States. The exports of St. Domingo and Hayti to the United Kingdom amounted to 53,216*l*. in 1895, and they received from the United Kingdom goods valued at 359,027*l*. The exports are principally logwood and other woods, coffee, cocoa, and cotton. The currency is the dollar, of the nominal value of 4*s*. 2*d*., but really 20 per cent. less. The French weights and measures are used.

The total population of the island is variously estimated at from 500,000 to 900,000. Hayti has a large floating debt, created by paper money issued at various times, the value of which is much reduced by repudiation and forgery.

The total indebtedness of Hayti is now estimated at 4,522,000*l.* Various financial operations, such as the establishment of the National Bank of Hayti in 1881, have taken place in recent years, but it cannot be said that the credit of the government has been improved, or the development of the country promoted.

A BIT OF KINGSTON HARBOUR.

CHAPTER V.

JAMAICA.

THE steamer stays but a short time at Jacmel, and then makes her way, hugging the coast, and passing capes and bays which have been famous as the scene of many encounters both with the enemies of England and with the privateers, who were not entitled to be called by the honourable title of enemies, and who were mercilessly dealt with when caught.

Past Cape Tiburon, the Cape of Sharks, the south-west extremity of Hayti ; past Navasa (where an outbreak, in which several whites were killed and in checking which a British man-of-war rendered good service, attracted general attention some little time ago), a volcanic islet containing valuable phosphates—a place claimed by the United States, according to their usual practice in the case of guano or phosphate islands, but claimed also by the Haytian Republic—the steamer is now in wider waters, and in twenty-four hours' steaming after leaving Jacmel, the 255 miles' run to Jamaica is effected. The steamer coming from the east will make her entrance into Kingston Harbour. This harbour is a large piece of water, bounded or inclosed by a narrow bank of sand, which runs out into the sea and forms a natural breakwater. This bank commences some miles east of Kingston, running parallel with the coast until it terminates about five miles to the west of Kingston in Port Royal. This sandbank is known as the Palisades or Palisadoes. The communication between Port Royal and the capital is principally by boat, few venturing to go along the sand, the negroes especially, it is said, having a superstitious aversion to it. The steamer, after getting a view of Port Morant, passes Port Royal and enters the landlocked harbour of Kingston; the crowning feature of the whole scene, which might have been noticed for some time previously, the Blue Mountains, being especially picturesque and grand. The former name of Port Royal was Point Caugway, and it was first called by its present title on May 29, 1661, when Charles II. was proclaimed King there. The place suffered from an earthquake on June 7, 1692, when a great loss of life occurred, and a large part of the town was buried beneath the sea; whole streets were swallowed up, and the harbour was covered with dead bodies from the burying place, which was swept by the sea. One, Lewis Galdy, was swallowed up by the earthquake, but another shock threw him into the sea, and he was saved by a boat. This legend is inscribed upon his tomb at Green Bay, which also states that after his adventure he lived for many years, beloved by all who knew him. One would like to have known Lewis Galdy, if only to ask him what his sensations were. But the calamity was terrible enough. The ruins of old Port Royal are still known to exist under the waves, and are even visible in clear weather. Nor was this the only disaster which befell the place. It was partly rebuilt where possible, but in subsequent years fire and hurricane have done their worst upon it. At one time, and especially in time of war, it was a great military and naval station, and no doubt it formerly possessed a reputation for great insalu-

brity, but it is now healthy. Its old importance in the buccaneering and war times, together with the conditions that produced and governed that importance, have gone. It is, however, still in high estimation as a naval station, the Imperial Government having purchased it as part of the scheme of colonial defence and coaling stations. The Apostles' Battery, Rocky Point, and Fort Augusta help to protect, with Port Royal itself, by means of new batteries for rifled guns, the entrance to the harbour, which is being made impregnable against a hostile fleet. In the cemetery at Port Royal, a spot dangerous from miasma, lie the remains of many a gallant fellow who was engaged in the defence of British interests and British honour in these seas.

Port Royal contains a dockyard and an official house for the Commodore and his staff, a well-appointed hospital, and other necessaries for a naval station. During the American War and the French occupation of Mexico, the British war ships on the North American and West Indian station were unusually numerous, and were constantly calling at Port Royal for coal and provisions. The ill-fated Archduke Maximilian, going to his doom in Mexico, was met at Port Royal by eleven ships of war. There does not seem any chance of the Panama Canal being completed; but if that water-way between two oceans should be at last effected, the importance of Port Royal must be very largely increased.

While the steamer is proceeding through the smooth water of the harbour, a reference to Tom Cringle's first experience of the Palisades might be interesting. 'We shoved off, and as the glowing sun dipped under Portland Point, as the tongue of land that runs out about four miles to the southward on the western side of Port Royal Harbour is called, we arrived within a hundred yards of the Palisadoes. The surf, at the particular spot we steered for, did not break on the shore in a rolling, curling wave, as it usually does, but smoothed away, under the lee of a small, sandy promontory, that ran out into the sea about half a cable's length to windward, and then slid up the smooth, white sand, without breaking, in a deep, clear, green swell, for the space of twenty yards, gradually shoaling, the colour becoming lighter and lighter, until it frothed away in a shallow white fringe, that buzzed as it receded back into the deep green sea until it was again propelled forward by the succeeding billow.' Tom and his party were in a small rowing boat, and were going to deliver despatches in Kingston from H.M.S. 'Torch,' lying some distance east of Port Royal, and opposite the Palisades. They therefore determined to cross the Palisades, dragging their boat across the sand, and launching it again on the other side in the harbour. 'We leapt with all our strength, and thereby toppled down on our noses. The sea receded, and before the next billow approached we had run the canoe twenty yards beyond high-water mark. It was the work of a very few minutes to haul the canoe across the sandbank, and to launch it once more in the placid waters of the harbour of Kingston. We pulled across towards the town until we landed at the bottom of Hanover Street; the lights from the cabin windows of the merchantmen glimmering as we passed, and the town only discernible from a solitary sparkle here and there. But the contrast when we landed was very striking. We had come through the darkness of the night in comparative quietness, and in two hours from the time we had left the old "Torch" we were transferred from her orderly deck to the bustle of a crowded town.'

But the steamer, having given the passengers a view of the Blue Mountains many miles away, having passed Morant Bay, the scene of the outbreak of 1865, and also having passed Port Royal and the forts opposite to it, is proceeding through the channel, which is about a mile wide at the entrance, varying from six to nine fathoms in depth, and is well buoyed and staked. In its narrowest part it is a little over a cable in width. Vessels are lying alongside the different wharves. Kingston is situated on an extensive flat plain, rising slowly and by small graduations from the sea. The steamer goes alongside the wharf, and passengers step immediately on land, amidst a crowd of rather excited negroes. Preparations are ready to coal the steamer, and a long line of men and women are waiting with baskets to be filled from piles of coal and carried on board on their heads. Amidst noise, and, it must be added, coal dust, the passenger takes guard of his luggage and proceeds to his destination in one of the vehicles in waiting, or in one brought by his friends.

Kingston has an area of about 1,080 acres. The streets run down to the sea, with intersections parallel with it. The centre of the town was originally King Street, running north and south, and Queen Street, running east and west. A square of ten acres in the centre of the town is now a Government garden. The soil of Kingston being gravelly, surplus water easily disappears and malaria is prevented. The city is well supplied with water from the Hope River, and also from the Wag Water. Kingston came into prominence as a commercial centre as a substitute for Port Royal, after the great earthquake of 1692 and the fire of 1703. In the middle of the eighteenth century it was proposed that it should be constituted the seat of Government, but the arrangement was not generally approved, and the official records were returned to Spanish Town. In 1802 it received municipal rights, with their outward and visible signs in mayor, aldermen, and common council. The city has unfortunately been subject to conflagrations, causing much loss of property. In 1866 the civic rights of the Corporation were transferred to a municipal board under the direction of the Governor in Privy Council and under the immediate management of a Custos. There is, however, at the present moment, a Mayor and Corporation of Kingston. In 1872, under the administration of Sir John Grant, the seat of Government was removed from Spanish Town to Kingston. The colonial secretariat became lodged in Head-quarter House, and the Bishop's residence in Liguanea Plain was converted into Government House. The city contains a population of 48,504. It is lighted by gas, but many of the public buildings have the electric light, and communication is rendered easy by street cars. A spacious and handsome market has been established, called the Victoria Market, at the end of one of the principal streets looking on to the harbour. Lord Rodney's statue was brought from Spanish Town and placed here, but has been again restored to the position where it stood for so many years in honour of the victory of the Admiral over the French fleet, commanded by Count de Grasse. In the upper part of King Street, and opposite to the principal entrance of the Parade Garden, the statue of Sir Charles Metcalfe, at one time a popular Governor, stands. On the eastern side of the Parade is the statue of the Hon. Edward Jordon, C.B., a Jamaica statesman and defender of popular rights. On the northern side of the garden is the statue of Dr. L. Q. Bowerbank, a

KING'S STREET, KINGSTON

JAMAICA. 45

distinguished physician and sanitary reformer. The deputation to Lord Carnarvon, Secretary of State for the Colonies, on sanitary and other matters in Jamaica, of which Dr. Bowerbank was one of the principal members, will be long remembered by everyone who took part in that representation. There is a good theatre in Kingston, which is occupied frequently by excellent theatrical companies from the United States. The public hospital is worthy of a visit. The Mico Institute at the north of the Race Course recalls a somewhat romantic story. Dame Jena Mico, widow of a knight who was at one time Lord Mayor of London, had a niece who was engaged to be married. Her marriage portion was ready. The marriage, however, did not take place. In the middle of the seventeenth century, when Lady Mico was alive, half of the intended marriage portion was diverted by her will to the cause of the Christian captives in Algiers. This lady died. There was then no occasion for the redemption of Christian captives in Algiers. The one thousand pounds destined for them was invested in freehold property in London. The value of the property increased in time to 120,000*l*., and, at the suggestion of Sir Thomas Fowell Buxton in 1834, the interest of the money was devoted to the Christian instruction of the children of West Indians. A charter was granted, and the British Government added a substantial sum for the purpose, which grant was stopped in 1841. With a portion of the money thus available the Mico Institute was formed in Jamaica and other Colonies. It celebrated its jubilee in 1887. The students are charged 5*l*. by way of fees, and the Colonial Government makes a grant. The management is undenominational. The building was for many years situated in Hanover Street, but in

1894 the trustees purchased Quebec Lodge, near the Race Course, where spacious premises have been erected at a cost of over 12,000*l*. It is a school, combined with a training college for teachers, and the general results are good.

The Jamaica Institute is the successor of the Royal Society of Arts and Agriculture in Jamaica, originally formed under the auspices of Governor the Earl of Elgin in 1843. It has an indefatigable secretary in Mr. Frank Cundall. It is an institute for literary and scientific purposes, with library, museum, reading-room, lectures, and all the appurtenances that belong to such an undertaking, in addition to which it now issues a well-edited journal dealing with various questions affecting the history and progress of the Island. To the Institute was granted the library of the old House of Assembly. The building in East Street, Kingston, called Date Tree Hall, contains the geological specimens collected by Messrs. Sawkins and Brown when they made the survey of the island. A fine collection of woods, grasses, ferns, and orchids is exhibited. There are, too, many specimens of Jamaica shells, of birds and fishes of the island, as well as of its general products. The bell of the old church of Port Royal, submerged in the earthquake of 1692, is also here. The Institute arranged for the display of the island products at the Exhibition of New Orleans in 1884-5, under its then chairman, Mr. D. Morris, who is now the Assistant-Director of the Royal Gardens at Kew. It sent a number of interesting exhibits to the Fisheries Exhibition in London in 1883, and it contributed a very good representation of island products to the Jamaica Court of the Colonial and Indian

JAMAICA: JETTY AT KINGSTON.

Exhibition of 1886, whilst in 1890 it undertook the preparation of a collection of samples of the products of the island for exhibition in the Jamaica Court of the Imperial Institute in London. Its library is one of the best in the West Indies, a special feature being a collection of books on Jamaica and the West Indies, in addition to volumes of scientific, historic and general literature. It has recently become a centre of the Cambridge Local Examinations, with very creditable results to the principal schools of higher education in the Colony. It was in the museum and public library that Mr. Froude saw what was erroneously supposed to be the identical bauble which Cromwell ordered to be taken away from the Speaker's table in the House of Commons.

Among the attractive and characteristic institutions are the Jamaica Club, which has a large and commodious house in Hanover Street, numerous cricket clubs, and the Royal Jamaica Yacht Club, with its annual regatta and other races, and the pleasant social intercourse to which it gives rise.

The Kingston Collegiate School, conducted by Mr. and Mrs. Morrison, should also be mentioned, as well as the Hebrew National Institution. There are many Jews in Kingston, highly respected and influential, the descendants of former emigrants to the island from Great Britain and the Continent. The Hebrew community is a real and noticeable element in the public and private life of the Colony. A splendid new synagogue was opened in 1888, the ceremony being attended by men of all classes and creeds, who took this means of showing their sympathy and goodwill. The Wesleyans, Baptists, Moravians, and other denominations are doing good work, as shown by their various educational and other institutions. The Young Men's Christian Association and the Women's Self-Help Society might also be mentioned.

The history of the Church of England in Jamaica is contemporary with that of the Colony. Many Acts of the Legislature have been passed in connection with the ecclesiastical organisation. In 1870 a law was passed regulating the disestablishment and gradual disendowment of the Church of England in the Colony. The government of the Church was vested in a Synod, together with all Church property. This body consists of bishop, clergy, and lay representatives. Under the energetic rule of the present Bishop the Church is increasing in influence and usefulness. The Rev. Enos Nuttall, a local clergyman, after being elected by the Synod, was consecrated Bishop in St. Paul's Cathedral, London, on October 28, 1880, by the Archbishop of Canterbury, assisted by numerous other prelates.

The mention of the Church of England suggests at once a visit to the old Parish Church of Kingston, with its comparative antiquity and its interesting historical memorials, among the latter being the tomb of Admiral Benbow, with the following inscription upon it : 'Here lyeth interred the body of John Benbow, Esq., Admiral of the White, a true pattern of English courage, who lost hys life in defence of hys Queene and country, November ye 4th, 1702, in he 52nd year of hys age, by a wound in hys leg received in an engagement with Mons. Du Casse, being much lamented.'

The arrangement of the streets in Kingston, the Central Park, which is a favourite resort of the inhabitants, the different public buildings in the city, the wharves and stores, the shipping in the harbour, all these have perhaps been sufficiently indicated. If the traveller is desirous, as a loyal subject of the Queen, of paying his respects to her representative, he will proceed to King's House, about four miles from town. The drive is made pretty by the number of private villas with verandahs, protected by the cactus-like leaves of a plant which grows to a considerable height. The road is rendered lively by negro women, going to or returning from town, with their baskets of fruit and vegetables on their heads.

A few days at King's House as the invited guest of his Excellency is an experience which cannot fail to be remembered. A large house with the blinds down, cool galleries for smoking, and other means of enjoyment; the early breakfast, the social lunch, the formal dinner in the saloon, built separately from the house—all these will pleasantly stimulate and yet soothe the mind. The polished floors, with centre mats, are inviting to walk upon, but perhaps dangerous for a dance. Tom Cringle's introduction to fashionable society was rendered noteworthy by his slipping on the floor 'and splitting his lower canvas' to such an extent as to necessitate borrowing a petticoat from his fair cousin before he could rise. The cool green blinds, the verandahs, the outlooks into the garden after dinner—all this will become part of the picture in the mind, and perhaps pleasurably idealised in time. Add to all this, the courtesy and refinement of the host and hostess, and nothing more can be desired. Imagine entirely new tropical surroundings to English social life of the best character, combined with the hospitable reception, and King's House in Jamaica is described. Within easy distance from town lies Up-Park Camp with its extensive ground and red-brick barracks, and the racecourse, adjoining which the exhibition building and gardens formed so great an attraction in the early months of 1891.

One of the first visits, on arrival at Kingston, will be to Spanish Town, the old capital of the island. It is an exceedingly quiet place, full of memories of the past.

A railway run of half an hour is sufficient for the thirteen miles' distance from Kingston. The red-brick cathedral, the massive King's House, which was the Governor's residence in former times, with its pretentious columns and porticoes, are to be seen. Bacon's marble statue of Lord Rodney in the Square at Spanish Town stands in its old position opposite King's House. In this square, too, are the old House of Assembly and other public buildings. Anthony Trollope found the place extremely quiet and deserted, although at the time of his visit it was the seat of Government. The Spanish Town pigs also attracted his attention, but not his admiration. Spanish Town, or St. Jago de la Vega, was named by the son of Columbus by that title to distinguish it from St. James of Cuba. It received its name of Spanish Town from the English in 1655. It is only about six miles from the sea. The first capital was Sevilla Nueva near St. Ann's Bay, founded by Don Juan d'Esquivel, under the direction of Diego, the son of Columbus, but this was abandoned subsequently for Spanish Town, which is now described as in St. Catherine's Parish, the latter deriving its name from the Queen of Charles II. This parish contains Spanish Town, Old Harbour, and Linstead. Spanish Town is situated on the Rio Cobre, one of the most interesting and important rivers of the island, deriving its name either from copper or snake. It contains a population of 5,019 souls. The old Governor's residence, with the old House of Assembly rooms, are transformed into a Government

JAMAICA: THE RODNEY STATUE, SPANISH TOWN.

Training College. This educational transformation by Sir John Grant has not been very successful. The two episcopal churches, and the churchyards adjoining them, contain the remains of early governors and settlers. From its former associations, Spanish Town is decidedly a place to visit, and in the newer times which are coming, it is hoped that the stores will be reopened and extended, and that the place will again take a position consistent with its old importance as the historical capital of the island. The Temple, in which the statue of Rodney stands, is in itself enough to redeem the principal square of the town from insignificance. The two brass 32-pounder guns which were captured by the Admiral in 1781 from the French fleet under De Grasse, are still to be seen, bearing the inscription, 'Louis Charles de Bourbon, Compte d'Eu, Duc d'Aumale, 4th May, 1748.' There are other guns and relics of the wars lying about. Altogether, Spanish Town, although very quiet and deserted nowadays, may be inspected with interest, especially as having been connected with the earliest discoveries of Christopher Columbus, who always tried to promote in the New World the reproduction of the older customs and spirit of Spain.

Before visiting other parts of the island we might take advantage of the quiet of its ancient capital to note some of its general characteristic features, and to consider shortly its history.

Xaymaca, the aboriginal name of the island, signifies the land of streams. Upon the authority of Bridges, the historian, the derivation of the word is thus explained : 'Chabauan,' the Indian word for water, and 'Makia,' wood, when compounded would be pronounced 'Cha-makia,' whence the name Jamaica, 'denoting a land covered with wood, and therefore watered by shaded rivulets, or in other words fertile.'

The island of Jamaica is one of the four islands which constitute what are known as the Greater Antilles. It lies between 17° 43' and 18° 32' N. lat. and 76° 11' and 78° 20' 50" W. long., about 5,000 miles to the south-west of England, 100 miles west of St. Domingo, and 90 miles south of Cuba, 445 north of Carthagena, and 540 miles from Colon on the Isthmus of Panama. Jamaica is bounded on the north and east by that part of the Caribbean Sea which separates it from Cuba and St. Domingo, the north-eastern part of these waters, before they merge into the Atlantic, being called the Windward Passage. On its other sides the island is washed by the Caribbean Sea.

The islands of Grand and Little Cayman, with Cayman Brac, are situated, the first about 156 miles and the two latter about 110 miles north-west of Negril Point. The Pedro Bank and Cays commence about 40 miles south of Portland Point, and extend westerly for 100 miles. This Bank is about three-fourths of the size of Jamaica. The Morant Cays are 36 miles from Morant Point in a south-easterly direction. These islands and cays, together with Turks and Caicos Islands, are all now dependencies of Jamaica. A question was raised by the Government of the United States, a few years ago, as to whether Pedro Bank did not belong to them under their law relating to guano islands, as it was uninhabited when they visited it, and apparently had not been claimed by Great Britain. But it may be assumed that this question has now been settled by diplomatic means. Certainly in 1884 a serious correspondence between the British and American Governments took place on this subject.

The extreme length of Jamaica is 144 miles. Its greatest width is 49 miles, right across the centre of the island, and its narrowest part is 21½ miles, from Kingston to Annotto Bay, the latter a very practicable and pleasant day's excursion for the visitor. Since the original division of the island into districts or parishes changes have been made. During Sir John Peter Grant's administration the number of parishes was reduced, in several instances two being amalgamated into one. No doubt by this measure the recognition of some places of historic interest might be rendered more difficult, although the conveniences of Government might have been facilitated. The island is divided into three counties and fourteen parishes, namely :

County of Surrey	Square miles	County of Middlesex	Square miles	County of Cornwall	Square miles
Parish		Parish		Parish	
Kingston . .	7⅛	St. Catherine	470	St. Elizabeth	462
St. Andrew .	166	St. Mary . .	249	Trelawny .	333
St. Thomas .	274	Clarendon .	474	St. James .	234
Portland . .	285	St. Ann . .	476	Hanover .	167
		Manchester .	302	Westmoreland	308
Total . .	732⅙	Total . .	1,971	Total . .	1,504

Or a grand total of 4,207⅙ square miles. The foundation or basis of the island is composed of igneous rocks, overlying which are several distinct formations.

The coast formation of the county of Surrey is of white and yellow limestone ; the interior consists chiefly of the metamorphosed and trappean series with carbonaceous shales and conglomerate. This county is mountainous, with the exception of the Liguanea Plain behind Kingston and the valleys of the Morant and Plantain Garden Rivers. In the mountain districts, mineral deposits are found, but are not extensively worked. The late Mr. Thomas Harrison, who was for several years the Surveyor-General, gives full particulars in the 'Jamaica Handbook.' Some of the points he mentions are as follows:

In the county of Middlesex the parish of St. Mary exhibits a great diversity of formation, consisting of white and yellow limestone, carbonaceous shales, metamorphosed, porphyritic, granite and conglomerate rocks, with many mineral-bearing rocks. The district of St. Thomas-in-the-Vale is of granite formation, overlaid considerably by cretaceous and white limestone and marl beds. St. Catherine possesses an extensive alluvial flat, stretching from Kingston Harbour to the boundary of Clarendon; the rest of the parish is of white limestone. In Upper Clarendon the metamorphosed trappean and conglomerate series prevail; the central districts are of white limestone, and the southern part, with the district of Vere, is alluvium and embraces an area of about 132 square miles, which is the largest continuous flat in the island. The mineral deposits of Upper Clarendon are considerable, and, it is believed, offer a fair field for mining enterprise. The parishes of Manchester and St. Ann consist almost entirely of white limestone.

The parish of St. Elizabeth, in the county of Cornwall, has an extensive area of alluvium from the boundary of Manchester to the boundary of Westmoreland, narrowing so considerably at Lacovia that the north and south limestones nearly meet; much of this flat is covered by swamp. In the north-east of the parish there is also an extensive flat called the Nassau Valley. The rest of the parish is white limestone with some patches of yellow. The parish of Westmoreland has large alluvial deposits and marl beds. In the north-western part of the parish are trappean rocks

1

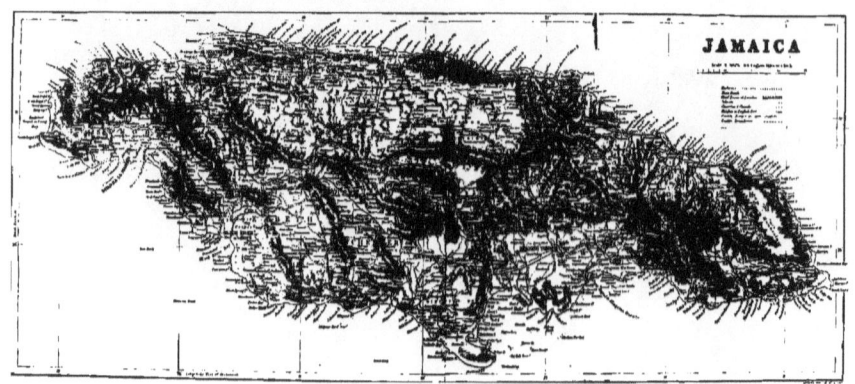

with yellow and cretaceous limestone. The eastern part is chiefly white limestone. Trelawny contains trap formation and white limestone, with some alluvial valleys, that called the Queen of Spain's Valley being a very beautiful and fertile region. St. James is of trappean formation with some yellow and cretaceous limestones. Hanover is chiefly white limestone.

The story of Columbus crumpling up a piece of paper in his hand and then showing it to Queen Isabella as a description of Jamaica is so good and apposite that it deserves to be historically true if it be not so. It is indeed a 'crumpled' country of most diversified beauty—hill and valley, mountain ridge and sheer precipice, rough fissure and romantic glen, the whole enlivened and animated with cascades, streams, and rivers of all sizes and forms. The different altitudes render the climate very diverse, ranging from 80° to 86° in the plains near the coast to 45° and 50° on the high mountains, where indeed ice has once been found. This variety of climate makes Jamaica particularly attractive and beneficial as a health resort for even the most delicate constitutions. The principal mountains run east and west through the middle part of the island, the highest point being Blue Mountain Peak, 7,360 feet above the level of the sea. The following are the principal elevations:

Names	Elevation in feet	Names	Elevation in feet
Blake Mountains, average	2,100	Belle Vue, Cinchona Plantation	5,017
Cuna Cuna Pass	2,698		
Blue Mountain, Western Peak	7,360	Arntully Gap	2,754
		Hagley Gap	1,959
Portland Gap	5,549	Morce's Gap	4,945
Sir John's Peak (highest point of Cinchona Plantation)	6,100	Content Gap	3,251
		Newcastle Hospital	3,800
		Flamstead	3,663

Names	Elevation in feet	Names	Elevation in feet
Belle Vue (Mr. Pinnock's)	3,784	Mount Diablo, highest point	2,300
Silver Hill Gap	3,513		
Catherine's Peak	5,036	Mount Diablo where road crosses	1,800
Cold Spring Gap	4,523		
Hardware Gap	4,079	Bull Head	2,885
Fox's Gap	3,967	Mandeville	2,131
Stony Hill (where main road crosses it)	1,360	Accompong Town	1,409
		Dolphin Head	1,816
Guy's Hill	2,100		

The chief rivers are the Agua Alta or Wag Water through the parishes of St. Andrew and St. Mary; the Hope River in the parish of St. Andrew; the Rio Cobre running through the parish of St. Catherine; the Plantain Garden, Morant, and Yallahs Rivers in the parish of St. Thomas; the Rio Grande, the Swift, the Spanish and Buff Bay Rivers in the parish of Portland; the Cave River, forming the boundary between the parishes of St. Ann and Clarendon; the Hector's River, dividing the parish of Trelawny from Manchester; the Rio Minho or Dry River and the Milk River in the parish of Clarendon; the Black River in the parish of St. Elizabeth; the Martha Brae River in the parish of Trelawny; the Cabaritta River in the parish of Westmoreland; and the Great River, dividing the parishes of St. James and Hanover. The Black River in the parish of St. Elizabeth is navigable for twenty-five miles of its course, the water being fresh from three to five miles up the river. None of the other rivers are navigable to any extent.

The ports are Kingston and Port Royal, in the parish of Kingston; Old Harbour Bay, in St. Catherine; Salt River, in Clarendon; Alligator Pond, in Manchester; Black River, in St. Elizabeth; Savanna-la-Mar, in Westmoreland; Lucea, in Hanover; Montego Bay, in St. James; Falmouth and Rio Bueno, in Trelawny; Dry Harbour and St. Ann's Bay, in St. Ann; Port Maria and Annotto Bay, in St. Mary; Port Antonio and Manchioneal, in Portland; Port Morant and Morant Bay, in St. Thomas.

The chief bays are Morant Bay, Old Harbour Bay, Carlisle Bay, Alligator Pond Bay, Black River Bay, Negril Bay, Montego Bay, St. Ann's Bay, Ocho Rios Bay, Annotto Bay, Buff Bay, Hope Bay, and Plantain Garden River Bay.

The principal capes or promontories are Morant Point, in the parish of St. Thomas; Portland Point, in Clarendon; Great Pedro Bluff and Parotte Point, in St. Elizabeth; Negril Point, in Westmoreland; Montego Bay Point, in St. James; and Galina Point, in St. Mary.

The many mineral springs in the island are especially noticeable for their curative powers. The hottest is the spring at Bath in St. Thomas. At the fountain head it is 126° F., but the water loses about 9° of heat in its transit to the baths. These waters are sulphuric and contain a large proportion of hydro-sulphate of lime; they are not purgative, and are beneficial in gout, rheumatism, gravelly complaints, cutaneous affections, and fevers. A cold spring flows from the same hillside, near the hot spring, so that cold and hot water are delivered alongside of each other at the bath.

The bath at Milk River, in the district of Vere, is one of the most remarkable in the world. It is a warm, saline, purgative bath; the temperature is 92° F. It is particularly efficacious in the cure of gout, rheumatism, paralysis, and neuralgia; also in cases of disordered liver and spleen. Some wonderful results are on record, and it is believed that if the beneficial effects of these waters were more generally known in Europe and America a large number of sufferers would be attracted to them.

The waters of the Spa Spring, or Jamaica Spa as it is called, at Silver Hill, in St. Andrew, surrounded by grand mountain scenery 3,000 feet high, and only fifteen miles from Kingston, are chalybeate, aërated, cold, and tonic, and are beneficial in most cases of debility, particularly after fever, dropsy, and in stomach complaints.

There is also a remarkable spring at Moffat, on the White River, a tributary of the Negro River in the Blue Mountain Valley. These waters are sulphuric, cold, and purgative, useful in itch and all cutaneous diseases. A similar spring exists near the source of the Cabaritta River, in Hanover.

The climate of Jamaica promotes longevity. During the day the refreshing sea breeze makes existence not only tolerable but exquisitely enjoyable. A moderate wind from the mountains keeps the nights deliciously cool. At a height of 225 feet above Kingston the mean yearly temperature is 78°, and it naturally falls according to the rise of ground. Dr. Phillippo, in his well-known book on the climate of Jamaica, says that even delicate invalids can live virtually in the open air, carefully avoiding, of course, chills and draughts. The few insalubrious spots in the island, or on occasional outbreak of fever in Kingston, do not detract from the remarkable general healthiness. Once on the upper ground, all fear of miasma is at an end. Nothing can exceed the bright life-giving influences of the air, to breathe which is an exhilaration. Nor is this account of the climate a theoretical exaggeration. The practical testimony of many who have derived real benefit from it could be brought forward. Those who would die if they remained in the fogs of London, or the snows and frosts of New York, obtain a fresh lease of life by spending the winter in Jamaica. For weak chests, unsound lungs, and bronchial disorders the climate is peculiarly suited. The testimony of many medical men might also reassure the patient. The late Dr. Bowerbank, the principal physician for many years in the island, said : 'There can be no doubt that where a predisposition to tubercular or scrofulous disease exists, a residence in Jamaica will completely check its further development ; and even during the earlier stages of tubercular consumption, if its progress be not arrested, life is often prolonged, and the disease divested of much of its suffering.'

Dr. Logan Russell, a well-informed witness, in a paper read before the Royal Colonial Institute in 1879, remarked that residence at the greater altitudes, say at Newcastle, 4,000 feet above sea level, would give fair hopes of recovery, even though softening and disintegration of the pulmonary tissue be in progress. Buoyancy of spirit, elasticity of frame, diminution of expectoration, absence of night perspiration, are among the benefits derived by those suffering from phthisis in these elevated regions. Even a more moderate altitude is also advantageous. The steady warmth is also good for gout, rheumatism, and calcareous affections. The climate of the Santa Cruz mountains, in the parish of St. Elizabeth, is highly recommended. The minimum temperature is $66\cdot8°$, the maximum $75\cdot3°$, and the mean $71\cdot1°$. Annual rainfall about forty inches ; all which indicates a state of things which corresponds to that which prevails in such a health resort as Algiers. It is opposed to the progress of tubercular diseases, which are often cured even after development has commenced. Dr. J. H. Clark, who knows the district well, gives the following instructions for tourists and invalids in Kingston. They can travel either by rail to Mandeville, one of the prettiest towns in the island, hiring a conveyance thence to the Santa Cruz Mountains, or by coasting steamer to Black River, and, hiring a conveyance at this seaport, after a pleasant drive of two or three hours, be located in very comfortable lodgings on the mountain top. It would be advisable always to engage rooms before coming. Visitors should communicate by letter, stating full particulars, addressed to 'The Postmistress at Malvern P.O.' This lady will supply information as to rooms, residences, and charges. The roads are in excellent order, so that carriage drives may be enjoyed. There is a large market at Malvern twice a week, where the delicious fruits of this country, and occasionally grapes, can be procured, with vegetables, beef, and mutton; fresh fish can be obtained three times a week. The Post Office is accessible; mails arrive and are despatched three times a week, and a Telegraph Office is within eight miles. Two churches and a Moravian chapel are open on Sundays for Divine Service. There are excellent schools, for boys and girls, within easy reach.

The climate of the hills of the parish of Manchester has also been strongly recommended. Mizpah is 2,400 feet above the sea level, with a greater range of temperature than that of Santa Cruz. Easterly winds are prevalent, and sometimes fogs occur after heavy rains in the lowlands. Although the atmosphere is rather moist (and getting wet should be carefully avoided), statistics of death-rate show the healthiness of the situation. Many other favoured spots, with their own peculiar advantages and picturesqueness, might be mentioned, but probably sufficient information has been given not only to remove all objections to the general climate of Jamaica, but to show the real attractions it offers to those who are in search of health or pleasure.

A few general words about the different parishes might be apposite at this point. Sufficient probably has been said descriptive of Kingston. St. Andrew contains many interesting spots particularly suitable for short excursions from Kingston. The three principal villages are Halfway Tree, Gordon Town, and Stony Hill. The first, three miles from Kingston, and easily reached by tram-cars, is the centre of a residential district. It has its Court House, Police Station, Market, and Parish Church, the latter dating from the time of Queen Anne, and containing memorials of Governors who died in the island, and other historical characters. It is close to King's House and Bishop's Lodge, the official residences of the Governor and Bishop respectively. Gordon Town is nine miles north-east of Kingston, and is the halting-place for visitors to the Newcastle encampment above, to which it is the picket station. Gordon Town may be reached by omnibus from Kingston, the charge for a return ticket being 5s. A visit to Newcastle is described later on. Craigton, the mountain residence of the Governor, is in the vicinity. The Jamaica Spa, on Silver Hill, is at no great distance from Newcastle. Stony Hill is on the road across the island to Annotto Bay, the tramway going as far as the Constant Spring hotel. The parish of St. Andrew also contains Up-Park Camp Barracks, a mile and a half from Kingston, whence a good view of the harbour can be obtained. This parish has been long celebrated for its coffee, which thrives on the hillsides. Here, too, are the Government and private plantations of cinchona. An experimental growth of the tea plant has also been attempted in these elevated regions. This infant industry may be successful, as experts in England have pronounced the tea very good. Some tobacco is also grown by planters from Cuba. Fruits in abundance are also produced, but very little sugar. The use of the word Parish might suggest to an English untravelled mind a small and compact area, but St. Andrew comprises just 166 square miles. It has 11,183 acres in cultivation, 3,070 acres are in coffee, 178 acres in tobacco, 5,521 in ground provisions, 3,283 in Guinea grass, 11,580 in common pasture, and 52,729 in wood and ruinate. The varied nature of the scenery—the combination of hill, ravine, and forest—the number of valuable products, make this parish interesting to the tourist, and perhaps attractive to the settler.

That part of the country now called the parish of St. Thomas is a very important sugar district. It is an old settlement, dating from the time of the early Spanish explorers, who were attracted by its natural beauty, its rich soil, and its easy access by Port Morant and Morant Bay. The sugar estates in Plantain Garden River district form one of the sights of the island, when viewed from a convenient standpoint. To the practical mind of a sugar manufacturer, this district might be regarded as offering a good site for a central factory to work up the produce of the estates. The rivers in St. Thomas are the Yallahs and Morant Bay Rivers, the Dry River, and the Falls River. The Morant Point lighthouse at the eastern end of the island has already been noticed by the visitor while on board the steamer. Morant Bay, the shipping port, was rendered very interesting to Englishmen at home by the fact that it was the centre of the disturbances in 1865. The execution of Gordon, and the subsequent controversy as to the conduct of Governor Eyre and the military officers engaged in putting down the disturbance, made Morant Bay a very familiar name throughout the United Kingdom. Port Morant lies seven miles eastward, and was once a busy commercial port. Easington, with its suspension bridge over the Yallahs River, is a village also to be noted. There are in St. Thomas 6,480 acres in ground provisions, 1,975 in sugar canes, 2,594 in coffee, 238 in cocoa, 1,740 in Guinea grass, 15,563 in common pasture, and 94,864 in wood and ruinate. During 1895-96, 1,186 puncheons of rum, 1,348 hogsheads of sugar, and 19,000 cwts. of coffee were produced in this parish, and the rum duties collected amounted to 4,737*l*. The pens for the rearing of cattle (for which there is a demand from the sugar estates) are reported to be doing well, and a country gentleman or farmer in England might, in these hard times, find a pleasant and profitable occupation as the proprietor of a pen or cattle farm in Jamaica. Sir Henry Norman once advocated the rearing of horses for the English cavalry in the Jamaica pens.

The parish or district of Portland recalls the Governorship of the Duke of that name in the early part of the last century. It extends from the sea coast on the north-east, and is bounded inland by the Blue Mountains, including Blue Mountain Peak. Port Antonio, Buff Bay, and Manchioneal are its principal towns or villages, all lying upon the coast at some distance from each other, Manchioneal being the most easterly. Port Antonio has two safe harbours, the westerly one capable of allowing vessels of large tonnage to lie alongside the wharves. From Port Antonio large quantities of fruit are shipped. The Maroon town, called Moore Town, on the banks of the large river the Rio Grande, over which a fine bridge has been erected, which is the longest in the island, and was opened by the Governor,

Sir Henry Blake, in 1892, recalls a time when the Maroons were an important and, at times, a very disagreeable factor in the social condition of the island. They are now peaceable and contented in their township near Buff Bay. They send their children to be educated in the Government Model School. Manchioneal, although possessing only a small harbour, is now an important fruit port. On its grazing properties many cattle and sheep are reared. Its mutton is pronounced to be excellent. Of the 12,708 acres under cultivation, the principal is in ground provisions, with some sugar and coffee. The uncultivated lands comprise 842 acres in Guinea grass, 15,064 in common pasture, 46 in pimento and common pasture, and 79,792 in wood and ruinate.

St. Mary contains Port Maria, Annotto Bay, and Oracabessa, which has recently sprung up as the result of the banana trade together with its having a good harbour. Annotto Bay is at the mouth of the Wag Water River, which name is explained to be a corruption of Agualta. There are three rivers running through the town of Annotto Bay. It has a fine church and some good public buildings. On going from Kingston to Annotto Bay, the Government gardens at Castleton should be visited. Sugar (and whenever this is mentioned, rum is also inferred), coffee, and cocoa are grown, and there is the usual large proportion of pasture, wood, and ruinate in this parish.

That part of the country now called the parish of St. Ann is a very productive and beautiful district. It has its hills and valleys, pastures and pimento groves. St. Ann's Bay is a town and port where considerable trade is carried on. The Spanish adventurers, coming to the north side of the island, were particularly attracted by the country of which St. Ann's Bay is the port. Here again, the fruit business to the United States is carried on. Close to St. Ann's Bay, just a trifle to the west, is 'Sevilla Nueva,' or, as it is now marked on the maps, 'Seville,' the original Spanish capital of the island, founded in 1509. There are still traces in this historic town of the earliest settlers. Slightly to the eastward is Drax Hall, where Christopher's Cove is situated, reputed to be the spot on which Columbus stranded two of his vessels on his last visit. Between St. Ann's Bay and one of the other principal ports of the district, namely, Ocho Rios, on the north side of the island, are the large Roaring River Falls. Roaring River is private property, but the Falls can be seen by any visitor on request. The town and port of Ocho Rios, a modern version of its old name, the 'Bay of the Waterfalls,' lies on the coast, a few miles east of St. Ann's Bay. It is becoming better known as a port of call. This part of the coast is known as the place where Cromwell's soldiers expelled the last of the Spaniards. Brown's Town, on the western extremity of the parish of St. Ann, verging on Trelawny, is a prosperous township. Its new market was opened by Sir Henry Norman. Dry Harbour, quite to the west of St. Ann's Bay, and called by this name because of its having no fresh-water springs or wells, is also to be noted for the number of trading vessels visiting its excellent harbour. There are also other interesting points, especially Moneague, with its handsome and comfortable hotel ready for the refreshment of man and beast. Sugar and rum, coffee and pimento, are grown largely in this parish. Bananas and oranges are now also important productions.

Trelawny derives its name from Governor Sir William Trelawny, who died in the island in 1772. Falmouth is its principal town and port, lying considerably to the westward, and near to St. James. The Court House of Falmouth is one of the largest and most splendid buildings of the island. It contains several portraits of former Governors. The Baptist Chapel, built by the exertions of the Rev. William Knibb, whose name is so well known in connection with Emancipation times, is one of the principal erections in the town, and bears its testimony to the religious movements of the past. The channel in the harbour is rather complicated and care is necessary to avoid the coral reefs. There are a number of towns in this parish, with a large number of sugar estates, and a particularly large area sown in Guinea grass. Altogether Trelawny is a very productive and valuable agricultural portion of the island.

St. James, still farther to the west on the north side, is a small parish, but it contains a very important town and port, Montego Bay. The position of this port is such that it attracts a large proportion of the trade of the island. A glance at the map will show at once this position. From Montego Bay Point the coast comes sharply down some distance, and in the indentation or corner thus caused, before the coast bends away again westward, Montego Bay is situated looking directly westward, the coast on the left in Hanover, with some irregularities, narrowing to the westward end of the island. Montego or Manteca Bay suggests the boiling of hogs' flesh into lard, and recalls the early domination of the wild pigs in Jamaica. The town has a supply of excellent water, and a company has been formed for the erection of an hotel, the building of which is proceeding; an electric light company has also been formed. The principal productions of St. James are sugar, rum, and coffee. The bay is an open roadstead. Like all the.

MONTEGO BAY.

principal towns of Jamaica, it has its convenient and extensive market. It is bounded on the west by the Great River, falling into the sea at the west of Montego Bay.

Hanover is also a very small parish, its principal town and port being Lucea. This parish is noted for the extent of its business in yams, formerly largely shipped for the use of the emigrants to Colon. Lucea is as healthy as it is attractive in natural scenery. The sea breeze is especially refreshing. Its harbour is a very good one, on the north-west corner of the island. Lucea is a favourite residential place, and has all the advantages of a sanatorium. The parish comprises Green Island, which is a port at the end of the island facing the west. The parish is mountainous, the Dolphin Head being a mark for mariners. The district is a productive one, sugar, rum, pimento, arrowroot, ground provisions and pasture occupying the usual proportion of the acreage.

Westmoreland is on the western end of the island and extends round the southern coast until it reaches its principal port, Savanna-la-Mar. In 1744 the town was devastated by a hurricane, and the sea swept over it, causing great destruction. There are many sugar estates in Westmoreland, to which Savanna-la-Mar affords a commercial centre. In the town itself is a handsome drinking fountain and horse trough, presented by Mr. E. J. Sadler, as well as a commodious market which was opened by Sir Henry Blake in 1892. Besides this town, Bluefields should be mentioned, the site of an old Spanish town. It was here that Gosse the naturalist lived when he resided in the island. There are many rivers and streams, including the Great River, which comes right into Westmoreland from near Montego Bay, and the Cabaritta River, which is navigable for some miles. Westmoreland also produces rum, coffee, and ginger, in addition to which there are many grazing pens, and the cutting and export of logwood is also carried on to a large extent. In the higher lands of the parish coffee is grown.

St. Elizabeth, the next parish on the southern side going eastwards from Westmoreland, is an important district both for its size and population. It has 471 square miles and 63,000 people. Black River is the principal town and port. This contains an interesting old church and other well-adapted public buildings, with of course the market place, where so much of the activity of the Jamaica population finds a means of expression. In this parish is situated 'Accompong,' the most important township in the island belonging to the Maroons. It is of very varied formation, containing level ground and mountains. The Santa Cruz Mountains go from north to south, ending in a precipice, known as the 'Lover's Leap,' rising 1,600 feet above the sea. These mountains have a dry and regular temperature, and the atmosphere is particularly invigorating and healthy. The parish contains a very fine area for raising cattle and horses. The Black River is one of its most noticeable features, not only for its alligators, but being navigable for a part of its course, is a good means of transport. The savannahs in this parish are greatly dependent on rain for their fertility, and in favourable seasons much corn is grown. The usual island productions, such as sugar, rum, coffee &c., are here to be observed, whilst large quantities of logwood are exported.

Manchester, named after the Duke of Manchester, who was governor for twenty-one years from 1808, is an interesting parish with aspects especially recalling agricultural towns in England. Its chief town is called Mandeville, from the second title of the dukedom; it is remarkably picturesque, being on the top of a hill and situated about the centre of the parish. Miss Roy's lodgings, where Mr. Froude stopped, and the Waverley Hotel are favourite resorts of visitors from England and America. The oranges of Manchester are a revelation to those accustomed to that fruit in England. The life and bustle of the town of Mandeville, with its many prosperous inhabitants engaged in fruit and corn growing and other pursuits, make it a pleasant epitome of Jamaica, while a month in its clear and healthy atmosphere is worth six months in any European resort, where the vital forces are wasted and burnt up over the excitement of gambling tables. Besides the articles already mentioned in connection with other parishes, ginger is produced in Manchester. To the east of Mandeville lies Porus, which for several years was the terminal station of the Jamaica Government Railway.

Clarendon, named after the English Lord Chancellor, who sat in the Long Parliament and afterwards became one of the chief ministers of the Restoration, is the next parish in this order of enumeration. The name of the historian of the Great Rebellion is one of the numerous links that connect the Colony with the stirring home events of the seventeenth century. Chapelton, a town of considerable commercial importance situated to the north of the Mocho Mountains, is the trading centre of the interior of this parish, which also contains the old district of Vere near the coast. In the shipping port of Carlisle Bay the Colonial forces repulsed the French under Du Casse in 1694 and sent them to their ships with heavy loss. The bow of Ulysses was in good working order on that occasion. Milk River runs into the sea through this parish, and a little way inland above this shipping-place is Milk River Bath, near the 'Rest,' a village on the river bank. The warm springs of the 'Bath' are good for rheumatism. Mineral deposits have been traced in Clarendon. The hills in the interior contain the locations of many small settlers. The parish, especially in the district of Vere, contains a number of sugar estates. The Rio Minho takes a devious course from the upper part of the parish and flows into the sea just to the west of Carlisle Bay. Coffee plantations and grazing pens are also to be found in this district.

St. Catherine, called after the Queen of Charles II., is another memorial of Stuart-Restoration times. Here are Spanish Town, Old Harbour, and Linstead. Near Old Harbour is the old church where settlers who came with Penn and Venables are buried. Linstead is in a hollow encircled by mountains. It is a thriving place for marketing and trade. Driving from Spanish Town to Linstead the visitor passes through Bog Walk, probably the most picturesque piece of scenery in the island, steep mountains on either side forming a long ravine, down which the Rio Cobre runs. The richness and variety of the vegetation in this famous spot are unsurpassed. It is one of those natural beauties of which Jamaica does well to be proud. The Rio Cobre discharges itself by Kingston Harbour near Passage Fort, where the English landed in their conquest of the island. Port Henderson with its mineral spring, Rodney's 'Look-out,' the Apostles' Battery, the Quarantine Station (Green Bay), and Fort Augusta are all in the vicinity. The Lazaretto is at the mouth of Kingston Harbour, on a cliff. It has an extent of ground of ten acres. It contains facilities for excellent sea-bathing, fishing, and other seaside amusements. The views are particularly good. At the same time

LINSTEAD, JAMAICA.

it is to be hoped that none of the readers of this book will be kept at the Quarantine Station by necessity and superior force, but will be able to visit it from choice.

We have thus obtained a passing glimpse of the various districts of the island, on both sides of the Blue Mountains, from Kingston and St. Thomas in the east to Hanover and Westmoreland in the west. We have noticed their characteristic productions, their various industries, their natural features, their numerous harbours. The corn fields and the cane fields, the coffee plantations and the cattle farms, suggest a mixture of the temperate and the tropical, a reproduction of English agricultural life bathed in the light and warmth of the tropics. The churches, chapels, schools and mission houses speak eloquently of the religious life of the people. The hospitals are witnesses of the care which is taken of the sick and needy. The Jamaica planter of the old magnificent days has passed away, but there is still the open door and the friendly welcome, showing that the old spirit of hospitality has not been killed by changing circumstances, while the municipal, or to speak, perhaps, more correctly, the parochial organisations show that the duty of attending to public affairs is recognised and efficiently performed. An interesting picture truly of what Jamaica is at the present moment—a suggestion of what she might become in the future when her resources are fully developed, and her utmost capacity of production utilised.

There is an excellent coast service. The steamer leaves Kingston every alternate Tuesday for both the eastern and western route, and these steamers make direct communication with the New York steamers.

For inland travelling the main roads are good, some of them being decidedly better than others for driving or horseback. From Kingston the main road goes right round the eastern end of the island, passing through the various port towns in succession until it reaches Annotto Bay, whence the junction road strikes across the island and connects the north side with Kingston. Leaving Annotto Bay the road runs to Ocho Rios, where the two sides of the island are again connected by way of Moneague, and then strikes east through Linstead and Spanish Town. From Ocho Rios the road runs close to the coast to Falmouth. Falmouth is also connected with the interior by the great interior road commencing at Moneague and passing through St. Ann and Trelawny. Continuing westward from Falmouth, Montego Bay is reached, whence a road branches off. A road from Montego Bay crosses the island, branches terminating at Savanna-la-Mar and Black River. From Montego Bay the western road goes to Lucea and Green Island—from Lucea striking across to Savanna-la-Mar. From this place it continues along the coast to Black River, and passing into the interior finally reaches Kingston. There is a main road from the Bog Walk Station across the island to Port Maria. Full details of travelling by railway, mail coaches, or hired carriages need not be given here. They can best be obtained locally, or from the 'Jamaica Handbook.'

The ascent of Blue Mountain Peak was formerly very difficult, but a good riding road has been constructed at the expense of Governor Sir Henry Norman. Leaving Kingston in early morning the Peak is reached before dark. Visitors, who are recommended to bring rugs, blankets, and refreshments, sleep in a hut which has been erected on the Peak, the keys of which hut are kept at the house of Mr. Duval at Gordon Town. After the enjoyment of the early morning on the Peak, the return journey on horseback can be leisurely pursued, carriages being available from Gordon Town.

One favourite excursion is from Kingston to Flamstead; carriages are available to the gardens, about 1,000 feet above the sea level; then, mounted on ponies, the hill is ascended. A wide prospect of country is enjoyed on the way to Flamstead, which is 4,000 feet above the sea level. The temperature gradually becomes lower as the height increases. Life takes a keener edge up these tropical heights. Port Royal can be seen, with the stretch of Palisades (along which not very many people have ridden, the communication between Port Royal and Kingston being by boat), and in the distance are Fort Augusta and the Twelve Apostles. On the northern coast Falmouth and Montego Bay should be visited. With the exception of Kingston, they are the busiest ports of the island. This was apparently part of Trollope's eastern tour, going across the island from Kingston to Annotto Bay, hence to Port Antonio, and through Portland and St. Thomas back to Kingston. In his western trip he went through Spanish Town and then westward by the northern road, passing on his way through the Bog Walk and then over Mount Diablo, near which is now the railway station at Ewarton. Trollope stops for a moment to philosophise upon the selfishness of the devil in taking to himself some of the loveliest points of scenery in the world. He (the Post Office official, not the other gentleman) much admired the view from Mount Diablo. The route led through the parish of St. Ann, on the northern coast of which are St. Ann's Bay, Ocho Rios, and Dry Harbour. The pens and sugar estates in St. Ann's present the most characteristic and attractive features of Jamaica life. Then

Trelawny with Falmouth for its port, and St. James with Montego Bay. Going still farther west, the extreme end of the island is reached through the parishes of Hanover and Westmoreland, the latter, as previously stated, being a very important sugar district. Then back to Kingston through St. Elizabeth, Manchester, and Clarendon. With hospitable houses open at every stopping-place on the route, good living, cheerful society, and comfortable beds, the traveller must be hard to please if he does not enjoy himself on his tour through Jamaica.

The latest visitor who has written an account of some scenes in the centre of the island is Mr. Froude. All readers will remember the glowing account he gave of Mandeville in Manchester. Mandeville from Kingston can nearly be reached by railway, the nearest station being Williamsfield, four miles distant. The English character of the town is noticeable. The parish church, parsonage, and school-house, the common, the farmhouses, the few shops, the blacksmith's forge, all are suggestive of English life and occupations. Miss Roy's lodging-house is a comfortable place in which to spend a few days. The temperature at Mandeville is ten degrees less than in Kingston. The air is exquisitely pure, and the oranges of the district particularly good. The park-like aspect of the country is grateful to the eyes of the English traveller for its similarity to the scenery at home.

If the visitor has friends among the officers at Newcastle he will have good escort from Kingston to that famous military station up high in the hills. The appearance of the streets through which the buggy passes is not particularly attractive, but getting out into the suburbs, where there are detached villas with cool-looking green

verandahs and pleasant gardens, the prospect improves. The hedgerows are of prickly cactus, which grows ten or fifteen feet high, and are an effective defence against trespassers. A two hours' drive from Kingston brings one to a halting place called the Gardens at Gordon Town, a kind of halfway house to Newcastle. Horses are here substituted for wheels. 'The scenery throughout the drive to Gordon Town,' said the late Lady Brassey, 'had been lovely, but just here the foliage on either side of the River Hope (from which the water supply of Kingston is derived) was superb. The effect of the great, broad-leaved, light-green bananas among the palms and the ferns on the other side of the river was wonderful; while the stream itself, rushing and brawling, and forming miniature cascades at the bottom, was in places almost hidden by great bushes of datura (or pondiflora, as they call them here and in Chili) completely covered with large trumpet-shaped fragrant flowers of the purest white.' On resuming the journey on horseback, wraps or waterproofs should be carried for protection against the sudden storms of rain which surprise the traveller. Getting wet through, the work of a minute without any protection, may mean fever or ague. Still proceeding in one never-ending ascent, which at times looks very perilous, the road often a mere ledge round the hills, overlooking fearful declivities, the principal danger is from the road being weakened by heavy rains. At 4,130 feet the camp is reached, and the rows of white huts are seen. The prospect from Newcastle excites the enthusiasm of all travellers. A wide expanse of mountainous region rugged with sharp declivities and deep ravines, or rounded and undulating, all covered with the most varied vegetation. Lying far below are Kingston, the bay, and a stretch of coast. On moonlight nights the view is perhaps more enchanting than in the blaze of sunlight. An excursion up Catherine's Peak (so called, it is said, from the name of the lady who first ascended it) may follow. Still higher is the central ridge of the Blue Mountains in all its massiveness and grandeur, the highest peak being generally invisible owing to the clouds and mist. Whilst in these upper regions, the fern walk, with all the marvellous variety of fronds, is another example of the multiformity of tropical nature. In these elevated places the finest coffee and cinchona are grown. A barbecue, which up in the hills has nothing to do with pigs, is a house for drying the coffee and getting it ready for market. The cultivation of cinchona has only been recently introduced into Jamaica. The story of how cinchona derived its name from its having been the means of curing the Countess of Cinchon from fever, is too well known to need recapitulation at length. It promises to be a thriving industry upon the sides of the Blue Mountains.

Bog Walk (a corruption of *boca de agua*, or water's mouth) may now be reached by railway. It is the next station to Spanish Town on the Ewarton line. The late Lady Brassey drove the five miles from Spanish Town to Bog Walk. She thus describes her impressions: 'Imagine everything that makes scenery lovely—wood, rock, water, and the wildest luxuriance of tropical foliage, mingled and arranged by the artistic hands of Nature in one of her happiest moods; and then picture all this surrounded by lofty and abrupt precipices, with a background of the most brilliant blue, illuminated by the brightest of suns (the heat of which on the present occasion was tempered by a gentle breeze which rippled the surface of the river). The Bog Walk is a gorge through which the Rio Cobre flows towards the sea. As we passed out, the sides of the ravines became less precipitous, and were clothed with all kinds of tropical trees, such as the sloth, bread fruit and bamboos, besides vast quantities of flowering orchids.' The Princes are not so enthusiastic, simply comparing it to a Welsh valley, and noticing that the bamboos grouped themselves like Prince of Wales's feathers.

From the Bog Walk, Lady Brassey drove to Linstead, and enjoyed the sight of the market which was being held, purchased oranges at twopence per dozen, delicious mangoes at fourpence a dozen, and pine apples at twopence each. Leaving Linstead, her ladyship had a long hot drive to Moneague, passing many carts loaded with oranges. She had gone through the pass of Mount Diablo to Moneague (or mountain of water), and thus well named, 'for it is completely surrounded by clear streams.' The inn's garden 'was full of tropical foliage, plants of the usual gorgeous reds, yellows, and browns, interspersed with the creamy spikes of the ginger plant, the shell-like blossoms of the Alpinia, and the snowy stars of various kinds of jessamine; while blue and scarlet ipomæas and wax-like stephanotis climbed and twined all over and about the rough fence that surrounded the little plot.' From Moneague the drive was resumed through the vale of St. Thomas. The fields of Guinea grass are observed, and the story is repeated of the accidental introduction of the seeds of this grass from the coast of Guinea in 1744. They were sent as food for parrots which had been forwarded from Guinea to Jamaica. The birds died, the seeds were thrown away, they took root and spread, and became in time a most important factor in the prosperity of the island Her ladyship had, too, a pitiful feeling over the well-known story of the cow who, neglecting the rich grass underneath, choked herself with an orange from a tree. In brilliant moonlight Lady Brassey passed through the Gully Road, and endeavours to describe its fantastic beauty: 'The variety of scenic effects was endless. Sometimes the rocks so nearly met over our heads that they formed a thick roof.' Then the Gully became more open, filled with most fantastic shadows. Leaving this scene of enchanting beauty, the carriage sped on to the town of eight streams—Ocho Rios— and thence to Belmont, where her ladyship and party passed the night. They drove by the coast road back to Ocho Rios in the morning, and embarked on board the 'Sunbeam,' which was waiting at that port. Thus concluded one of the most memorable excursions across Jamaica, which could not fail to leave the most pleasant impressions and fill the mind with pictures which could never lose their colour, freshness, and beauty.

Columbus gave a new world to Spain—but not to Spain alone. Great Britain has shared in the results of these discoveries, and the fortunes of these possessions have become intertwined with the main lines of British history. The voyages of Columbus are probably, when viewed from this period of time, among the most important events that distinguished the early years of colonisation. The idea that Cuba was the extreme eastern point of the Asiatic continent seems unacceptable now, but in this impression lies the origin of the name of the West Indies. Columbus, when he arrived, was received by the aboriginal inhabitants of Jamaica with welcome. An eclipse of the moon was the foundation of his influence over the natives. After various adventures he seems to have maintained his ground. Diego Columbus, the son of the great discoverer, was confirmed in the government of these territories. Diego's marriage with a great lady in Spain extended, so far as regards his connections at court, his practical influence regarding the Indies. When he was at Hayti, the adventure he entrusted to Esquivel will be remembered. Peter Martyr's connection with Jamaica is also to be noticed, although perhaps personally he had little to do with the island. The early Spanish discoverers endeavoured to find locations in Jamaica, and many interesting traces are found at the present day of the manner in which they lived and worked. Upon these matters of earlier history the work of Sir Hans Sloane, who accompanied the Duke of Albemarle, the Governor of the Colony in 1687, may be consulted. It is quite clear that after the arrival of Columbus, for many years, the difficulties were with the aboriginal population. There is no doubt that for a long period the island was in Spanish occupation; and although Spain committed many cruelties, she carried out her principles of empire in a way that may enlighten, and probably shock, the conscience of the nineteenth century. At all events, we have here the discovery by the Spaniards, the early occupation by them, the manner in which they treated the natives, the real desire to establish themselves, and form, in these islands of the New World, the reproduction of what they were acquainted with in the Old—all these points are to be noted, and their contemplation brings about a feeling of admiration at the adventurous spirit of those who were thus the pioneers of empire, however some of the records may appear to be stained with unnecessary cruelties and with blood uselessly spilled. Even the English, perhaps, would have pursued a similar course, for in America the red man has disappeared before the white, and the location of the Maoris in New Zealand has been confined to native forests and to primitive areas outside the influences of what may be called, for want of a better term, the boundaries of civilisation.

No doubt, then, the original Spanish occupation of the West Indies may be condemned in regard to some of its incidents by the modern conscience, but it is recorded as an historical fact that Jamaica was sighted first on its north side near Dry Harbour by Columbus in his second voyage, May 1494, as he was coming eastwards from Cuba. Then the proceedings of Juan de Esquivel, who was sent by Diego from Hispaniola to take possession of Jamaica in opposition to Alonza d'Ojeda, have to be noted. Sevilla Nueva can still be traced in fragmentary indications on Seville Estate. The account of Peter Martyr, the abbot of Seville in Jamaica (although it is not clear whether he ever actually resided in the island), might be referred to for particulars of its earlier history. Following the establishment of the Spaniards in the island, there is no need to record in detail the careers of the Spanish governors; or how the freebooters compelled the Spaniards to retire more into the interior, and collect themselves in the town of St. Jago de la Vega, known since as Spanish Town. Of all places in the British West Indies, probably this town bears the greatest traces of the original Spanish occupation. The visitor who looks upon the square as it now stands is reminded of old colonial Spain. The town gave the title of Marquis de la Vega to the grandson of Columbus when he gave up his hereditary rights in the New World for a home pension. In the beginning of the seventeenth century Portugal became interested in Jamaica, and at this time the Jewish emigration from Europe began to exercise an influence upon the island. In 1597 an English buccaneer visited Jamaica and committed some ravages. Some years later Colonel Jackson landed with 500 men at Passage Fort. He plundered Spanish Town, and, as it would seem, laid the foundation of the British conquest, which was effected later. In these early times, swine were produced, and their lard was an article of export. The grazing facilities of the island are also suggested by the fact that hides were exported. Indeed, hides were probably the first of the articles exported from the island. The native woods were also utilised for commerce. Fruits were grown, but not to any great extent. Of sugar and tobacco there was at this early time very little, but maize or Indian corn was familiar to the settlers. On the plain of Liguanea thousands of cattle and horses fed on the rich grass. In the districts to the east, the Yallahs, there were vast herds of cattle. Morant abounded in hogs and horned cattle. But in those days large portions of the island were uninhabited, and roads or other means of communication were few and far between. The historian Gardner says there was a settlement at Porus, and a Spanish Well may still be seen there. Some copper was found in the Healthshire hills, from which it is said church bells were cast. The result of the Spanish occupation was, that industries were established in isolated districts, principally of a simple, agricultural character, but no real homogeneous interest was created to form, if the word may be consistently used in this connection, the backbone of a new country.

In the meantime what became of the original inhabitants? Jamaica was not the home of the fierce Caribs, although these latter made incursions from South America. Esquivel treated the natives with great humanity; his example was not followed, for of the 60,000 to 100,000 Indians no descendants existed in 1655. The coppercoloured native denizens of the Jamaica woods (Arawaks)

G

are described as a beautiful race, although the nose was flat and wide, and the compression of the forehead led to an undue elevation of the back part of the head. When Columbus saw them on the coast on his arrival, he was struck with the absence of clothing and the variety of paint. They dwelt in primitive habitations covered with palm leaves, and slept in hammocks made from the twine of the cotton tree. Plates on which to dry cassava constituted their principal culinary requisite. They were acquainted with the potato, cassava, and maize. Fruit, fish, and birds were also part of their food, and even a lizard (the iguana) was not despised. The Spaniards were astonished at the practice of smoking tobacco, and when tubes were attached to the nostrils, the inhalation having naturally an immediate or early effect, the consequence was not particularly graceful or æsthetic. It must be added that the agricultural ideas of the native Indians were of the most elementary character. They were not bad fishermen. They could use the hook or manage the harpoon with great dexterity. Now and then the natives found gold in a rapid stream, but nothing beyond personal adornment (or disfigurement, according to taste) came of the discovery. They were ruled by chieftains or caciques, but little is known of the authority thus exercised and the legislation thus propounded. Books on Mexico, with their half-mythical and highly coloured stories, suggest a magnificence on the South American continent which is absent from the local records of the West India Islands.

An idea of the Spanish occupation has thus been obtained, with its leading aspects of conquest, pride, profit, and (it must be confessed) hardship to native races. It might be thought that if Englishmen instead of Spaniards had been the adventurous pioneers, things would have been different, and the native Indians have been now a flourishing race. But who knows? European ideas of humanity in a particular century are pretty much the same. And modern civilisation is perhaps as ruthless, working, no doubt, in different methods, as the old sword of Imperial Spain.

After the Spanish occupation, the next historical point is connected with Cromwell. The last word has not yet been said about Cromwell's administration. Opinions differ now as they did in Dryden's time, and the sentiments of the 'Heroic Stanzas consecrated to the Memory of his Highness' and the greatly different views put forward by the same author in the 'Astræa Redux' are represented in contemporary literary discussion. At all events, there was no 'horrid stillness' to invade the ear. The foreign policy of the Protector was undoubtedly vigorous, and his Colonial policy was equally peremptory. On May 3, 1494, Jamaica was discovered by Columbus. For 161 years it was in Spanish occupation, and an English expedition, under Admiral Penn and General Venables, obtained possession of the island on May 11, 1655, after their failure at St. Domingo. No great confidence was felt in the above leaders. Political feeling ran so high that Penn and Venables were committed to the Tower on their return home. The pen of Milton was employed to set forth the wrongs endured by Englishmen in the West Indies. Religious principles were advanced in opposition to the Spaniards. Barbados and other islands sent volunteers in aid of the English forces. St. Domingo was the original destination of the expedition; but through the blundering of the leaders and disease among the men, the demonstration against that island failed. On May 3, 1655, the British fleet rounded Port Royal (then called Caguaya) and anchored off Passage Fort. The weakness of Venables and the suffering of the troops are important elements of this story. On May 11 capitulation was agreed upon. Subsequently alterations were made in the command. The soldiers found themselves in a very sorry plight. The Spanish Governor of the island was Don Arnoldi Sasi. He was a respectable old gentleman, but not quite quick enough to deal with a serious situation. The consequence was that the English troops took possession of the island. These troops were badly served, being on one occasion forty-eight hours without provisions. The swamps near Passage Fort, the want of food, clothing, and medicine, were telling on their health. Both Penn and Venables, the admiral and the general, were, as above stated, imprisoned for the manner in which they had conducted the expedition. But the fact remains that the island became, as a consequence of their operations, a British possession.

When Cromwell knew of the repulse at St. Domingo and the capture of Jamaica, he took measures to confirm the possession of the island. Colonel Edward D'Oyley, who commanded the troops on the death of General Fortescue, was appointed President of what was probably the first Executive or Legislative Assembly called together in Jamaica under British rule. It was in 1660, when the news arrived of the Restoration, that the English official record of the island took a new development. General D'Oyley in 1660 is the first Governor recognised in the official list. Then followed a number of Governors, all engaged in settling matters, providing means of justice, and generally laying down the foundations of English rule. The first General Assembly was held in the island under Lord Windsor's administration, Sir Charles

Lyttelton being Deputy-Governor, in 1664. The meeting took place in a building in the town originally founded by Diego Columbus, St. Jago de la Vega, known since as Spanish Town. The arrival of Sir Thomas Modyford from Barbados, bringing with him 1,000 settlers, as Governor in 1666 (the 'Annus Mirabilis' of Dryden) is the next important event recorded. Political questions, especially in relation to finance, arose. Quarrels of a deplorable character, and in one case with fatal results, took place. A member was imprisoned for not returning to the House of Assembly when directed by the Speaker. Sir Thomas Modyford, no doubt getting tired of local dissensions, commissioned the privateers of the Caribbean Sea to engage in acts of war against the Spaniards in the West Indies. The order was given and the work of pillage was begun, but Sir Thomas was ordered home, and no doubt thought himself very badly treated for doing what he could against the traditional enemies of his country. In 1671 the planting industry of the island was, after many struggles, fairly established. Probably no one can realise now the aspirations of these early settlers, the difficulties they had to contend against, or the heart-breaking results which too often followed. In 1675 a number of the inhabitants of Surinam came to Jamaica. In 1678 the Assembly was in opposition to the Governor on the question of finance. England at that time wanted to get the utmost profit out of the Colonies, in the form of direct Imperial revenues, duties on produce, and facilities in connection with home manufacturing industries. In fact, the mercantile or Colonial system established by Cromwell was being developed. In 1687 the Duke of Albemarle arrived as Governor, bringing with him as his medical attendant Dr. Hans Sloane, whose observation as a naturalist is recorded in one of the most beautiful books connected with the island. Under the reign of the Duke political matters became very excited, as may be inferred from the fact that one of the members of Assembly was fined 600*l.* for saying that the voice of the people was the supreme law. In due course of time the news respecting James II. and the assumption of William and Mary reached the island. The Earl of Inchiquin, who arrived in 1690, was not more successful as Governor than many of his predecessors. Freebooters, owing to the war with France, were particularly active. Rich prizes were brought into Port Royal, a place then described as the 'richest spot in the universe;' ruined, however, by the earthquake which so soon after occurred. The year 1693 was an anxious time, especially when the fleet of Admiral Du Casse came in sight, and his men ravaged some of the districts of the island. But, as already recorded, the marauders were met by the Colonial Militia at Carlisle Bay and sent to their ships. In 1702 war was again raging between England and France. Admiral Benbow encountered Du Casse, but after an engagement the former died of his wounds in Kingston. His monument in the church has been already described.

It might be permissible here, as the earthquake of 1692, which destroyed Port Royal, was one of the most important events in the island's historical records, to quote Gardner's account of that occurrence. 'The day was exceedingly sultry, the sky glowed like a furnace, and the ocean was unruffled by a single breath of air. The harbour was well filled with ships. The Legislative Council had adjourned. At twenty minutes to twelve o'clock, a noise not unlike thunder was heard in the hills of St. Andrews, to the north of Port Royal; then three shocks were felt, the last being very severe. Not only did the earth tremble, and in some parts open beneath the feet of the terror-stricken inhabitants, but the horrors of the event were intensified by the mysterious, awful sounds that at one moment appeared to be in the air and then in the ground. Houses built by the seaside were the first to fall. Morgan's Fort, to which many fled as a place of security, was next observed to disappear, the sea rolling completely over the place where it stood. The wharfs loaded with merchandise, and most of the fortifications, together with all the streets near the shore, sank into the harbour and were completely overwhelmed. For three weeks successive shocks were felt. The heat was insupportable, for the usual sea breeze failed to come. In different parts of the island, especially in St. Andrews, the severity of the shock was experienced. The courses of rivers were changed, old springs disappeared, and new ones burst out.'

The above account of the great earthquake, quoted directly from Gardner, is really founded, as he acknowledges, upon the works of Sloane and Long. It must not be assumed that Jamaica, any more than other countries, is peculiarly subject to earthquakes. The very importance attached to this one in 1692 shows that such convulsions are rare, and need not be feared by the most timid traveller.

In this hurried review of Jamaica history, we are brought down to the end of the seventeenth century. From the date of the Treaty of 1671, by which the English possession of the island was confirmed by Spain, sugar grew to be a most extensive industry. The eighteenth century was remarkable for the productive development of the island. Its early years were characterised by violent controversies, especially as to passing a permanent Revenue Bill. The Duke of Portland, who died in 1726, was succeeded by Major-General Hunter, and under the administration of the latter the permanent revenue was granted and the question for the time set at rest.

For a number of years the Maroons had caused anxiety by their depredations and warlike habits. These people, the result of the intermixture of races at the time of the old Spanish occupation, under an able leader named Cudjoe, became very formidable about the year 1734. Military operations against them were difficult, because they were so familiar with the mountainous region. But a conciliatory policy was adopted by Governor Trelawny in 1738 ; special districts for settlements were assigned to the Maroons, and a very serious danger to the general peace and security of the Colony was thus averted, although only for a time, as on several occasions later on these wild mountaineers gave much trouble.

Quarrels between the Executive and the Assembly broke out again about 1750. The Legislature assumed rights in passing Bills which trenched upon the prerogative of the Crown. Another source of disagreement was the proposal for the Legislature to meet in Kingston. The Assembly seemed, at this period, to be in a perpetual state of dissolution, and the height to which political feeling rose may be judged from the fact that Governor Knowles was burnt in effigy.

The slave insurrection of 1760 pointed to another danger to which the island was subject. Negro slaves had been imported in large numbers from Africa, and the manner in which they combined and fought considerably taxed the power of the authorities in coping with them. The rebels seized the arms and ammunition at Port Maria. Much blood was shed on both sides in this deplorable outbreak, which at first rapidly extended in area. Murders of whites occurred in different parts of the island. The rebellion was ultimately suppressed, many who took part in it were killed in the field, and 600 were transported to Honduras and sold to the logwood cutters.

In 1762 the war between England and Spain allowed an expedition to be despatched from Port Royal, resulting in the capture of Havana and much booty and prizes. In 1777 there was another outbreak of the slaves, the discovery of a far-reaching conspiracy among them causing great alarm. In 1778, when war was declared against France, the latter country having recognised the United States, Jamaica armed herself with great spirit against an expected attack by the French fleet under D'Estaing. But it was in 1782 that the principal event in the history of these wars occurred. The French fleet, under De Grasse, was on its way to join the Spanish fleet in a combined attack upon Jamaica, when the great battle took place off Dominica which saved the Colony and added much to the lustre of British empire in these seas. Home politics (in England) were divided as to this expedition. But Rodney went to Barbados through storm and stress. He was even followed by a command from the Home Government to strike his flag and come home. That order he providentially never received, and the critical, the 'epoch-making' battle was won. De Grasse, when he came from Martinique, thought that the whole New World was before him, and that England was to be deprived of these possessions. It was a question of Imperial interest, for matters connected with the Empire were fought out in these seas, and the existence of England as a great naval power was at stake. England, of course, without her navy and her naval stations would be nowhere in the world's contentions and concerns. The 'Ville de Paris' was imagined to be the herald of conquest. The Windward and Leeward Islands were practically in the possession of the French. Only in St. Lucia and Barbados the banner of England flew. From St. Lucia the French fleet was seen by Rodney. For days the fleets were in sight of each other. Broadsides were naturally in the operations that followed. The critical moment of the fight was when a British ship was alongside the 'Ville de Paris,' which ultimately surrendered, and Rodney received the sword of De Grasse on the 'Formidable.' Jamaica, as representing the fact, and it may be said also the principle, of Empire, was saved by his victory. There was great joy among the inhabitants, and the Colony voted Rodney a magnificent sword as well as the famous statue.

In the succeeding years, towards the end of the century, what with fire in different districts, hurricanes, want of food owing to the restriction of trade with America, the dreaded effect of French revolutionary ideas in St. Domingo, the disastrous British expedition against that island, and the very serious anti-slavery discussions which were being raised both in the West Indies and in England, the island was in a depressed and anxious state, which was not improved by another Maroon war. In 1795 there was an expedition against the Maroons. These latter had necessarily the advantage of their settlements in the hills. Ambuscades were frequent, and many English soldiers were shot. The result was that many of the rioters were transported to Nova Scotia. In 1804 there was war against France and Spain. Jamaica was again in a state of alarm. The Colonies had to bear their usual burden of Imperial necessities. Under Nelson the British fleet did their part in resisting the enemy; a victory was gained over the French off St. Domingo, and Port Royal was again made jubilant with prizes. In the early part of 1808 the Duke of Manchester commenced his long rule as Governor. Questions between the Governor and the Legislature arrived again at an acute stage. The Chief Justice was ordered to be 'released from custody,' he having been confined for refusing to attend as a witness before the Assembly in a case which had come under his own judicial cognisance. The Duke of Manchester's government was particularly signalised by the restrictions which were imposed on trade with America. The discussions on the slave trade were continued, and naturally excited the greatest interest and anxiety. The slave code in the island itself was also a matter of debate. The slave population became in a very excited state. Property to a large amount was destroyed. The position was complicated by the quarrels of the Assembly with the Governor. The question seemed to be as to the right of the Assembly to pass laws that were not consistent with Imperial laws, and were assumed to be against the policy of the Government at home. Of course, the slave trade had been abolished in 1806, but the great question of the emancipation of the slaves in the Colonies had become a very urgent one. Twenty millions of pounds sterling were supposed to have been awarded by Parliament in compensation for emancipation. Only about sixteen millions were actually awarded. Lord Mulgrave had closed his career in Jamaica, and Lord Sligo had undertaken the management of affairs, with the assistance of a number of stipendiary magistrates whom he brought with him.

In 1836—that is, in the very middle of the Emancipation and Apprenticeship period—Sir Lionel Smith arrived. The Jubilee of Her Majesty's happy reign was celebrated in Jamaica in 1887. The changes during fifty years were remarkable. An interesting book by Mr. W. A. Feurtado, of Kingston, furnishes particulars of the 'Island story' during that period. It does seem like an old world record that the brig 'Velocity,' Tatem, master, in thirty-nine days from London, with a general cargo consigned to Messrs. Harvey & Darrell, arrived at Kingston on August 2, 1837, bringing the intelligence of the death of William IV. and the accession of Queen Victoria. It was not until seven days later that the steamer 'City of Kingston,' bringing the official intelligence, arrived. The oaths of allegiance to the new Queen were taken on August 11, at King's House, in Spanish Town. The 64th Regiment was paraded in front of the Court House, and Rodney's Temple was surrounded by troops. The principal actor in this scene was Governor Sir Lionel Smith. The paper containing the signatures of the principal inhabitants was read in the portico, and what with the excitement, the loyal cheering, the roll of the guns in salute, the old square in Spanish Town must have been lively that day. Sir Charles (afterwards Lord) Metcalfe was sent in 1839 on a mission of peace, and closed an administration in which reforms were promulgated, in May 1842. During this period the marriage of the Queen (1840) took place. It was announced in the House of Assembly on April 8, 1840, by a message of Sir C. Metcalfe. A humble address was presented by the House of Assembly to the Queen congratulating her upon her marriage, and ' expressing the sanguine expectation that under the blessing of Divine Providence this event will be conducive to your

Majesty's personal happiness, and to the welfare of your Majesty's kingdom at large.' The Earl of Elgin arrived immediately afterwards, and for five years carried on the government. His lordship founded the Royal Agricultural Society, and encouraged many proposals for developing the agricultural resources of the island. The cattle industry had been a very important one, and at this time new breeds were introduced. Railway schemes were projected, and to some extent carried out. But the home legislation of 1846, involving the equalisation of the duties on free-grown and slave-grown sugar, practically put the Colonial productions at a great disadvantage in European markets. The sugar production fell to a point from which it has never recovered. Estates worth their thousands a year became valueless. Some estates that had to go into Chancery because the proprietor was unable to manage them, through incompetence of mind, dwindled away from their thousands of annual income to a position in which they could not pay a small merchant's commission. Many profitable properties were thrown up, and large districts of the Colony returned into bush. The Mother Country had obtained every possible advantage from the Colonies in previous years. The Colonial system simply resulted in Great Britain for 200 years receiving the halfpence, and then distributing the kicks. Coolie immigration was established after many years of struggle, but the system never really throve in Jamaica, although the ten or twelve thousand coolies now in the Colony are probably better off than any body of men in a similar position, and engaged in the like pursuits, in any part of the world. The shrinking of the productive wealth of the Colony led to further controversies between the Assembly and the Council and Executive. Upon these questions of revenue Bills, however exciting they might have been at the time, there is no necessity now to express an opinion. The Assembly thought that they were standing up for their constitutional rights, and the Crown was equally determined to assert its prerogative. The laws of the Imperial Parliament were of course supreme, but the question had been often raised as to the effect in the island itself of a local Act in relation to the power of the Crown, through the Minister in London, to disallow it when it had been passed without a suspensory clause. These matters are, however, rather academic than practical at the present time. They only serve to illustrate the position of a conquered Colony assuming, from the first, representative institutions and the command of its own affairs. In 1853 Sir Henry Barkly commenced a reign which lasted for four years. This gentleman, the son of a West India merchant in London, had been a member of the House of Commons, and was appointed from that body to a Colonial Governorship, that of British Guiana, in 1848. He retained, curiously enough, his seat in the House (for Leominster) until February 1849. His career as Governor, in the different Colonies it became his duty to administer, is interesting as matter of history. He has been a man of 'affairs,' and has taken part in the settlement of many really important questions. When he was in Jamaica in 1853 he endeavoured to utilise the representative institutions he found in existence there, prompted, no doubt, in this course by his experience in the House of Commons. His public speeches in the Colony had a Liberal tendency. He recommended 'a strong Executive Administration, consisting of upright and intelligent men, chosen from among her own citizens.' In point of fact, responsible government was proposed. It was carried out in a modified degree. Those who remember the time between 1853 and 1865 will be able to call to mind a number of able men who had responsible charge of the business of State Departments in the Legislature. In Mr. Eyre's time, from 1862 to 1865, questions as to the power of the Assembly arose (as they had done so frequently before), and there was undoubtedly a good deal of friction. In the meantime Gordon's agitation became important. In October 1865, rioters at Morant Bay openly showed themselves and declared for 'war.' The struggle, which took place in front of the Court House at Morant Bay, was a noteworthy event. The volunteers were overpowered, Captain Hitchins was killed, and the custos of the parish, the curate of Bath, the inspector of police, magistrates, and other white people met with a similar fate. These proceedings alarmed the Colony and fixed the attention of Englishmen at home. The Maroons, under Colonel Fyfe, were called out. Other measures were taken, and within a short time the outbreak was confined within practicable limits. The trial by court-martial of Gordon, and his execution, followed. As soon as the report of these proceedings reached England, the Secretary of State for the Colonies (Mr., afterwards Viscount Cardwell) was approached. He promised in the name of the Government every protection. At that time there was no telegraph. People were anxious for their friends, and all the letters from the Colony were full of the alarm (perhaps exaggerated, but naturally so) which was felt there at the outbreak. Sir Henry Storks was appointed Governor. There was a Royal Commission of Inquiry, consisting of the Governor Sir H. Storks, Mr. Russell Gurney, and Mr. Maule. The panic was so great that the Legislature gave up the island constitution, and Jamaica became a

Crown Colony under Sir John Peter Grant, a former Lieut.-Governor of Bengal, who was appointed Governor in 1866.

It is not desirable to try to kindle dead ashes. The Eyre controversy may be allowed to remain extinct. The prosecution by Mr. John Stuart Mill, on behalf of the Association he represented, the charge of Chief Justice Cockburn, the verdict of the Grand Jury, were the final incidents in an exciting drama. And although it is possible that some injustice may have been done, on one side or the other, the matter has lost its interest. The administration of Sir John Peter Grant was vigorous, and in many respects beneficial. Sir Anthony Musgrave's rule was fairly good, but there was a growing feeling in the Colony that there should be some return to the old system of representative institutions. The scare of the disturbances had passed away. Accordingly, Lord Derby, when Secretary of State for the Colonies in 1884, announced the now famous 'new departure.' This was the institution of a mixed Council, partly elected and partly official, with the Governor in the chair. When closing in November 1888 the first Council constituted under this system, which had lasted nearly its natural term of five years, Governor Sir Henry Norman spoke in high praise of the legislative work which had been done and the public spirit displayed. By a subsequent order in Council (1893) the Governor ceased to be a member of the Legislative Council, and a President was added, to be appointed by the Queen or by the Governor under instructions from Her Majesty, but in the following year a further order was issued replacing the Governor as President, taking away his deliberative vote, and leaving him a casting vote only. In 1895 further alteration took place, and the Council now consists of the Governor as President, the Senior Military

Officer, the Colonial Secretary, the Attorney-General, the Director of Public Works, the Collector-General, and such other persons not exceeding ten in number, together with fourteen unofficial members elected by a fairly low suffrage. Mr. Froude did not approve of this principle of suffrage in the tropical colonies. He preferred the somewhat arbitrary rule of Crown government; but so far as the present constitution has worked, it has undoubtedly been successful.

There is also a Privy Council consisting of officials and members nominated by the Governor, subject to the approval of the Queen. But the Governor may act in opposition to the advice and decision of the Privy Council, reporting his reasons for doing so to the Secretary of State. In cases, therefore, of emergency, such as any question requiring immediate action, or involving the public peace and safety, 'the Captain-General and Governor-in-Chief' is supreme.

The Colony has, therefore, been under four distinct systems of government. First, the military jurisdiction of the opening years of its career as a British possession. Then came the period of general assemblies, which lasted for 200 years (subject, of course, to different modifications). Then in 1866 Crown government, the Legislature consisting exclusively of official and nominated members; and in 1884 the mixed system of official and elected members came into force, and this system is the one which at present exists. For the purpose of election of members to serve on the Council, the island is divided into fourteen electoral districts. The qualification is one of an extremely liberal character—that is, males over twenty-one years of age, who are British subjects or naturalised, or who pay poor rates for a house of 10*s.* annually, or parochial taxes on property of

H

1*l.* 10*s.*, or are in receipt of a salary of 50*l.* a year or upwards, are qualified to vote. The number of voters on the register for 1896-97 was 30,442. The total population in 1891 was returned at 639,491.

The general revenue for the year 1895-96 amounted to 646,103*l.* Of this sum more than half, or 360,886*l.*, was raised by import duties, in accordance with the principle of indirect taxation which prevails in all the Colonies. As might be supposed, the customs tariff is an extensive one, containing about fifty specific duties on provisions and other articles in general use, and an *ad valorem* duty of $12\frac{1}{2}$ per cent. upon all goods unenumerated. There is, however, a fairly good list of exemptions from duty. The next largest item of revenue is the excise duties, amounting to 138,725*l.*, principally on rum manufactured and consumed in the island. Appropriated revenues, such as poor rates and other parochial taxes, are also included in the general revenue of the Colony, and amount to 129,602*l.* The total expenditure for the financial year 1895-96 amounted to 626,934*l.* The charges of debt (interest and sinking fund) run up to the very considerable sum of 102,539*l.*; the public debt being 1,666,177*l.*, of which 763,119*l.* was on account of the railway purchase, reconstruction, and extension, 126,500*l.* on account of the Rio Cobre Canal, 167,220*l.* for the erection of new bridges, and 146,000*l.* for reconstruction and conversion of parochial roads into main roads.

The imports in 1895-96 were valued at 2,288,946*l.* and the exports at 1,873,105*l.*, making together a total trade of 4,162,051*l.* It is interesting to note the countries trading with Jamaica. Thus the United Kingdom sends goods of the value of 1,099,324*l.*, or 48·1 per cent. of the imports ;

JAMAICA. 99

Canada and other British possessions, 196,660*l.*, or about 7·5 per cent.; the United States, 954,783*l.*, or 41·8 per cent.; and other foreign countries, 38,179*l.*, or 2·6 per cent. Of the value of exports above stated, the greater portion was island produce, the small amount of re-exports showing that Jamaica has yet to regain its old importance as an entrepôt of commerce. The proportion of exports to the different countries was, in 1895–96, to the United Kingdom, 27·6, or less than the average per cent.; Canada, 1·6; United States, 57 (a growing proportion); other countries, 13·8. It will thus be noticed that the trade with the United States is of greater bulk and importance than that with the United Kingdom—indeed, more, perhaps, than is represented by the figures; for while the United States offer a better market for sugar and take nearly the whole of the fruit, the Colony is dependent upon them for a large proportion of its food supply. In illustration of this latter point the item of food stuffs may be taken. The United Kingdom sends only 115,000*l.*, British possessions 172,000*l.*, and the United States 493,000*l.*; and the United States take in return the largest proportion of the sugar crop, or 19,000 hogsheads out of a total export of 23,000 hogsheads. The principal items (value in sterling) of island produce exported in 1895–96 are as follows: Sugar, 195,459*l.*; rum, 164,600*l.*; coffee, 284,800*l.* Pimento shows a considerable increase, viz.: 90,046*l.*, as against 84,000*l.* in the previous year. Dyewoods, both in weight and value, are slightly decreasing, their value being 362,322*l.* for 1895–96; but still there are two sides to the question of cutting down trees, because there must naturally be a limit to the industry, unless one tree cut down is immediately replaced by another being planted. The value of fruit exported in 1895–96 (almost entirely to the United

States) was 531,812*l.*, being a great increase upon the previous year, and showing a very wide difference as against 51,316*l.* exported in 1880. Minor items (including ginger) amounted in 1895-96 to 137,920*l.*, which, with 98,089*l.* worth of foreign produce re-exported, brings the total value of exports to 1,873,105*l.* The following is a summary in tabular form of the trade of Jamaica for 1895-96 :—

IMPORTS.

United Kingdom	£1,099,324
British Possessions	196,660
United States	954,783
Other Countries	38,179
Total	£2,288,946

EXPORTS.

United Kingdom	£517,504
British Possessions	47,613
United States	1,067,186
Other Countries	240,802
Total	£1,873,105

For a country with such a large population and so full of agricultural resources as Jamaica, such a small export value is remarkable. It may be added that Jamaica continues to afford a good market for the Manchester cottons and other materials for clothing, no less than 586,563*l.* value of these articles being imported, principally from the United Kingdom, from whence also the hardware and furniture principally come.

Of the smaller exports from Jamaica, there are 7,648*l.* worth of tobacco and cigars, only 388*l.* of horse kind, and no cattle. Now, surely there must be a big future for all these industries, if only the necessary enterprise, by means of emigration from England and the United States, were brought to bear. Other facts may also be noted. Sugar is not an increasing industry, nor does coffee cultivation appear to be rapidly extending—in both of these particulars there is great room for supplying in a much larger degree the ever-increasing demand for these two important articles of food of the world's consumption. No doubt, an improvement in the quality of the cane from which the sugar is extracted is a matter that demands attention, although experiments seem to show that the old Bourbon cane is probably the best. The propagation of sugar cane from seed, so likely to result in an improved plant, is referred to in another chapter. Mr. Fawcett, the Director of the Botanic Gardens, says that it is alleged the rum distillers permit the molasses, when diluted, to spontaneously ferment, instead of adding yeast to promote fermentation. 'It is computed that about forty per cent. of the sugar used is lost in the process through its conversion into other bodies than alcoholic and carbonic acid during the prolonged fermentation.' The yeast, of course, would have to be imported and kept sound for use, respecting which there might be some difficulty in a country like Jamaica. With regard to coffee, M. Pasteur, in his report upon the specimens shown at the Colonial and Indian Exhibition, speaks highly of the Blue Mountain coffees, both in appearance and taste. In some coffee-growing districts, better curing houses, better choice of seed, and generally better cultivation, should be adopted. A great deal depends, too, upon the careful manner in which the coffee is finally prepared and packed for market. The fruit industry is the one which has made great strides in recent years, and is likely to be of ever-increasing value. In this case the manner in which it is shipped, whether bananas, pines, or oranges, is of the utmost importance, and requires the greatest care. Otherwise, the fruit would be spoilt, to the disappointment and loss of all parties concerned. Fruit is now being sent to England in cool chambers by the Jamaica Fruit Company, but the experiment cannot be said at present to have been a success. With more experience it is possible that a considerable trade may be established.

With regard to the different industries of the West Indies, the following remarks may be quoted from an interesting address delivered by Dr. D. Morris, C.M.G., before the London Chamber of Commerce, in March 1888 :—'Although the native flora of the West Indies includes many valuable plants, it is remarkable that nearly all the vegetable productions of these islands at present are derived from exotic plants introduced from elsewhere, and kept under cultivation. The sugar cane itself is of Asiatic origin. Its introduction to the West Indies is clearly traceable in historic records. What is called Otaheite cane, also known as the Bourbon cane, was introduced to the English islands at the end of the last and the beginning of the present century. Captain Bligh brought the sugar cane and bread fruit from the Pacific in His Majesty's ships in 1796. These and other plants on arrival were carefully tended, and distributed from the Jamaica Botanic Gardens by Wiles, a gardener selected by Sir Joseph Banks. The introduction of coffee to the West Indies we owe to the French. Logwood was brought from British Honduras to Jamaica by Dr. Barham, a botanist, in 1715. The export of logwood from this island now exceeds that of British Honduras, and amounts to 190,000*l.* annually. (This has now considerably increased, and in 1895–96 amounted to 362,322*l.*). Dr.

Clarke, the first island botanist, brought with him to Jamaica the jujube tree and the camphor tree. The first mango plants were brought by Lord Rodney; while Dr. Marten in 1788 introduced the clove and black pepper. Jamaica ginger had its origin in the East Indies. Cacao is indigenous to none of the islands, and in Jamaica, at least, owes its recent increase in culture to the action of the Botanical Gardens. The first seeds and plants of cinchona and tea cultivated in Jamaica were sent out from Kew. Numerous fibre plants, cardamoms, peppers, india-rubbers, and spices have been supplied to the islands through the instrumentality of Kew and distributed by the local gardens. The records of these and similar introductions are easily accessible. They are mentioned here only for the purpose of indicating the important part which introduced plants generally have taken in establishing successful industries in the West Indies. With the exception of pimento and some timber and dye woods, it may be generally assumed that all the industrial plants of the West Indies, as we know them at present, have been brought from other countries. Hence we realise the useful character of the duties assigned to the Botanic Gardens, specially charged with the work of introducing and distributing such plants. It is only by such means that the islands can be supplied with the best sorts and kinds of plants suited to their circumstances, and they can be so equipped as to hold their own amidst the keen competition of other countries.' Dr. Morris has been instrumental in establishing a system of botanical stations throughout the West Indies, so as to allow of the collection of important information, and to provide the means for its useful distribution.

The following is a graphic description extracted from an article written by Governor Sir Henry A. Blake, in the *Nineteenth Century Magazine*:—'With such a variety of soil and elevation it is evident that Jamaica offers great advantages for the investment of capital, whether in the form of money and brains or labour and brains. Here, where even the tropical heat of the plains is assuaged by the sea breeze that blows by day and the cool land breeze that flows down from the hills at night, the new-comer may choose his climate through the sub-tropical temperature of the lower ranges to the bracing air of the higher mountains. Where I now write, at the botanical station of Cinchona, situated at an elevation of 5,000 feet, on one of the southern spurs of the Blue Mountain Range thrust boldly out into the great valley of the Yallah, dividing the Blue Mountains on the north from the Port Royal Hills on the south, the temperature in the middle of July is 63° at midday, and the climate is that of the early English summer. In the evening we find a cheerful wood fire comfortable to sit round, and at night, with a temperature of 55°, a pair of blankets is necessary. In the close-cropped sward in front of the house, smooth and green as an English lawn, are formed beds of roses, petunias, fuchsias, verbena, and geraniums, while the mountain roads are gay with masses of beautiful pink and white begonias, and here and there fringed with English gorse. Everywhere the banks are laden with wild strawberries, and the woods around are fragrant with the scent of flowers. A great portion of the hill sides is planted with the famous Blue Mountain coffee, which commands the highest price in England, but large areas are devoted to the cultivation of potatoes, yams, and scallions for the Kingston market, or bananas for home consumption, as the absence of roads for wheeled traffic prevents their being sent down for exportation. These pro-

OX-CART WITH LOAD OF BANANAS.

vision lands have either been purchased, or are held by tenancy from year to year at an average rent of one pound per acre. The cultivation is most carefully carried out, and the thorough weeding might be copied with advantage by some farmers in Ireland. The mixture of temperate and tropical crops is sometimes striking, carrots and cassava, sugar cane and scallions growing side by side.'

His Excellency further observes:—'Here in Jamaica there is room and welcome for men of the proper stamp. It is not the country for a young man without capital, however energetic he may be. By a man with 3,000*l*. to 5,000*l*. properties may be bought, in many cases with houses ready built, that would afford him a comfortable income. To the man with a family, success is equally probable. A floral farm for the preparation of perfumes would afford pleasant and remunerative occupation for the ladies of the family, nor would it interfere with the regular working of the property. To such men, industrious, sober, and moral, the black people would give a hearty welcome and willing respect; for men without these qualities Jamaica is no fitting place. The value of all property is increasing rapidly, and will in the near future still further advance. The extension of the railroad through the centre of the island, connecting the ports of the northern shore with the interior, will enhance the value of lands hitherto neglected, and the additional annual expenditure of 18,000*l*. for the improvement of parochial roads will still further assist in the rapid expansion of the banana trade. The value of the banana as food for working men has been recognised in the United States, and it is found peculiarly sustaining for those engaged in heavy labour in warm situations, such as blacksmiths and ironfounders. The operatives in cotton factories also use it largely.'

The total number of acres under cultivation or care in the island, with the exception of fruit, the acreage of which cannot be obtained, is estimated at 691,967, divided thus—sugar 30,971, coffee 23,643, ginger 84, arrowroot 7, corn 384, tobacco 230, cacao 1,687, vegetables 44, ground provisions 95,808, Guinea grass 126,877, common pasture and pimento 395,593. Including the fruit, the above figures, given on the authority of the 'Jamaica Handbook,' suggest a picture, not indeed of the productive capability of the island, but of the rather disappointing extent to which that capability is now developed and utilised. Jamaica has a great future, but in order to secure it people in England must wake up to the fact of the value of this great possession, and must send their sons, invest their money, exercise their influence, and enlarge their sympathy, so that the prosperity of the country may be assured, that it may contribute its proper proportion to the wealth of the world, and that the old bad days of struggle, selfishness, disaster, and cruelty may be forgotten in the dawn of a day the light of which shall shine upon a happy and contented people, living under fairer auspices and juster conditions than were ever known or enjoyed before.

The vital statistics of the island have already been indirectly referred to. It might be useful to give here the following particulars:—The population in 1881 was 584,281, the sexes being pretty evenly balanced, females being slightly in excess. A natural yearly increase, ranging from 6,000 to 10,000, brought it up in 1891, the date of the last census, to 639,491, showing the presence of 14,692 white persons, 121,955 coloured, 488,624 black, 10,116 East Indian coolies, 481 Chinese, and 3,623 not stated. The estimated population on March 31, 1896, was 694,865. The births registered in the year 1895-96 were 26,842, giving a rate of

38·8 per 1,000 of the population. The male births exceeded the female births by 397. The deaths registered in the year were 15,716, or 22·7 per 1,000. The rate for the previous year was 21. The sanitary condition of the island compares favourably with that of previous years, and it must continue to improve with better ventilation, food, and cleanliness, and less overcrowding, together with a better supply of good water.

At this point, before passing away from Jamaica, a few words respecting the West India Regiment, the principal depôt of which body of troops is in this Colony, would be opportune. The distinction between the 1st and 2nd Regiments has been abolished, and a 3rd battalion recently decided upon, and all three will be incorporated into one, called the West India Regiment. The smart Zouave dress, with the white turban, the scarlet jacket, and the loose full breeches, will be remembered by all who listened to the band of the then 1st West India Regiment at the Colonial and Indian Exhibition of 1886, which was in charge of Captain R. J. Norris, D.S.O., and by those who witnessed the recent Jubilee procession.

This force, recruited principally from the African race in the West Indies, and being placed under the command of English officers, has been a most valuable supplement to the white troops who are engaged in the defence of the West India Colonies. It was about the close of the last century, during the stress of the war with America, that this plan of a local Colonial army was established. It consisted originally of twelve battalions of negro troops; in the course of years these, for some reason or other, were so far disbanded that only two regiments remained, and these two, with an additional one recently ordered to be raised, as has been stated, have now been merged into one. These troops have received the highest encomiums from every British commander under whom they served, including Sir Ralph Abercrombie in 1796, Sir John Moore in 1797, and other distinguished generals of a later period. Coming to more recent times, so late as 1873, the 2nd West India Regiment bore for six months the entire brunt of the Ashanti attack, and had actually forced the invading army to retire across the Prah before a single line battalion arrived. The black men do not become good shots, but their bravery is unquestionable. A private named Hodge won the Victoria Cross for conspicuous courage at Tubarcolong on the River Gambia in May 1866, and only two years ago Sergeant Gordon was also awarded this coveted decoration for saving his commanding officer's life during further operations on the Gambia. In the Ashanti war just mentioned, when it was reported that the enemy had retired across the Prah, two soldiers of the 2nd volunteered to go on by themselves to the river, to ascertain if the news were true. On their return they reported all clear to the Prah, and said they had written their names on a piece of paper and posted it up. Six days later, when the advanced party of the expeditionary force marched into Prahsu, this paper was found fastened to a tree on the banks of the river. It was in circumstances of peculiar danger that these two men went nearly sixteen miles into an unknown forest, to follow up an enemy who never spared life, and whose whereabouts was doubtful. Certain it is that in the Ashanti war of 1873–74 the West India troops rendered most valuable assistance. Without them the advance on Kumasi must have been delayed, and its difficulties very much increased.

Of the many actions in which these troops have taken

part in different countries, including America (the campaigns in the Carolinas), Africa, and the West Indies; of the many useful services rendered by them to the Empire; of the hardships which they have undergone and the steadiness and fortitude they have displayed—a record may be found in an interesting book, 'The History of the 1st West India Regiment,' written by the late Colonel A. B. Ellis. There is probably no island in the West Indies where, during the wars with France, these troops have not been conspicuous for their fighting qualities, and they have rendered no less important services in repressing disturbances within the Colonies themselves. They have had a most creditable and distinguished past, and in estimating the military strength of the Empire abroad at the present time the organisation of this force cannot but be regarded as an important element of that strength. England need not fear the future when all her sons, of whatever race and colour, are ready, like these West Indian troops, to devote themselves to her defence.

CHAPTER VI.

PANAMA.

LEAVING Jamaica, the ocean steamer proceeds to Colon, or, to give it its American name, Aspinwall; the influence of the United States being in the ascendant in these quarters, and the Monroe doctrine not unknown. The distance from Jamaica to Colon is 550 miles, and the trip takes 1 day 18 hours. The crossing of the Isthmus of Panama, the manner in which the railway was built, the canal intended to unite two oceans—a work thought of for hundreds of years (for it is not Lesseps' own idea), grand in its conception, and equally great in its present misfortune—all these points will instantly occur to the mind. It is not, however, now intended to dwell at any length upon the associations of the place, or to detail the geographical and natural features it presents. Colon is the terminal port of the ocean steamer. Passengers are here disembarked for Panama and ports on the west coast of South America. The splendid inter-oceanic position of Panama will be seen by a glance at the map. The territory of the Gulf of Darien and Panama is within the limits of the most northerly of the South American Republics, New Granada, which was originally only a portion of the Republic of Colombia. This latter country, in the old Spanish days, was important and valuable. The town and port of Cartagena on the

Atlantic, and Panama on the Pacific, were strongholds. Whether the country has thriven since the Republican system was introduced is a question that need not be discussed here. The house, near Santa Marta, in which Bolivar died in 1830, is shown to visitors, or was so shown a few years ago. A story is connected with Cartagena. It was taken by the English in a curious way. After much fighting, a number of sailors dragged a gun up a hill which commanded the town, and so possession was obtained. There is certainly humour in the story even if it be not true. The railway line across the isthmus, under fifty miles, runs through a tropical bush, which has to be constantly kept clear of the track. Panama used to be a considerable Spanish town, with cathedral, public buildings, and forts; but it only now practically exists as an outlet for the traffic of the isthmus. Many schemes of transit by canal between the Atlantic and Pacific Oceans have been proposed in years gone by. The only alternative scheme, however, to that of Panama which has survived discussion is the one through Nicaragua. Waterways were already connected with the great inland lake of Nicaragua, the principal point of discussion being where the outlet into the Pacific should be. Napoleon III. had a grand scheme of canals through Nicaragua, but it came to nothing, as it would have been too imperial in its cost. As an alternative route to the Colon and Panama one, the scheme just mentioned seems to be the best and most practicable. An amusing account is given by Trollope of M. Belly's Nicaragua canal scheme, the ornate eloquence with which it was recommended by its inventor, and the curious correspondence with the British Government, in the course of which Lord Malmesbury, as Foreign Secretary, gravely informed M. Belly that the Clayton-Bulwer

Treaty would be applicable to his project. This flourish of trumpets was not succeeded by business, and the work has yet to be done. It will probably be done under the auspices of the United States, sooner or later—probably later, but it may come in time.

The transit trade across the Isthmus of Panama is estimated at fifteen millions sterling per annum, two-thirds being from the Pacific to the Atlantic, and the remainder in the reverse direction. Some activity is being displayed in the gold industry, but the results in bullion shipments have not yet been encouraging. Mining enterprise met with success in the old Colonial period, and recently a quantity of machinery has been laid down to utilise the former workings. A vein of gold has been found near the line of the Panama Railway, but apparently a supply of water is wanted for the necessary washing operations. The labourers who were attracted in such large numbers from Jamaica and other British Colonies by prospects of high wages on the canal works, have now all left for their respective homes—at least those who survived, for there was a very considerable mortality.

DEMERARA: WHARF AT GEORGETOWN

gas and the electric light. The houses are of wooden construction, and are usually raised several feet from the ground on pillars, to allow a free circulation of air beneath, and to prevent damp. The houses have the usual West Indian balcony and Venetian blinds. The trenches used for the drainage of the town will be observed on the road sides. Coolie men and women, immigrants from the East Indies or their descendants, are numerous in the streets. These men are thin in build, but bear themselves in a graceful and independent way, very different from the frightened and abject appearance they present on their first arrival from India. The coolie women have their proportion of good looks, and their prosperity is displayed in the silver armlets, necklaces, rings and earrings with which so many of them are plentifully adorned. The clothing of the men is a loose shirt with short sleeves, and a strip of cloth round the waist. The women wear short dresses with a bright-coloured loose jacket, and scarf for the head. The coolie men carry the formidable hackia stick, which they sometimes make so effective over the heads of foremen and overseers. The 'bucks' who visit Georgetown for the purchase of necessaries are plump and brown, showing in many instances the narrowest ideas with regard to clothing. The Chinese (many of whom have achieved success in trade), with their quiet industrious ways, go about with the somewhat sad and far-off look upon their faces that might be considered characteristic of men who are exiles from their native land, and who have brought the piece of Chinese soil with them to hallow the earth in which they will be buried. In the gardens of the houses the pink flowers of the oleander are prominent.

The Government building is a large, fine-looking edifice; the Law Courts cover a considerable area; and the new

Town Hall is an ornamental structure. The many churches are pleasant and picturesque, the new Cathedral which was built to commemorate the Jubilee of the late Bishop Austin, the Roman Catholic cathedral, and the Anglican church of St. Philip being especially noticeable. There is an appearance of prosperity associated with cleanliness (if such a juxtaposition of ideas may be pardoned) which makes this town one of the very nicest in the West Indies. The ample stores and commodious offices in Water Street and the two imposing bank buildings tell plainly of the prosperity of the place. The hospitality afforded to visitors shows the kind spirit which commercial success does so much to encourage. The 'swizzle' is ideally perfect. Notions of relaxation and of luxury are suggested by the Georgetown Club, with the refreshing trade wind blowing full upon it and through it. Extending towards the sea wall is Main Street, in and near which many of the principal residences in Georgetown are situated. Mr. Boddam-Whetham, in his work on 'Roraima,' thus describes this quarter: 'Main Street is broad and picturesque; a series of wide trenches (as there is no natural fall of water, these open trenches, which are seen everywhere in the country as well as town, are necessary to carry off surface water to prevent flooding in the wet season—by sluice gates the town trenches can be flooded when required) with green sloping banks divides it, and on each side runs a fine road. The residences which line it are all detached, and of various styles of architecture, from a three-storied edifice, with towers and cupola, to a low, wide-spreading structure with but one floor above the basement. But all are built for coolness as well as comfort, and their wide, shady verandahs are the favourite resorts of the family. Many of the gardens are brilliant masses of colour, resembling a rich oil-painting rather than a delicate water-colour of those of European lands, the tints are so gorgeous and heavy; there are bushes of the crimson hibiscus, scarlet cordias, flaming poinsettias, trailing corallitas, the bright flowers of the bois immortelle, the drooping clusters of the red quisqualis, the vermilion blossoms of the flamboyant, all vying in splendour with saffron petræas, deep blue convolvuluses, abutilons, and the white trumpets of the datura. In one garden I remember seeing a resplendent mass of bougainvilleas, and on a neighbouring tree some equally showy blossoms of a magnificent crimson orchid—*Cattleya superba*. Between them crept pale clusters of English honeysuckle, not a bit abashed by their grand neighbours, but rather exulting in the fragrance denied to their bright-coloured companions. Marbled crotons and purple dracænas are tipped by strange-looking papaws, whose wax-like blossoms grow direct from the trunks and branches, and above these tower shade-trees and tall palms. Very conspicuous are the royal palms, standing either singly or in groups, and near them bend the cocoa-nut trees as if in acknowledgment of the superior majesty of their kings.'

The above is an eloquent description of one of the most picturesque streets or thoroughfares in the West Indies. In the Public Gardens are some specimens of the famous lily, the *Victoria Regia*; but these are not the largest specimens. On Leonora Estate, for instance, there is a plant with leaves six feet in diameter.

Schomburgk visited the interior about the years 1837 to 1840. His travels were directed by the Royal Geographical Society of London, aided by the British Government. The following extract contains his description of the discovery of the *Victoria Regia* in the Berbice River : ' It appears as if the productive powers of nature, on receding from the poles, had collected themselves in their greatest strength near the equator, spreading their gifts with open hand, rendering every scene more imposing and majestic, and manifesting the abundant fertility of the soil. Gigantic trees raise their lofty crowns to a height unknown in the European forests, and display the greatest contrasts in the form and appearance of their foliage. Lianas cling to their trunks, interlace their wide-spreading branches, and having reached their summit, with aërial roots descend again towards the ground, and appear like the cordage of a ship. Clusters of palm trees, of all vegetable forms the most imposing, rise in grandeur above the surrounding mass, waving their pinion-like leaves in the soft breeze. Nature, as if not satisfied with the soil allotted to her, richly decorates the trunks and limbs of trees, the stones and rocks ; even the surface of the water is covered with a carpet of plants, interspersed by magnificent flowers. Nothing can give a better idea of the luxuriance and richness of vegetation in Guiana than the splendid *Victoria Regia*, the most beautiful specimen of the flora of the western hemisphere. The calm of the surrounding atmosphere, when frequently not a breath of wind agitates the foliage, not a cloud veils the azure vault of heaven, contrasts strongly with the hum of animated nature. The colibri, with its metallic lustre, passes rapidly from blossom to blossom, sipping the nectar of fragrant flowers, or sporting with the dew-drops which glitter on their petals. The ancient forest of noble trees re-echoes with the notes of feathered songsters. The plumage of the splendid macaws and parrots, perched on boughs, perhaps illumined by the beams of a setting sun, richly mingles with the brilliant and bright green foliage. Night approaches, and displays the firmament with all the southern constellations; the musical notes of birds give place to the chirping voices of crickets, the sounds of the tree-frog, lizard, and reptiles. Thousands of phosphorescent insects flutter among the leaves, emitting a light which, if it does not illuminate, tends to increase the characteristic features of a tropical night, and to realise the idea which imagination sketches when impressed with the most splendid descriptions in the Arabian tales. During our ascent of the River Berbice we met with difficulties of no common nature. The river being broken up by numerous rapids and cataracts, our progress was but slow, and having been deserted by a party of Wacawais, we could not muster a sufficient number to man our canoes, and had, therefore, to abandon one. After we had passed the cataracts, which extended for nearly fifteen miles in almost an uninterrupted line, the river narrowed considerably, and numerous trees, which from age or the undermining effects of the current had fallen across, disputed our advance, so that we were obliged to cut our passage through.

'Such thoughts were passing in my mind when we arrived at a point where the river expanded and formed a smooth basin on its eastern bank, while the current directed its course along the opposite shore. Something on the southern point of the basin attracted my attention: I could not imagine what it might be; urging the crew to increase their rate of paddling, in a short time we were opposite to the object of curiosity—a vegetable wonder! All calamities were forgotten; I felt as a botanist and was rewarded. A gigantic leaf, from five to six feet in diameter, salver-shaped, with a broad rim of light green above, and a vivid crimson below, rested upon the water ; quite in character with the wonderful leaf was the luxuriant flower, nearly four feet in circumference, and consisting of many hundred petals passing in alternate tints from pure white to rose and pink. The smooth water was covered with them, and I rowed from one to the other, constantly finding something new to admire. When the flower first opens in the morning it is white with pink in the middle, which spreads over the whole flower as the sun in his daily course proceeds towards the western horizon, and is generally found the next day of a pink colour. As if to enhance its beauty it is sweet scented, and chiefly so in the morning when it first opens, but even the heat of the day does not entirely overcome its fragrance. An account of this plant having been transmitted to England, Dr. Lindley found it to be a new and well-marked genus, and her Majesty, having graciously consented that it might be dedicated to her, gave permission that it should be known by the name of " *Victoria Regia.*" '

The interior of British Guiana is not yet thoroughly well known. The magnificent dreams of Raleigh have invested it with a splendid mystery. Traces of the golden cities he wrote about have not been discovered, although unquestionably the soil in many parts is auriferous. The gold-mining industry promises to be a large one in time. Adjoining British territory is that portion of Venezuela which contains the El Callao gold mine, long reputed the richest in the world. Although there are many delays and hardships to be endured in travelling through the interior, yet the ever-changing scenery, the rivers and the cataracts, the wonderful vegetation, the traces of the Indians, make it an interesting occupation for those who are strong enough to bear it.

KAIETEUR FALL, ON POTARO RIVER.

Roraima in its highest peak is described as about 8,000 feet above the sea, the tableland from which it rises being about 3,500 feet above the sea level. Its peculiarity is, that out of a mountain clothed with vegetation rises a perpendicular wall of red rock, 1,500 feet in height. Cascades add to the beauty and impressiveness of the scene.

The chief rivers of this Colony are the Essequebo, the Demerara, the Berbice, the Mazaruni, the Cuyuni, and the Corentyn; the last mentioned dividing the British and Dutch possessions. The Essequebo, having its origin in the Acarai Mountains, 41 miles north of the Equator, has a course, including its windings, of not less than 620 miles, exceeding in length any river in France, and vying with the Vistula in Poland. After receiving many large tributary rivers it continues its northern course, growing gradually wider, until at its mouth it forms an estuary nearly 20 miles wide, with numerous fertile islands, several of which are from 12 to 15 miles in length, and are under sugar-cane cultivation. In consequence, however, of interruptions caused by cataracts, it is not navigable by large vessels for more than fifty miles from its mouth. During inundations its waters rise from 25 to 30 feet above its banks. Local steamers ply along the coast and for some distance up the chief rivers.

On the upper branch of the River Potaro, a tributary of the Essequebo, is situated the now celebrated Kaieteur Fall, or the Old Man's Fall, which in point of height far surpasses Niagara. It was discovered by Mr. Brown, of the Geological Survey, on Sunday, April 24, 1870. Quoting the words of that gentleman : 'The Kaieteur Fall is situated in latitude 5° 8′ N., longitude 59° 19′ W., and is produced by the Potaro River flowing over a sandstone and conglomerate table-land into a deep valley below with a total fall of 822 feet. In the first 741 feet the water falls as a perpendicular column into a basin below, from which it continues its downward course over a sloping cataract in front, 81 feet in height, and through the interstices of great blocks of rock to the river below. The head of the Fall is 1,130 feet above the level of the sea. The width of the Fall varies from 240 feet to 370 feet, according to the season. The width of the river, 200 yards above the Fall, is about 400 feet.'

Mr. Everard F. im Thurn, C.M.G., late curator of the British Guiana Museum, and now Government Agent of the North-Western district, who visited the Kaieteur Fall for the second time in March 1879, describes it as follows: 'Crossing the savannah and coming to the edge of the cliff over which the Potaro falls, we once more lay down, bodies along the top of the cliff, heads over its edge. It was a very different scene from the last time. Then it was beautiful and terrible; but now it was something which it is useless to try to describe. Then a narrow river, not a third of its present width, fell over the cliff in a column of white water and was brought into startling prominence by the darkness of the great cave behind; and this column of water, before it reached the small, black pool below, had narrowed to a point. Now an indescribable— almost inconceivable—vast curtain of water—I can find no other phrase—(some 400 feet in width) rolled over the top of the cliff, retaining its full width until it crashed into the boiling water of the pool which filled the whole space below; and of the surface of this pool itself only the outer edge was visible, for the greater part was beaten and hurled up in a great high mass of surf and foam and spray.'

The lonely Roraima Mountain, with its sheer wall of red rock (thought to be inaccessible, but conquered by Mr. im

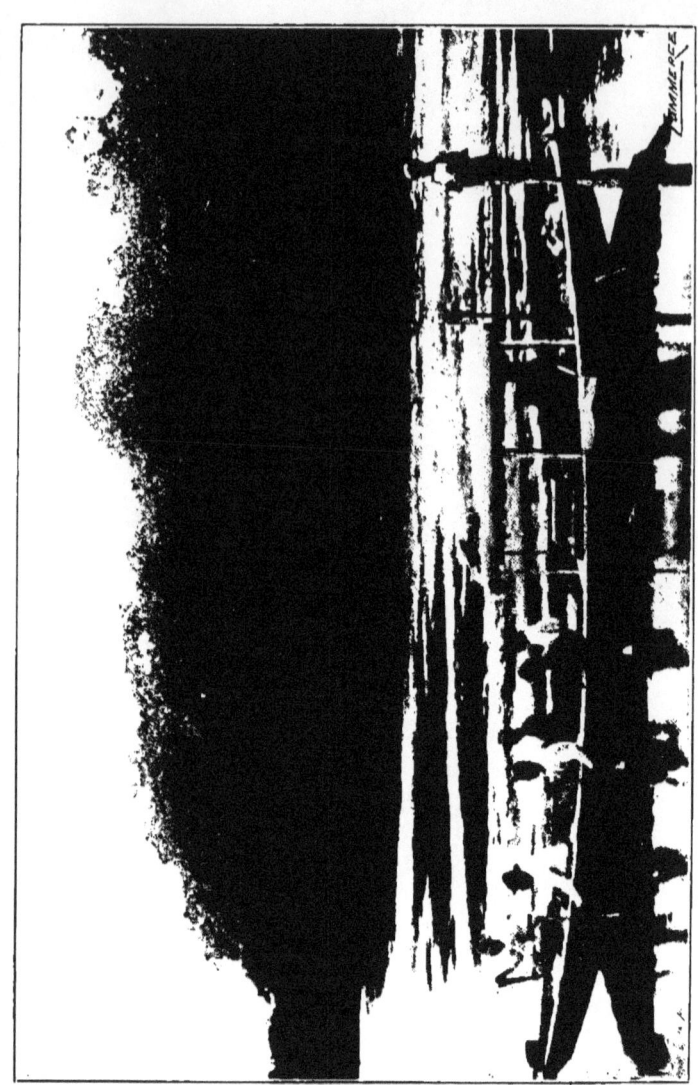

TRAVELLING ON THE DEMERARA RIVER.

Thurn in December 1884), the beautiful scenery of the Potaro River, with its wonderful Kaieteur Fall, the mountains, savannahs, and forests, the rivers, cataracts, and cascades, suggest a picture all the more striking to the imagination because so little is known about it. It is a mystery, with its legendary fabulous wealth, its inexhaustible stores of gold. A large silent country, waiting to be understood and known.

But a few more particulars as to the rivers of British Guiana might be here given. The upper part of the Demerara River is unknown. It widens until, when it enters the sea, it is a mile and three-quarters across. It is navigable for vessels of considerable size for about 70 to 80 miles from its mouth. The Berbice River in its upper course approaches within nine miles of the Essequebo in lat. $3° 53'$ N. It occasionally narrows to 30 feet, and at times spreads into lake-like expansions. About lat. $4° 19'$ N. the cataracts commence. Vessels of twelve feet draft can ascend 105 miles, and of seven feet, 175 miles, the influence of the tide being perceptible to nearly that distance. It is two miles and a quarter wide at its mouth.

The Corentyn takes its rise about 25 miles east of the source of the Essequebo, probably in $1°$ N. It is impeded in its course by the same tract of boulders which crosses the rivers Essequebo and Berbice, in lat. $4° 20'$ N., forming a series of cataracts which, until the discovery of the Kaieteur Fall and the Falls of Roraima, were supposed to surpass in grandeur all others in British Guiana. It is navigable for small vessels to about 150 miles from its mouth, which is variously estimated to be from 10 to 18 miles in width.

The Canje Creek, as it is termed, falls into the Berbice River, near its mouth. The Abary Creek, the Mahaicony Creek, and the Mahaica Creek, all streams of considerable size, though inferior to the great rivers, fall directly into the Atlantic between the Berbice and Demerara. The Boerasirie Creek divides the counties of Demerara and Essequebo; and between the rivers Essequebo and Barima are the rivers or creeks Pomeroon, Moruca, and Wai-ni.

The Rupununi, a large river, has its source in a savannah at the western foot of the Carawaimi Mountains. It forms a cataract in 2° 30′ N. latitude, and meandering through the savannah, it passes the Saeraeri Mountains, and flows northward through the Canucu, until the Sierra Pacaraima, in the vicinity of the mountain Annai, turns it to the east. It receives previously, in 3° 37′ N. latitude, the stream Awaricura from the south-west, by which, and its tributary the Quattata, the Pirara may be reached, which latter river belongs to the basin of the Amazon. Having passed the southern foot of the mountain Wakarapau, the Rupununi receives from the south its largest tributary, the Roiwa or Rewa, and joins in latitude 3° 59′ N. the Essequebo. The course of the Rupununi is about 220 miles; it flows mostly through savannahs, and its waters are light in appearance.

Although internal communication is carried on almost exclusively by means of the rivers, there is a railway from Georgetown to Mahaica, a distance of about 20 miles, owned by the Demerara Railway Company, Limited. A contract has recently been signed for the extension of the railway from Mahaica to Blairmont, which will bring the whole country between the points mentioned within reach of the markets of Georgetown and New Amsterdam. In the interior a railway connecting the Demerara and Essequebo

THE ESSEQUEBO EXTENSION RAILWAY.

Rivers has been recently opened, and gold-miners and timber workers in that district have now an easier and a quicker route to the port of Georgetown. A survey has also been completed for a proposed tramway or light railway between New Amsterdam and Skeldon on the Corentyn coast.

The range of sandhills about twenty miles inland from the coast seems to show that at one time, before the comparatively artificial formation of the coast was produced, the sea came up. The ground which has been cultivated between these sandhills and the sea is flat and alluvial. This part of the country where the Europeans live, with its canals, sluices, and dams, resembles Holland, and may be considered as the practical memorial of the Dutch occupation. Journeying into the interior, a gradual rise of ground is noticed. Hills, dales, and rocks are interspersed among the wide and far-reaching savannahs. The plantations are ranged on the banks of the great rivers or along the coast, running parallel to each other, and extend like immense garden slips from the sea to the forest, in properties of 500 to 1,000 acres. Humboldt and Waterton (the famous ride of the latter upon an Essequebo alligator will be remembered) have described the vegetation of the interior. Everything is gigantic—mountains, rivers, and the mass of vegetation. The coasts, washed by the Atlantic Ocean, are covered with mangrove and courida bushes.

A casual reference having been made above to Waterton, it might be interesting here to interpolate a few remarks from a paper in 'Timehri,' a British Guiana journal, by Mr. James Rodway, F.L.S. This writer says: 'In Demerara we see around us the beautiful scenes which the traveller and naturalist so vividly described, and in a walk along the west coast may observe the descendants of the curri-curris, egrets, and spurwings which he admired so much. In a few hours' journey up the Demerara River we may reach Camouni Creek, pass through its affluent, the Warratilla, and follow the windings of that little stream into the Mibiri, where Waterton spent many happy days in the enthusiastic study of the forest creatures he loved so much. The house is gone, and there is nothing remaining of the wood-cutting establishment, but the forest remains, and the fauna is still the same. The howling of the red monkey, the barking of the toucan, and the screaming of flocks of parrots overhead may be heard and appreciated to-day as they were eighty years ago. At night, when lying in our hammocks, we can compare the voices of the owls and goatsuckers with the description in the "Wanderings," and listen to their weird cries of "whip poor will," "who are you," and that other wailing series of notes which he so well describes as like "the departing voice of a midnight murdered victim." Daddy Quashie is gone, but there are plenty of his successors to guide the traveller through the forest, and help the huntsman in finding out the lurking places of the acourie and labba. At Soesdyk, the descendants of that Louisa Backer who prepared Waterton's dose of castor oil are doing business as boat-builders, while some of the older people still remember having heard of the traveller. Charles Waterton sailed from Portsmouth in the ship *Fame* (Captain Brand) on November 29, 1804, and arrived in Stabroek after a passage of about six weeks—that is, in January 1805. His uncle, Christopher Waterton, was proprietor of the two plantations, La Jalousie and Fellowship, on the west coast, and his father having lately bought an estate for the benefit of his younger children, Charles was sent out to superintend the property. His uncle appears to have gone to England soon afterwards, leaving his nephew in charge of La Jalousie and Fellowship as attorney, in which capacity he acted until 1812, with the exception of short intervals during which he made one or two trips to England.'

The general idea of the country has perhaps been sufficiently suggested—its largeness, vagueness, variety, mystery, and loneliness. But a reference to the geological survey of Messrs. Brown and Sawkins in 1867 may lead to a little more definiteness of impression. Means of travelling in the interior have since that date been improved, but not very much. The ascent of the rivers, the haulage of the boats at cataracts, the penetration through dense forests, the winding ways through Indian paths, the heavy rains and floods, present pretty much the same difficulties as were experienced twenty years ago. The geological surveyors were particularly struck with the great grass plains or savannahs stretching eastward from Brazil. 'The views from the savannahs have a beauty and singularity of their own, and it stirs one with a sense of boundless freedom to stand upon a knoll midst one, and view the grassy plain fading away to the horizon in the distance, and melting gradually, as it were, into the atmosphere.' There are two great parallel mountain systems crossing the Colony from west to east, the greater being that of the Pacaraima and Merumé Mountains, and the lesser the Canucu, Camucumu, and Coratamung Mountains.

Reverting again to the coast country, lying at the foot of the higher portions, the following may be quoted from the above authorities. 'The sea is kept from these lands by a line of dams along the coast and side dams between each estate, the drainage being effected by sluices or kokers when the tide is low. The drainage of the swampy lands behind the estates has to pass through the trenches of the estates, and in wet weather the supply of water being very great it accumulates rapidly when the tide is high, so that dams have been erected in the rear of each estate. With the exception of the cultivated portions nearly all this land is covered with high forest trees and dense jungle, chiefly of courida (*Avicennis nitida*), mangrove (*Rhizophora Mangle*), and corkwood, near the coast, and mora (*Mora excelsa*) upon the slightly raised portions. Small areas are also covered with coarse grass and rush in the immediate vicinity of the estates, and are termed floating savannahs. From the coast line seawards the ocean deepens very gradually, and at low tide extensive mud flats and sandbanks are left bare.' There is a very regular and sloping formation of this alluvial portion up to the sandbanks already mentioned. The above reference to the water at the back of the estates, suggests the questions which have been raised during many years past as to its storage for the use of the estates, especially in times of drought. A service canal (as it is called) has been made running along the back dams of the estates on the east coast. This canal is fed by the back water, and in order to store this back water an inland lake, to be formed by dams or raised embankments, was at one time proposed, but this scheme has been only partially carried out, the estates deriving their supply by certain streams and water paths with which they are more immediately connected. The matter is stated here only for the purpose of showing the peculiar difficulties arising from the construction of the estates. To guard against water from the back in wet weather and ease it off through the trenches, and to endeavour to keep it by a method of storage for use during the not infrequent seasons of drought : this vital question has not been settled yet.

It is, perhaps, not necessary to enter into any detailed description of the geological formation. The fluvio-marine alluvium extends along the whole sea coast of the Colony, stretching inland to distances varying from five to thirty-five miles. The thickness of this deposit is about 100 feet, and it is composed of layers of sand and bluish clay, containing portions of decayed wood and vegetable matter. The soil above it (on the estates) is a dark loam, of great strength and productiveness. The sandstone formation constitutes the greater portion of the northern part of the Pacaraima Mountains, extending westward into Venezuela. The surface of a very large part of the Colony is formed of gneiss, which is noticed particularly in the beds of the rivers. Greenstone, schists of various kinds, granite rocks, and other formations are to be noticed. The white sandhills on the Demerara and other places are well adapted for glass-making, although this industry does not appear to have received any attention. The white clay is also available for porcelain and earthenware. Every variety of building stone is found in the interior, except limestone, but owing to the cost and difficulty of transport it is very little used. The same remark may be made as to the supply of granite in the quarries at the mouth of the Mazaruni River and other places. Jasper rock occurs in layers in the sandstone of the Pacaraima Mountains. Impure ores of iron are extensively diffused throughout the interior in beds in alluvial deposits, and on the surfaces of the greenstone masses. Near Darunow village, on the upper Rupununi savannah, there is a large patch of fine specular iron ore in greenstone.

K

With regard to gold, apart from the adventures and speculations of Sir Walter Raleigh, it is recorded that in 1721 the Council of Ten in Holland granted privileges for the working of mines. But the operations consequent upon this, apparently of a very limited character, were not successful. Within the last thirty years, steps were taken by a British company to obtain gold about forty miles up the Cuyuni River, but this also was unsuccessful. After many years of anxious effort, the industry has now become an important one, and bids fair to develop largely but gradually. All the writers on Guiana, from Raleigh to Schomburgk, are agreed as to the presence of gold, although Raleigh's Manoa, a city paved with gold, containing a lake with golden banks, was but a dream. Since 1880, search for gold has been made in the districts contiguous to the Cuyuni, Mazaruni, Puruni, and Potaro Rivers. In a recent Report on the Blue Book of the Colony, the Governor states that 'the steady growth of the gold industry has been of undoubted benefit to the Colony. There has been no rush to the diggings, occasioning a dislocation of everyday life, although in some districts the withdrawal of labour has been felt ; and while the revenue contributed by the royalty on gold has carried with it the necessity for a large expenditure in administration, yet there is evidence on all sides that the wealth extracted from the soil is being largely spent in the Colony.' In the Report on the Blue Book for 1895-96 the Acting Governor (Sir Cavendish Boyle, K.C.M.G. states :—

'The gold production of the Colony for the year under review amounted to 121,285 oz., and yielded a royalty of 22,740*l*. The following table, showing the rise of the gold industry during the last 10 years, is interesting :—

MAZARUNI RIVER.

				OZ.
1887	...	...	...	10,986
1888-1889	...	...	...	20,216
1889-1890	...	...	...	32,332
1890-1891	...	...	...	66,864
1891-1892	...	...	...	110,555
1892-1893	...	...	...	134,124
1893-1894	...	...	...	138,527
1894-1895	...	...	...	132,994
1895-1896	...	...	...	121,285

'It would be a mistake to regard the falling off in the last two years as indicative of the general condition of the industry. In 1893-4 practically the whole of the available capital in the Colony was devoted to placer mining, but since then a large proportion has been withdrawn for the development of quartz reefs, and the flotation of companies to work them, which so far have not yielded any return. An unremunerative interval of two years in the case of mines assaying richly and full of promise may seem long to those unfamiliar with the natural difficulties to be overcome. The dense forests, broad creeks, and strong currents which must be cleared, crossed, and stemmed before one ton of machinery can be taken to the spot where its work is to be done, have offered obstacles perhaps as great as miner ever knew. But they have been surmounted, and at the time of writing one mill of twenty stamps has been crushing for some weeks in the heart of the North-West District, while two others are in course of erection. From the former there has been a steady yield of about an ounce per ton. These pioneer works carried on in a virgin forest with but a scanty supply of technical and scientific aid have been costly, and the financial resources of the people have been severely strained. In these circumstances it is a matter for congratulation that the placer yield has maintained its position so well as to be only some 9 per cent. less than in the previous year. In the meantime it has been demonstrated by local enterprise that rich quartz exists in large quantities within reach of the pickaxe and the mill, and with the influx of English capital which must follow a wider knowledge of the possibilities of the country a prosperous future may well be predicted.'

The climate has been subject to much animadversion, especially by people who know nothing about it. It is hot, but certainly not unhealthy, a fact proved by the vigorous health enjoyed by many English planters who have spent a great portion of their lives in the Colony. Men advanced in years have been known to retain all their physical and mental energy, together with all their capacity for work of all kinds, up to the very last. There may be an occasional epidemic of yellow fever, as there are analogous periods of fever, smallpox, and cholera in England. But this application of the law of diseases, from which no country in the world is free, does not militate against the general excellence of a particular climate. The bland, warm, and moist atmosphere is particularly adapted to cases of threatened or incipient phthisis (consumption); and even in a more advanced form of the disease, life would be prolonged in British Guiana. Dr. Hancock, who knew British Guiana well, said: 'Guiana is most favourably situated of any part of the world, perhaps, with respect to the winds and sea breezes. It lies in the main track of the equinoctial current, whilst hurricanes, so terrific and destructive amongst the West Indian Islands, are unknown here, and the equinoctial gales are extremely steady and uniform.' Again he says: 'In the interior parts of Guiana the purity of the air is such that in the dry season the stars appear like brilliants in the deep azure sky at night, and we not unfrequently perceive planets in the daytime. At the same time the splendour of the moon and the zodiacal light contribute to make the nights most pleasing, and to throw a charm on every object. The testimony of the woodcutters constantly assures us that the wooded parts and inland forests are never found to be unhealthy to either Europeans or others. These are facts which I can vouch for, and, to show they are not contrary to reason, let it be considered that it is not the absolute degree of temperature that determines the salubrity of any climate, but, as everyone knows, it is the great and sudden changes from heat to cold and from cold to heat which chiefly render any country unhealthy. Now, there is probably no country on the globe where the temperature is more uniform than in Guiana.'

Sir R. Schomburgk, whose knowledge of the climate is beyond dispute, affirms that 'the salubrity of the interior is proverbial, and there are many instances of longevity among the settlers on the banks of the rivers Demerara, Berbice, and Essequebo. The natural drainage is here so perfect, that all impurities are swept off by the torrents of rain, and the purity of the air is so great that the planets Venus and Jupiter may be seen in the daytime. While descending the Upper Essequebo in December 1838, we saw, one afternoon at three o'clock, the sun, the moon, and the planet Venus.'

In a country depending upon tropical produce, the 'seasons' are all-important. In all the West Indian Colonies, too much rain at one time, or too much dry weather at another, would be sufficient almost to destroy the crop. A drought in Demerara would perhaps mean a loss of thirty or forty thousand tons of sugar, which would be represented in money value, taking the cost of production (without considering loss of profit on the sale) at 10*l.*, at from 300,000*l.* to 400,000*l.* on a single crop. And, on the other hand, too much rain would prevent the cutting of the cane, would stop the mills, and seriously hinder the operations of manufacture. The corn and fruit crops of Great Britain depend almost entirely upon seasonable weather, but this dependence is practically absolute in a tropical country where seasons are exaggerated beyond the experience of Europe. In British Guiana there are two wet and two dry seasons. In the latter part of April the long wet season is expected to begin, and to last for three months or a little more. It is a mistake to suppose that the wet season is one continuous downpour. A day rarely passes without fair weather and sunshine. This is succeeded by a dry season, from August to November. December and January are wet, and these rains are always hailed with satisfaction by the sugar grower. February and March constitute the short dry season. The sea breezes prevail throughout the dry season. The temperature is very equable, ranging only from 75° to 90° F. Georgetown has a mean annual temperature of 80°, and the average rainfall is ninety inches. The death rate among the whole population compares favourably with many European towns, being about 30 per 1,000. Upon this point the following paragraph contains a further reference.

The population of British Guiana according to the census of 1881 was 252,186. Since that time, by means of a continuance of coolie immigration from India, and also by natural increase in the Colony itself, the population has risen to very nearly 300,000. The result of the census of 1891 shows that the total population numbered 278,328, made up as follows: Europeans other than Portuguese, 4,558; Aborigines, 7,463; East Indians, 105,463; Chinese, 3,714; Portuguese, 12,166; Africans, 3,433; Blacks, 112,155; Mixed Races, 29,029; Race not stated, 347. The estimated population at the present time is 283,278. In Georgetown sanitary improvements are steadily going on, with beneficial influence on vital statistics.

The aborigines are the relics of the old Indians. They are slowly decreasing in number. The history of these aboriginal tribes is associated with many theories, and is certainly to the present day, notwithstanding the researches of Humboldt and Schomburgk, marked by much obscurity. The possibility of an early emigration from Asia to America has been suggested. The following are the names of the tribes or nations represented by the Indians of Guiana: Arawâks, Warraus, Caribs or Caribisi, Acawais or Waccawaios, Macusis, Arécunas, Wapisianas, Atorais or Atorias, Tarumas, Woyowais. These people live in small settlements mainly in the interior, though a few are to be found in the coast regions. In size and appearance they average about five feet four inches in height. The forehead is lower than in Europeans, but it is sufficiently formed to bespeak intelligence above the lowest order. The females are almost equal in size to the males, but their embonpoint prevents them from appearing graceful. Their colour is a brownish olive, varying according to tribe and to location. Some are almost as fair as Spaniards, while others are dark brown. They have straight, luxuriant black hair; their features are small and their limbs well proportioned. They paint lines on their faces and bodies, and a few tattoo their faces slightly. They like to deck themselves out in glass beads or seeds and shells strung together round their arms, necks, and ankles. Their dress is a piece of cloth covering their loins, or in the case of the women an apron of glass beads. Their dress and habits still indicate the peculiar characteristics of their different tribes. They live in huts, forming small villages. Each tribe has its own hunting ground, and each family its own plantation. They make their own earthenware vessels, sometimes ornamenting them with designs. Waterton gives a long description of the blow-pipe or tube through which poisoned arrows are blown by the Indians to kill birds. Indeed, the whole habits and ways of life of these people, as described by travellers such as Waterton and Schomburgk, are full of interest, but it would take a volume by itself to reproduce the results of their researches and observation. One of the tribes, living high up the Essequebo, was formerly addicted to cannibalism. Dalton, with the endeavour to throw some light upon the Eastern origin of these people, points out the similarity of many words used in the Carib language, in sound and meaning, to words in the Oriental dialect, and he gives a list to illustrate his point. Schomburgk thought that these Indians were in his time capable of progressive improvement. The late venerable Bishop of Guiana and Metropolitan of the Anglican Church in the West Indies (Dr. Austin) was clearly of the same opinion, and he tried to bring them (or rather those who could be reached a little way up the rivers) within the influence of civilisation and Christianity. The Rev. W. H. Brett's book on the legends of the Indian tribes of Guiana, and Schomburgk's account of the picture writings (Timehri), deserve a few words.

The following lines are from Mr. Brett's own introduction to his rendering of the Legends of the Arawâks:

ESSEQUEBO RIVER.

'Twas long ago, yet still I view
The scene to me then fresh and new,
   Where two fair rivers flow ;
Where stately moras tower above,
And palms wave gently in the grove,
   As pleasant breezes blow.
I see, as natives pass me there,
Bright copper skins and jet black hair,
While one, whose face is kind and fair,
   The forest trees lays low.

There painted Caribs in our view
Would pass us in their light canoe,
   And slowly glide away.
We saw grim alligators sleep,
And languid lizards near them creep,
   In the meridian ray.
And there—while no sweet breeze above
Would stir the leaves and cheer the grove
And water lilies scarce could move—
   Would wait the cool of day.

The ceiba, or silk cotton tree, was invested with religious associations by the Indians, as it is also by the Africans.

With regard to the 'picture writings,' the following is from Schomburgk : 'In about the fifth parallel of latitude, two ranges of mountains, the Akaiwanna and Twasinki, project into the River Essequebo on each side, and cause its general direction for about six miles to assume the form of an S. In this distance are three falls, the most formidable of which, named Yukurit, or Cumakatoto, is caused by a dyke of stratified granite, crossing the river in a north and south direction, over which the water hastened by previous rapids, and narrowed by projecting rocks, precipitates itself with violence. The Comuti or Taquiari Mountains have received their name from a remarkable pile of large granitic boulders, so placed as to resemble a water jar, called Comuti by the Arawâk Indians, and Taquiari by the

Caribs. Upon a large granitic block some Indian picture writing was observed. The lines were more symmetrical than those which had been observed in other writings.' These figures bore a resemblance to the sculptures found in Siberia, and also near Boston, in the United States of America. The granite was decomposing, but the drawings made by Schomburgk at Comuti, on the Essequebo, were fairly complete. Rude pictures of boats, ships on the sea, animals, and diverse irregular lines. There is great uncertainty as to the origin of these monuments of bygone races; but upon this point the following extract from Schomburgk will be opportune: 'I myself traced these inscriptions through 700 miles of longitude and 500 of latitude. I have copied many of them, and although they do not denote an advanced state of civilisation, in my opinion they have a higher origin and signification than that generally ascribed to them, namely, the idle tracings of hunting nations. But two vessels under sail, figures of birds, animals, and men are observed. Who conceived these strange, yet natural, devices on the rock, where the ideas came from, what was the origin of the rude artistic skill displayed, no one can explain, although it is possible that many have cited them in support or contradiction of racial or ethnological theories.'

There are at the present moment more than 115,000 coolies in the Colony who have been introduced from the East Indies or who are the children of those who have been so introduced. Upon the steady labour afforded by these people the Colony has thriven. Without coolie immigration the present cultivated portion would have been a land of swamps and ruined embankments, or perhaps washed over by the sea. The system of immigration established about 1850 and elaborated through successive years to its present efficiency and completeness, has been amply demonstrated as beneficial to all parties. It is a relief to the famine-stricken districts of India ; it is good for the coolie because it makes a man of him by giving him an adequate reward for his industry ; it is good for the planter because he obtains that command of steady labour upon which all his operations depend ; the shopkeepers increase their business by the presence of a new large wage-earning class ; the negro has his share of the advantage because he has opportunities of well-paid work which he would not have if the estates had not been continued or fresh ones set going ; and the Government and all the institutions of the country are better supported in consequence of increased revenues which follow an expansion of production and trade. The Colony has an agent in Calcutta, who employs sub-agents and recruiters in certain districts of India. Before an emigrant is allowed to leave his district he is taken before a magistrate, who carefully sees that he has not been deceived, that he knows where he is going, and that he understands the terms and conditions which are offered to him, and that he is in all respects a free man so far as the paternal supervision and inquisition of the Indian Government can ascertain and secure. He is taken to Calcutta and placed in a large building (which he can leave at any moment before embarkation, if he wishes), he is medically examined, and an official appointed by the Indian Government, called the Protector of Emigrants, steps in and takes him in hand and sees that all is right, administering, as he is bound to do, a most rigorous, particular, and elaborate set of rules made by the Indian Government to regulate the system and to protect the emigrant. The voyage lasts about three months, during which the good food and sea air bring to him much physical benefit. Upon arrival he finds himself still under the protection of the British Government. Responsible officials (the head of whom has a seat in the Legislature) are there to see him properly located, and to look after his comfort. He enters upon an indenture for five years to one particular estate. This secures to him work, wages (which cannot go below a minimum), house, and hospital accommodation, for it binds the employer to grant him, under penalties, all these facilities. If the employer fails to do his duty the Government have power to remove the indentured coolies from the estate, which means great loss and perhaps ruin to the proprietor. A great Government Medical Department is available to secure that the sanitary conditions of the property and its hospitals are all that could be required. The coolie may be accompanied by his wife and children, and these of course are lodged with him. There must be forty women to every hundred men on board each coolie ship. At one time, no doubt, the males largely preponderated over the females, especially in the earlier years of this system, but coolie children born in the Colony are constantly improving the balance of the sexes. After five years the coolie is free to choose any employer that he pleases, and work for him for as long or short a period as he may desire. He becomes a competitor in the general labour market of the Colony, or he may take to other occupations, such as shopkeeping, or going about the country selling rice in small quantities, or lending out money at interest, or even speculating in racehorses. The principal race in Trinidad has been won before now by a horse belonging to a coolie. In short, the coolie population is industrious and thriving. For the first year or so the immigrant is, perhaps, not of much value to his employer, but as soon as he gets accustomed to the work and becomes thoroughly acclimatised, his labour is worth the expense of bringing him from India, for the planter pays two-thirds of the expense of his introduction (the total of which may be put at about 20*l.* per adult), and the public revenue, recognising the general advantage to the community of this immigration, contributes the remaining one-third. It should be added that after remaining for ten years in the Colony he becomes entitled to a free return passage to India, with his wife, and children born in the Colony. This right of back passage he always retains, whatever the length of time, above ten years, he may have been in the Colony. That his sojourn is productive may be gathered from certain facts. At the close of the year 1895 the amount to the credit of the Indian immigrants in the Government Savings Bank of the Colony was 103,540*l.* In the same year 408 Indian immigrants were licensed as shopkeepers, 1,620 as hucksters, 44 as owners of mule carts, 45 as owners of cabs, and 249 as owners of donkey carts. There were three ships in 1895 carrying to India, under the right of back passage, men, women, and children, equal to 2,071 adults. They took with them savings amounting to 20,791*l.*, and the value of the jewellery they carried amounted to 4,062*l.* The fact that so large an amount is remitted, and that about a fourth of their total savings is dedicated to personal adornment, may be taken as a happy criterion of the prosperous days the Hindu spends whilst in British Guiana. A considerable number of people, after returning to India, re-emigrate to the Colony—many at their own expense.

The next class of the population is that known as the Portuguese, natives of Madeira, who emigrated in large numbers to the Colony after the disaster to the vine industry in their native country. They form, having left their original agricultural work, one of the principal trading classes of the Colony. As shopkeepers they have been eminently successful, and possess a large proportion of the retail trading business of Georgetown. A number of them have risen to affluence—they become landed proprietors and possessed of considerable influence.

The Creoles [1]—that is, for purposes of present description, people born in the Colony belonging to the African race—are not perhaps increasing in number to any extent, but by the introduction of coolie labour and the consequent maintenance of estates, they are provided with work suitable to their wishes and capabilities. A planter remarked to Anthony Trollope, 'Give us as many coolies as we want, and we will supply the world with sugar.' Formerly coffee and cotton were largely grown, but through the influences of competition in other countries these have practically disappeared, and sugar is now the one staple of the Colony. A number of the Creoles have acquired plots of ground, especially in certain villages laid out for them under Government supervision. One village *Plaisance* contains upwards of 4,000 people. Attempts have also been made to induce them to become growers of cane, to be worked up into sugar at an agreed percentage on neighbouring estates. Neither the village system, nor the small cane planter system, has been particularly successful. The difficulty consists in the expense of draining the lands, taxation for which purpose being willingly agreed to in theory, but materially objected to in practice. However, the village system in Demerara is one which has taxed the

---

[1] A Creole is a person born in the colony, of whatever parentage; but the term is used above, as explained, in a more limited sense.

energies of different governors, who have tried to make it a success, and there are many reasons which show that such a scheme is not to be disapproved. In the first place it cannot be helped, because the people will congregate in villages, and the Government are bound to look after their sanitary condition and the proper administration of their affairs. And in the next place, if they are properly located, when their provision grounds fail, as they occasionally must through stress of seasons, they have the advantage of engaging in their districts in the main industry of the Colony as it is carried on by the estates. They find employment also in cutting timber, and many now go to the gold-fields in the interior. It does not cost much to live. The trenches and ditches abound with fish; plantain, sweet potato, pumpkins, yams, can be produced all the year round in exhaustless quantities. Not only ordinary dress, of a somewhat scanty character, is obtainable, but some idea of the prosperity and resources of the black population may be gathered from the Sunday costumes which are exhibited in the Georgetown churches. Bonnets of Parisian shape, expensive dresses, and high-heeled shoes are not suggestive of general poverty.

Upon the whole, therefore, although not an increasing race in British Guiana, the people of African descent are prosperous, and not by any means the least intelligent as compared with similar communities of the West Indies.

As an agricultural labourer the Chinaman, when he is really industrious and capable, is the best and most successful in money-making of all the immigrants. But sometimes men have come from the Chinese towns, belonging not to the best class of labourers, and not from the sugar districts of China, where whole families, children and adults, may be seen working in the cane fields. But the Chinaman, by his thrift and carefulness, by his desire to earn money, by his calculating and reserved disposition, is not at all bad as an immigrant. The conscientious Chinaman always wishes to get on. He does his work well in the field, he is invaluable for certain services in the buildings, he takes to huckstering and shopkeeping when he is free from the estate, and some of the best of these men have adapted themselves readily to the European habits of the Colony. Of course, a number are addicted to opium, and to other peculiarities, which are not in themselves agreeable (every class of men has its particular weakness); yet the Chinese in British Guiana (whatever may be said against them, and they have had many hostile criticisms) are to be respected as a body. They have so thoroughly adopted English commercial principles as to make use of the Insolvency Law. Half a million of Chinese would quadruple the sugar crop, and the increasing prospect of gold in British territory in the interior ought to attract large numbers, to the immediate or certainly ultimate advantage of the sugar production on the sea coast and river banks.

With regard to the British population, what could be said in addition to Trollope's words, written many years ago?—'The men in Demerara are never angry, and the women are never cross. Life flows along on a perpetual stream of love, smiles, champagne, and small talk. Everybody has enough of everything. The only persons who do not thrive are the doctors.' It might be mentioned that the doctors even now sometimes complain to the *Lancet*, although the members of this profession, as a Government institution, have salaries, pensions, and holidays which make the mouths of unprofessional people water. The Demerara doctors have always been noted for their ability and conscientiousness, and also for their success in winning the confidence of the community after the lapse of time necessary for them to appreciate their surroundings there. Many distinguished doctors, whose fame and writings have been known in Europe, have been especially connected with this Colony. No better sphere of work for an able, ambitious, and yet open-minded, medical man could be found than British Guiana. Of course, he would have to take the country as he finds it, for its natural and social conditions could not be altered in a day to suit the requirements of a specialist, or of a man whose thoughts run in a narrow groove and lead to conclusions which may or may not fit in with the circumstances in which he finds himself.

The Surgeon-General, the head of the Public Hospital in Georgetown, gets a salary of 1,200*l.* a year, in addition to his consulting practice; the Medical Inspector of Estates Hospitals 800*l.*, and private practice; the medical officers in charge of districts, salaries ranging from 300*l.* to 1,000*l.* (travelling allowance additional), according to their length of service and the importance of their respective districts, and of course are all entitled to their private practice. The late Medical Inspector receives a pension of 480*l.* a year, the late surgeon to the Berbice Hospital 660*l.*, and some district medical officers from 200*l.* to 480*l.* respectively.

After population the next point is production. Without losing sight of the gold and timber industries, British Guiana may now be considered almost exclusively a sugar Colony, or, in other words, a British sugar farm, which, but for the accidents of soil and climate, might have been placed in the centre of England, and occupy an analogous position to

Louisiana in the United States. The West India Colonies are sugar, cocoa, cattle, and fruit farms, belonging to England as much and truly as any agricultural industries in Surrey and Essex at home. Between 1846 and 1856 the fortunes of the Colony of British Guiana were at their lowest ebb. Cotton and coffee had practically disappeared, sugar estates were abandoned, and the country, in the expressive Jamaica phrase, was fast becoming 'ruinate.' But by means of coolie immigration the corner was turned. A new class of proprietors sprang up, possessing capital and enterprise, and a boundless faith in the resources of the Colony; the result is now apparent. The following is a return, taken from the official blue books, of sugar and other exports, during the years 1892 to 1896.

The production of sugar during recent years has been very much less than it was during the 'eighties,' but this is on account of unfavourable seasons and other misfortunes, which will no doubt be remedied by larger crops to follow. The quantity of sugar sent to the United States will be noticed. This is only another proof of the important character of the American market to the West Indies. But, of course, the exports to the United States are subject to variation. At times the market there is better than in England, all these considerations being determined by telegraph. A great deal depends upon the operations of American Sugar Trusts, as the refiners in New York and Baltimore have the command of the market of their continent. Lord Derby once said that the United States was the natural market of the West Indies. It is quite true that without that market, in the face of the European bounties, the sugar Colonies of the British Empire could not have preserved their existence.

BRITISH GUIANA.

Table of Produce Exported 1892-1896

	1892-93	1893-94	1894-95	1895-96
SUGAR.	Tons	Tons	Tons	Tons
U. Kingdom	38,730	39,760	51,688	33,951
United States	70,115	61,616	48,762	63,460
British Possessions	3,856	6,289	1,965	3,723
Other Countries	179	108	87	26
Total	112,880	107,773	102,502	101,160
RUM.	Puns.	Puns.	Puns.	Puns.
U. Kingdom	34,061	25,422	23,390	28,991
United States	5	—	—	1
British Possessions	1,784	1,378	1,136	1,246
Other Countries	1,346	1,179	1,757	1,173
Total	37,196	27,979	26,283	31,411
MOLASSES.	Galls.	Galls.	Galls.	Galls.
U. Kingdom	14,000	10,000	—	11,200
United States	—	—	—	—
British Possessions	153,500	107,100	83,549	127,000
Other Countries	850,100	1,085,600	1,054,411	599,650
Total	1,017,600	1,202,700	1,137,960	737,850
TIMBER.	Cubic feet	Cubic feet	Cubic feet	Cubic feet
U. Kingdom	290,527	226,119	216,038	138,523
Other Countries	35,336	8,751	22,955	36,997
Total	325,863	234,870	238,993	175,520
Shingles (No.)	2,426,350	1,192,850	2,744,150	1,880,000
Charcoal (bags)	54,927	57,246	54,849	54,644
Cocoanuts (No.)	62,600	77,037	1,200	—
Gold (ounces)	134,124	138,527	132,994	121,285

The value of the exports of raw sugar (the finest crystals are always accounted raw) from British Guiana in 1894-95 amounted to 1,246,894*l*., whilst in 1895-96 it had decreased by 200,734*l*., the total for the latter year being 1,046,160*l*. These figures are subject to annual alteration.

The total value of the trade of the Colony as represented by the imports and exports was in 1894-95, 3,708,651*l*.— viz., imports, 1,668,750*l*.; exports, 2,039,901*l*.; whereas in

1895-96 the total trade fell to 3,213,053*l.*—viz., imports, 1,443,553*l.*; and exports, 1,769,500*l.*

The imports (1895-96) were: United Kingdom, 789,817*l.*; British Colonies, 204,516*l.*; United States and small imports from other foreign countries, 449,220*l.*

The exports were thus distributed (1895-96), including produce and manufactures of the Colony, and British, foreign, and other Colonial produce and manufactures: United Kingdom, 968,252*l.*; British Colonies, 61,854*l.*; United States, and small exports to other foreign countries, 739,394*l.* The following table summarises the trade in 1895-96:

	Imports from.	Exports to.	Total trade.
United Kingdom ...	£789,817	£968,252	£1,758,069
British Colonies ...	204,516	61,854	266,370
Foreign countries...	449,220	739,394	1,188,614
	£1,443,553	£1,769,500	£3,213,053

That portion of the revenue of the colony raised from import duties was in 1895-96, 254,104*l.*; wine and spirit duties, 27,359*l.*; excise duty on rum, 54,266*l.*; retail spirit licences, 84,515*l.*, making a total revenue, including other items, of 567,749*l.* The total amount expended was 596,493*l.*, including all Government and judicial establishments, one-third of the total cost of immigration for the year, public works, roads and bridges, steam communication, subsidies to mail communication and telegraph, charge of public debt, clergy list and missionaries, and all the various amounts that make up the expenditure of a great and growing Colony, such expenditure and taxation being carefully adapted to be as little burdensome as possible to the population and resources of the country

The history of British Guiana may be shortly summarised. There are apparently three claimants to the discovery of Guiana : Columbus in 1498, Vasco Nuñez in 1504, and Diego de Ordas in 1531. Columbus, perhaps, may be credited with the discovery, for in August 1498 he made the island of Trinidad, and experienced much difficulty in the mouth of the Orinoco. In the following year (1499) Alonzo de Ojeda, attended by Amerigo Vespucci (whose name is still preserved in that of the American continent), set sail from Seville. They are reported to have made for the land at Surinam, and in this way to have seen the coast of Guiana. Vincent Janez Pinzon in 1500 became acquainted with the mouths of the great rivers. But all this early history is vague. The footsteps of the original Spanish explorers are difficult to follow. They leave no very definite traces upon this wonderful land of Guiana. Titles and patents were granted by the Crown of Spain, but nothing practical seemed to result from them. Attacks upon the natives were not always successful. But the imagined city, with its golden palaces and streets paved with precious stones, the El Dorado, could not pass out of the imagination. The geographical limits of Guiana were practically unknown to these Spanish explorers. They were making an empire in those days, and no one can say what they did was wrong, although, in the light of modern times, exception may be taken to the manner in which they often carried out their work in regard to native races.

Vague possibilities resolved themselves into a practical solution by the Dutch, who, so early as 1580, effected a partial settlement. In 1613 the Dutch had made good their position to such an extent that they required African slaves for their settlements on the Pomeroon and Essequebo.

They gradually maintained their ground. The alleged grant to Lord Willoughby by the English Crown in 1662 need not be mentioned except in passing. In 1669 the whole of Dutch Guiana (now Surinam) was transferred to the Dutch West India Company. It was through the agency of this company that the settlement of the country was first partially made in 1580, as above mentioned. From this time various possessors came to the front. British Guiana was in the possession of the Dutch in 1802, but in the following year was retaken by Great Britain, to whom it was finally ceded in 1814. Under the Dutch, Demerara and Essequebo constituted one government, and Berbice another. This arrangement continued in force, under the British administration, to the year 1831. A general idea may then be taken. The efforts of the early Spanish explorers, seeking things they could not find; the repeated endeavours of Raleigh; the persistent approaches of the Dutch; the varied occupation until the final cession. If the same energy as was shown by the early explorers were put forward now, the interior would not be such an unknown land. And no more wonderful interior could be imagined by the mind of man.

The political history of the country may also be shortly discussed. To the present day the Dutch institutions, involving the old Roman Law, exist. The Court of Policy of Demerara was established in 1773. In 1789 the Essequebo Government was merged into it, and the seat of Government for the United Provinces was established at Staebroek, the site of the present Georgetown. Political differences as to the management of the Colony at once arose. Up to the end of the eighteenth century the States-General largely influenced the political fortunes of the Colony; but its capture by the

British in 1796 is to be noted : it was restored to the Dutch in 1802, and retaken by Great Britain in 1803, the articles of capitulation stipulating that the laws, usages, and institutions of the Colony should be maintained as before, a fact to which, no doubt, the Colony owes its present Constitution. So the Dutch marched out with flying colours in September 1803 ; the first signature to the agreement was that of A. Meertens, Governor-General of Essequebo and Demerara, and it was countersigned, 'by command of the Court of Policy,' by P. F. Tinne, Secretary.

These arrangements with the Dutch, by which the old constitutional system should be continued, have been faithfully carried out. There has been occasionally much straining of the Constitution, but the present political arrangements are a standing proof of the efficacy of the provisions of the agreement of 1803. The present and long expected change in the political constitution of the Colony took shape in a Bill entitled 'An Ordinance to alter and amend the Political Constitution of this Colony,' which was passed in 1891, and which came into force in January 1892. The principal features of the new Constitution may be briefly stated thus :—The functions and powers of the Court of Policy and Combined Court will be unchanged, except that the administrative functions of the Court of Policy have been transferred to an Executive Council, and the duties of the former become purely legislative, it being freed from the consideration of many trivial and routine matters which have hitherto engaged a large share of its attention. The Combined Court retains its two-fold power of (1) imposing the colonial taxes and auditing the public accounts ; and (2) discussing freely and without reserve the items on the annual estimates prepared by the Court of Policy. The first of these powers is the birthright of the Combined Court, having been bestowed in 1796, when Governor Beaujon called the financial representatives into being 'with a right of voting only for the raising of colonial taxes and not further,' while the second is conferred periodically by Her Majesty's Order in Council after each renewal of the Civil List and is co-existent with the Civil List. The Court of Policy, which has hitherto consisted of the Governor, four official members, and five elected members, under the new Constitution consists of the Governor, seven official members, and eight elected members. The number of the financial representatives, who with the Court of Policy form the Combined Court, remains unchanged. The qualification for membership of the Court of Policy which hitherto was restricted to ownership of 80 acres of land, 40 of which had to be under cultivation, has been extended to ownership of immovable property of the value of not less than 1,562*l.* 10*s.*, or of a house, or house and land, of the annual rental or value of 250*l.* The qualification for election as a financial representative is the same as that for membership of the Court of Policy, with the further qualification of clear annual income of 300*l.* arising from any kind of property not mentioned in any other property qualification, or from any profession, business, or trade carried on in the Colony. The College of Electors, which has hitherto elected members of the Court of Policy, has been abolished, and members will henceforth be elected by the direct vote of the people.

The franchise has been slightly lowered as regards the income qualification and extended as regards the property qualification, and, under the new Constituton, is as follows:—
For a *Country Voter*: (1) Ownership, during the six months

previous to registration, under a title by grant from the Crown, transport, letters of decree, inheritance *ab intestato vel ex testamento*, devise, or marriage, or possession under a license of occupancy from the Crown, of not less than three acres of land actually and *bonâ fide* under cultivation ; or (2) Ownership, during the six months previous to registration, under any such title as aforesaid, of a house, or of a house and land, of the annual rental or value of not less than 20*l*. ; or (3) Occupation or tenancy, during the six months previous to registration, of not less than six acres of land actually and *bonâ fide* under cultivation, secured by lease or any document in writing for three years or upwards, such lease or document being deposited or recorded in the registrar's office of the county in which such land is situate ; or (4) Occupation or tenancy, during the six months previous to registration, of a house, or of a house and land, of the annual rental or value of not less than 40*l*., secured by lease or any document in writing for one year or upwards, deposited or recorded as aforesaid ; or (5) Possession or enjoyment of an annual income or salary of not less than 100*l*., coupled with residence in the district or division, such possession or enjoyment and residence having subsisted during the six months previous to registration ; or (6) Payment, during the twelve months previous to registration of direct taxes to the colonial revenue of 4*l*. 3*s*. 4*d*. or upwards, coupled with residence in the district or division during the six months previous to registration, provided that no license duty of any kind shall be deemed to be within the meaning of the term 'direct taxes.' For a *City Voter* the new conditions are : (1) Ownership, during the six months previous to registration, under a title by grant from the Crown, transport, letters of decree, inheritance *ab intestato vel ex* *testamento*, devise, or marriage, of a house, or of a house and premises, of the value of not less than 104*l*. 3*s*. 4*d*. as appraised for local taxation ; or (2) Occupation or tenancy during the six months previous to registration, of a house or of a house and premises, of the annual rental or value of not less than 25*l*., secured by lease or any document in writing for one year or upwards, such lease or document being deposited or recorded in the registrar's office of the county in which the city or town is situate ; or (3) Possession or enjoyment of an annual income or salary of not less than 100*l*., coupled with residence in the district, such possession of enjoyment and residence having subsisted during the six months previous to registration ; or (4) Payment, during the twelve months previous to registration, of direct taxes to the colonial revenue of 4*l*. 3*s*. 4*d*. or upwards, coupled with residence in the district during the six months previous to registration, provided that no license duty of any kind shall be deemed to be within the meaning of the term 'direct taxes.' Aliens who had hitherto acquired the political rights of citizenship after three years' residence are now debarred from such rights while they remain aliens. A direct result of the revival of interest in the political constitution of the Colony has been the addition to the list of registered voters of 377 names, the majority of whom must have possessed the necessary qualification before, but not sufficient interest in political matters to register themselves as voters. At the close of the year 1896 there were 2,479 voters, as against 2,388 at the close of 1895.

British Guiana, therefore, in its history, so much mixed up with the Dutch ; in its one dominant industry ; in the coolie immigration by which alone it has re-established and maintained that industry; in its constant endeavour to keep out the sea; in its human relics of the old Caribbean Indians (formerly perhaps kings, but now mere hunters and fishers and small customers of shops); in its large unknown interior as contrasted with the cultivated land behind its sea wall; in its artificial dykes and dams and trenches; in its combination of prosperity and work; in its labour gangs, and its luxurious club house; in its perspiration and its swizzle—in all these things it makes up a very varied and interesting whole.

But Sugar! It is impossible to pass away from this without a further reference. The smoking chimneys, the imposing buildings, the acres of sugar cane stretching away as far as the eye can reach, are all in evidence. The sugar cane is perhaps the most valuable 'grass' in the world. How to plant it, whether in short or long distances, has always been a question; what cane to select, Bourbon or other, has equally stirred the anxiety of the planter. How to cross the canes, if possible, so as to get the best qualities of different breeds or growths, has been a matter demanding consideration. What manures to use is also a point for the planter who desires to obtain profitable returns; and where is the planter who does not?

Look for a moment at some of the more picturesque aspects of this country of sugar estates. At first sight the sea wall or river embankment, the long straight roads and trenches, may savour somewhat of monotony, and suggest the desirability of some variety of hill or dale to please the eye. But a drive along the road on the seaward edge of the estates reveals features which are interesting—the fringe of trees, the mangrove and courida bushes, the ferns and water-lilies near or on the dykes. Courida resembles a straight willow, and the number of the trees and thickness of the scrub assist in protecting the plantations from the sea. Animated nature is to be observed in the numerous beautiful birds that fly about. Nor can the villages, where many estates' labourers and provision growers live, escape unnoticed. The regularity with which the estates are laid out ; the front, back, and side dams; the straight canals, look like a piece of Holland brought over and laid down by enterprising Dutchmen. The cultivated land is divided technically into 'depths.' One long even 'depth' comprises an estate, as a rule, but new land at the back, called a second 'depth,' is not infrequently taken in. Some questions have occasionally arisen as to whether this land at the back is common to anybody, or is the property of the Crown. Taking a particular estate as an example, a raised dam or 'middle walk' running right through the centre is to be noticed, and on each side of it a deep canal or irrigation trench. These canals are supplied with fresh water, sea water being considered injurious to the canes, although in times of drought, when there is little or no water coming from the back, salt water has become a necessity. The names of the estates are often not the least interesting point about them. What can be more attractive than Cornelia Ida or Leonora, Diamond or Golden Grove, Hope and Enterprise, Annandale, Belair, Lusignan, and Industry, Anna Regina, Golden Fleece, Cane Grove, and Eliza and Mary? Some French, and, as might be expected, many Dutch, appellations are to be met with. Apart from the poetry of the names, and the beautiful appearance of the cane pieces, especially when this wonderful 'grass' is at its fullest and most luxuriant period, all is business-like and practical. When the canes are cut they are brought in punts along the canals and deposited. They are put between large and heavy rollers, and the juice crushed out. The liquor, having been boiled to a certain density in the coppers, is put into a reservoir, and drawn thence by suction into a vacuum pan. It then goes into the centrifugals, the rapid revolving movement of which cleanses the sugar and makes it bright and dry, fit for immediate use. It is not necessary at this point to enter into any technical details. Suffice it to say that every possible experiment has been tried to increase the yield of the cane and improve the quality of the sugar, until now the Demerara crystals have a world-wide reputation. One interesting fact is that the sugar cane has not hitherto been reproduced from seed, although experiments have often been made in this direction with more or less success. Propagation is effected exclusively by cuttings from the stems. The question, however, of propagating sugar cane from seed has recently been brought nearer to a practical point by the very able and assiduous researches and experiments conducted in Barbados by Mr. J. B. Harrison, M.A., of Christ's College, Cambridge (late Island Professor of Chemistry in Barbados and now Government Chemist of British Guiana), and Mr. Bovell, of the Dodd's Reformatory, Barbados. These gentlemen have embodied the results of their works in certain papers, showing conclusively that this important means of improving the cane, by blending the best qualities of all varieties, is now within reach. Of course, a planter in his estates' operations could not himself provide the seed for planting, but he could be supplied with plants of an improved quality grown from seed, and from this general improvement in the natural plant he would be able gradually to increase the yield of his fields. The value of the cane as a food-yielding product has been distinctly raised to a higher level by the labours of the gentlemen above mentioned. Spikelets of fertile seeds and germinating seeds, and seedlings preserved in glycerine, have been distributed to Botanical Gardens, Agricultural Societies, and individuals throughout the West Indies, and successful results are being announced at frequent intervals. In the meantime the propagation exclusively by cuttings is carried on; every part of the cane stem having a perfect 'eye' or bud will put forth a new plant. The soundest canes must always be chosen for this purpose. They must be planted in even rows or lines, at about three feet distance from each other, and the utmost vigilance and care are necessary in weeding and trashing, the latter term meaning the removal of dead leaves. Plenty of light and air is necessary. Canes are cut, and the stole or stool is left in the ground, and when this is the case, another growth of canes, called ratoons, to distinguish it from plant canes, comes up. Like all plants, the cane is subject to certain enemies and diseases. Rats are a great plague, but the useful little animal, the mongoose, has been introduced from India to extirpate them. It does its work almost too thoroughly, for after killing off the rats it takes a fancy to poultry. Another enemy is the ant, against which petroleum is said to be a good preventive. There are also numbers of insects, cane 'borers,' grubs, caterpillars, moths, and pests of this description. With regard to the yield of an acre, it varies much. In Demerara an average of $2\frac{1}{2}$ to 3 tons of sugar may be expected from an acre of canes. Upon estates particularly well situated, the yield is greater. From the cells of the cane the juice is crushed out by the mill. This juice contains about 81 per cent. of water, 18 of sugar, and

0·6 of organic matters and 0·4 of inorganic (mineral) matters. But while the juice contains 18 per cent. of sugar, the whole of this cannot be transformed into crystallisable sugar. Ten per cent. of crystallisable sugar from the juice is a fair average, notwithstanding all the exertions which have been made to extract as much sugar as possible from the juice. Reverting to the earlier operation of extracting the juice from the cane, there are different methods, which may be divided into three heads, viz. : crushing by roller mills ; disintegrating or tearing the cane ; maceration, and diffusion. The first of these methods is easily understood, and the manner in which the canes are put into the mills and crushed is well known. The canes are introduced into the mill from the feeding table, and are crushed between the top and bottom rollers, and are then crushed again between the rollers. The damp and fibrous mass remaining is called megass. It is laid out for drying, and is used for fuel, thus utilising the remaining sugar that may be in it for purposes of heat.

But it has often been suggested that by disintegrating the cane, or tearing its fibres, a greater quantity of juice could be extracted. The cane might be reduced to a pulp after being cut up, and then subjected to hydraulic pressure. Faure's defibrator, which is a system of teeth to tear the canes and transform them into a kind of fibrous broom, to be then passed through the cane mill, has been tried. M. Bonnefin introduced a rasper, by which the cane was made into thin shreds, but no responsible details of this plan are to hand at the moment.

Then comes the plan of maceration ; that is, subjecting the canes to hot water or steam, so as to sweat the juice out as far as possible, and then to crush out the remainder by the rollers. Mr. William Russell and Mr. Risien, both of Demerara, are credited with any success that belongs to this system. But in this case, it will be observed, the action of the mill is necessary to complete the process of extracting all available juice from the cane. The main characteristic, however, is the application of steam and water. The evaporation of the water in the process is of course necessary, and the whole question resolves itself into one of expense. To obtain an increased supply of sugar at a more than proportionate cost is obviously not to be considered. But the maceration process, taking into account the extra yield, and, on the other side, the extra fuel used, may or may not be adaptable to the most economical working of the cane. On this point no opinion need be here expressed, beyond recording the fact that the experiments by Messrs. Russell and Risien, in connection with this process, were among the most important of any which have been made in the scientific study of sugar extraction from the cane.

The process of diffusion has recently been attracting much attention, especially from the success which it has secured in the beet sugar factories of the continent of Europe. It might be thought at first sight that to cut a root like a turnip into slices was an easier thing to do than to cut a fibrous plant like the sugar cane. But this difficulty has been overcome by scientific skill, especially in the construction of the knives to be used. The cane being cut into slices, and soaked in water, the crystallisable sugar in the juice will pass through the cells into the water, while the uncrystallisable part of the juice remains in the cells of the cane. This separation of the contents of the cane is the diffusion. When the cane is sliced it is automatically put into a series of open diffusors, the liquor flowing by simple gravity from one to the other, and connected with each diffusor is a steam chamber, by the effect of which the sugar is separated from the non-crystallisable elements of the juice in the cane. It is indeed a principle of purification at each step of the process; and as these steps progress, the identity of the sugar becomes more marked and recognisable, and capable by further process of being transformed into marketable produce. M. Robert's system has been known for many years in connection with the beet, and it is also the subject of experiment in different cane countries. In describing this method Messrs. Lock, Wigner & Harland, in their valuable work on Sugar Growing and Refining, say: 'The cane cutters are four, each consisting of a revolving disc of cast-iron, 4 ft. 6 in. in diameter, on which are fastened in the line of radii six knives, which, in their rotation, pass rapidly and in close proximity to another knife fixed horizontally near the disc. The canes are cut in slices by being pressed against the discs or knives by means of a hopper. The thickness of the slices is regulated by the distance between the knives on the disc and the fixed knife.' In the earlier experiments in the West Indies some difficulty was found in the necessity of cleaning and sharpening the knives at frequent intervals, but this difficulty has not been found insuperable. Several forms of knives have been seen in London, the object being to 'produce as many chips as will expose the largest possible number of the central cells to the action of the liquids in the diffusion vessels.'

In the British Guiana magazine 'Timehri,' for June 1890, Mr. Lubbock says: 'Sugar cane contains about 87 per cent. of its weight in cane juice. Where single mills are used the expression of juice during a crop rarely exceeds 66 per cent. of the weight of the cane. In the case of double crushing about 72 to 74 per cent. of juice is obtained. . . . It is contended that an extraction from the cane equivalent to 85 per cent. of juice can be obtained by means of diffusion.' What is then the relative cost of diffusion as compared with double crushing? 'In the case of diffusion we have (1) the cost of the plant; (2) the increased cost of working it; and (3) the cost of increased quantity of fuel,' and other items of additional cost to set against the larger quantity of sugar. After going into details, the author says: 'There does not appear to be any advantage in adopting diffusion on estates where a satisfactory double-crushing plant already exists. In the case where no plant exists, diffusion would compare rather more favourably, as the required machinery could be somewhat more cheaply erected than in the case where it must be in the form of additional machinery. The difference, however, would not be very appreciable. . . . Further experience will, however, shortly be forthcoming, and prudence suggests that it would be wise to await this experience before embarking capital in diffusion.'

From the above it will be seen that British Guiana is certainly in the front in sugar making. There is no new process but what has been tried there. This is the only way in which the beet industry can be kept pace with. Sugar is the staple of Demerara. The cost of producing a ton of sugar has been much reduced of late years, but this limit has now practically been reached. Without the foreign bounties, the extra richness of the cane will tell, and the prosperity of this Colony be secured. As has been said above, all classes of the community depend upon sugar, and if this industry were, from any cause, allowed to decline or be destroyed, the consequences must be disastrous to the Colony, and certainly embarrassing to the Mother Country, for she would have to support the expenses of Government out of the Imperial Treasury. Demerara is Sugar ! It fulfils its destiny in being sugar. It is exactly fitted for that production, and anything which hinders that production must be detrimental not only to the Colony, but to the British Empire of which it is an integral part.

CHAPTER VIII

SURINAM.

THE title at the head of the last chapter might be continued for this one, for we are still concerned with a portion of the wonderful land of Guiana. Dutch Guiana or Surinam lies alongside of British Guiana, on the coast to the eastward. It extends from the River Corentyn (the British boundary) to the River Mariwini in 54° W. long., the latter river being the boundary which separates Dutch from French Guiana or Cayenne.

There is direct steam communication between the United Kingdom and Surinam, Messrs. Scrutton & Sons despatching a steamer at irregular intervals from London for Paramaribo *viâ* British Guiana. Connection with Europe is maintained by the Royal Netherlands Steamship Company to and from Amsterdam every three weeks. The same line of steamers also maintains communication with New York monthly, touching at Demerara, Trinidad, a couple of Venezuelan ports, Curaçao and Port-au-Prince (Hayti). There is also a monthly service to and from St. Nazaire by way of Martinique, Guadeloupe &c., by the Compagnie Générale Transatlantique.

The route that we shall take, however, will be with Mr. Palgrave, who went by land and coasting steamer on an expedition from Georgetown, Demerara, to Paramaribo, the capital of Dutch Guiana. The above-mentioned traveller is apt in his poetical quotations, and he seeks to describe the coast of Surinam by quoting four lines from Mr. Morris :

> Then, creeping carefully along the beach,
> The mouth of a green river did they reach,
> Clearing the sands, and on the yellow bar
> The salt waves and the fresh waves were at war.

It may be said, at the risk of repetition, that Surinam, geographically speaking, is an easterly slice of Guiana between British Guiana on the one side and the French possession of Cayenne on the other. From Georgetown, Demerara, towards the eastward there is a good carriage road running parallel to the coast, although some little distance inland. It is a pleasant drive through sugar estates and busy villages. The western bank of a full and strong river is reached—the Berbice. Taking boat for 150 miles, the distance between the harbour of Berbice and the mouth of the Surinam River is traversed. But first the steamer anchors off the little town of Nikerie, or Nickerie, lying immediately to the east of the river Corentyn, which marks the boundary between the British and Dutch territories. Here are situated a few sugar estates, behind the shelter of the mangroves which fringe the river banks. The town of Nikerie has suffered much from the inroads of the sea, and the breakers now roll over the site of former streets and buildings. The ground, however, rises more rapidly here than in British Guiana, and the further progress of the sea may be stayed. It is interesting to hear the negroes speaking Dutch. Nikerie district contains about 10,000 acres of good land, but not more than a fourth of it has been utilised. Labour is much wanted, and endeavours have been made to supplement it by immigration from India and Java. Along the coast to Caronie, past the joint estuaries of the Coppename and Saramacca rivers, past the leper settlement near the former river, past the settlement of European labourers (a much more pleasant sight) on the latter river, the signs of industry and cultivation are noticed. The tall chimneys, the buildings, all look pleasant beneath the bright sky. The Surinam River is navigable for 100 miles, and is the main artery of the Colony. The River Commeweyne has a shorter course, but when it joins the Surinam it is a broad and deep stream. Nearly at the point of junction the fort of New Amsterdam was built in the middle of the last century. Past this fortress, which is well situated to command the river and guard the approach to the capital, going south up the river, the quaint and picturesque town Paramaribo is reached at last. The air is warm and moist and still, unstirred by sea breezes or bracing mountain winds, but it is not unhealthy. It has a population of about 32,000, whilst its streets are wide, its gardens well laid out, its shady and regular avenues of leafy trees attractive, its houses lofty, and its public buildings splendid. It is Holland under a tropical sky, and there are the usual evidences of Dutch energy, industry, and enterprise. It has a town hall, with a high tower looking over the river. Mr. Palgrave sees in Paramaribo a perfect image of the Dutch character. 'The well-planned and carefully kept canals that intersect the town in every direction, the neat bridges, the broad riverside quays, the trim gardens, the decent cemeteries, the entire order and disposition of the place, tell the same tale, witness to the same founders, reflect the same image, true to its original on the North Sea coast; all tell of settled order and tasteful method.'

Discovered in 1499 by Amerigo Vespucci, Surinam was not colonised by any nationality until many years had passed away. It was visited, of course, by adventurers. The first attempt was made by an English captain, Marshall, in 1603. The old Indian village of Paramaribo marked itself out by its situation as the proper site for the capital, a position to which it was raised by Lord Willoughby of Parham in 1650, and the Dutch retained it as such when they obtained definite possession later on. Lord Willoughby founded many a Parham in the New World, and it has been thought by some that Paramaribo was a rendering of that well-known name, but the Indian origin of the word seems now to be generally accepted. Under the Dutch rule the town was gradually built and improved, and the resources of the Colony generally developed. In the course of its history it has suffered from the same causes as those which have produced those many periods of depression and loss which are so common in the annals of West Indian agriculture and production. Paramaribo has suffered from two disastrous fires, one in 1821 and another in 1832. From this last misfortune it has now fully recovered; and since the labour troubles connected with emancipation have been outlived, the Colony, if it has made no progress, has endeavoured to hold its own as a sugar-producing country. The character of the population has been described as follows : steady in business, methodical in habit, economical in expenditure, liberal in outlay, hospitable in entertainment, cheerful without flightiness, kindly without affectation, serious without dulness. It must, however, be acknowledged that Surinam now contains a less number of Dutchmen, or Europeans of any kind, than it did formerly. What are called the Servile Wars, which lasted to a more or less extent during the greater part of the eighteenth century, have left no bitterness behind. A disturbed state of things was probably inseparable from slavery, which was not finally abolished until 1863. While the Creole quarters of the city are becoming more extensive, the neglected stores where the European merchants carried on their business tell a tale of decadence. The Colony was drained of its money in the troublous years at the end of the last and the beginning of the present century. The hostilities between France and Holland had a prejudicial effect upon the Colony. Java in the East has been a more profitable possession of Holland than Surinam in the West. The principal means of communication are the rivers and canals. A number of negroes live on the water in wide flat-bottomed boats. The cocoa plantations are busy scenes in crop time, and the industry has been attended with fair success. The names of the sugar estates have not always such a pleasant sound as those in British Guiana, although there are many happy ideas conveyed. 'Labour and Sorrow,' 'Discordia,' and other appellations of an equally dismal character, take the taste (if the metaphor is in order) out of one's mouth. Still the country, flat though it is, shows in the canals and chimneys, the coolie houses, the fields of cane, and other signs of agricultural work—that there is, or may be, a basis of prosperity and hope in this quiet and comparatively unknown country.

The most distinguished Governor in the history of the Colony was Van Sommelsdyk, who in 1683 owned a great portion of the land. He had been engaged in service at the Court of William II. of Orange, and knew the prince who was afterwards William III. of England. His negotiations with the aboriginal Indians required skill and delicacy,

SURINAM. 169

and the Caribs were equitably treated and settled. There are very few Indians now in the Colony. The above-mentioned Governor is credited with the introduction of the cocoa plant. A great canal and the principal fort already referred to still bear his name. His rule was disliked by some disaffected spirits whose interest was against reform, and he was killed in a mutiny in 1688. His son accompanied the new Governor, and assisted in repelling an attack of the French, who were uneasy neighbours in Cayenne. Up the Cottica River true Guiana forests are seen. In these up-river settlements the bush negroes, who caused so much trouble in the last century, are principally to be found, distinguished by their tribal divisions. The story of these events is given in much detail in a once well-known book, Stedman's 'Surinam,' an author who knew the country well. The bush negroes are strong athletic men of well-modelled stature.

The yearly average of temperature is 79°; the noon-day heat in town is very great; this is a time during which all Paramaribo sleeps.

Mr. Palgrave quotes the following sentence from the 'Saturday Review': 'It would be interesting to know the secret of Dutch Colonial management, which presents to an outside observer the aspect of minding one's own business and inducing other people to mind theirs.' Like most epigrammatic sentences this one may not be wholly true, but it throws a certain light upon the character of the people. From small beginnings in the Colony the Dutch have minded their own business, but this habit has not been instrumental in any unusual degree in preventing the interference of other persons with their affairs. There is a certain slowness about their operations. The Dutch West

India Company did little good with Surinam before Sommelsdyk began his career as Governor in 1683. He established the Court of Policy and the Court of Justice. The present Legislature is a House of Assembly partly official or nominated, and partly elected on a suffrage. The administration of justice is regulated by Dutch law and custom. Some years ago part of the revenue was raised by a poll tax, a relic of the old slave times when a planter was taxed according to the number of his slaves. Now-a-days, in a country like Surinam, a poll tax would be very difficult to collect. The system of export duties, too, except for the exclusive purpose of introducing labour, is not a sound one. The Moravians and Roman Catholics are the most active among the religious sects, and there is an influential, though not a particularly large, community of Jews. The acres under cultivation, about 30,000, are pretty evenly divided between sugar and cocoa. The production of cotton has gradually disappeared. Coffee is steadily increasing. Altogether about 400,000 acres are available for cultivation, and, as above stated, only a very small portion has ever been made of productive value. 'Estates there certainly are,' says the traveller from whom we have already quoted, 'but how small, how thinly scattered; rare islets in a trackless ocean of unreclaimed bush, marginal lines by the winding river courses, desultory fringes to a boundless expanse of wilderness behind.' This is true, no doubt, but in the large distances of Guiana the picture is a usual and characteristic one. In British Guiana the Dutch originally settled up the rivers, and so they apparently did in Surinam, and it is no proof of decadence that the sites of the earlier settlements were subsequently abandoned.

The United Kingdom supplies Surinam with hardware

goods. But Germany is pressing closely on Sheffield in this trade. The Germans send cheaper wares, not so serviceable, but more attractively got up than the British. Mr. Consul Wyndham says in a recent report: 'The immense amount of foreign cutlery &c. of an inferior quality which finds its way into the foreign market, marked with English names and marks, is a serious drawback to the hardware trade.' The English mercantile custom of sending out goods on commission is not to be encouraged. On the contrary, good commercial travellers, of the same stamp as those sent by American and German firms, would prevent England from being completely elbowed out of the trade in these distant parts of the world. Manchester goods fairly hold their own, but there is much competition with the German manufacturers. The provision trade is entirely in American hands. Building timber is brought from America, and bricks from Holland. There may be a demand for quartz-crushing machinery when the gold industry becomes more extensive, and British manufacturers should keep their eyes on this market. A good machine for cocoa-drying is also in demand. The coal-ships from Cardiff afford opportunities for shipments of machinery, as all the coal for the war-ships on the station, for the mail and other steamers, and for the sugar estates, comes from the Welsh port under an open yearly contract.

The value of sugar exports from Surinam (muscovado and vacuum pan) in 1895 amounted to 80,000*l.* Rum is made in proportion. The production of cocoa advanced from 112,354*l.* in 1891, to 181,000*l.* in 1895, and it is expected that yearly more cocoa will be exported as the young plantations are developed, the crops having been for the last three years very good ones. The balata industry is in a progressive state, hundreds of British subjects from Demerara being employed as balata bleeders or as collectors. Most of the gum is exported to the United States. It was only in 1890 that this industry was considered of sufficient importance to be regulated by special laws. Laws have now been made, and consequently the balata industry has attracted foreign capital and labour, English, American, and local firms having taken out leases of land to prospect for and to bleed the 'bullet' tree. Regarding the gold industry Mr. S. A. Churchill, the British Consul at Paramaribo, in a Report dated March 1896, says :—'The state of the mining industry in 1895 was not very satisfactory. Enthusiasm was wanting. The principal obstacle is want of capital and the lack of experienced mining managers. The mining operations are, as a rule, of a most primitive nature. Pan and sluice washing is the sum and total of the system adopted by most of the mine owners. The absence of sufficient capital to secure the services of men as managers who shall be beyond the suspicion of disinterestedness, and of known competence in mining, results in disappointment. Of the gold produced in 1894 over 100,000*l.* was shipped to the Netherlands, over 15,000*l.* to the United Kingdom, 13,000*l.* to Cayenne, and over 5,000*l.* to the United States. How much more was exported unofficially it is impossible to say, though the amount thus sent out of the country is said to be far from inconsiderable.' The total imports into Surinam in 1895 amounted to 433,585*l.*, the proportion of direct borne traffic from the United Kingdom being about 46,640*l.* The exports amounted to 421,738*l.*, and the shipments to the United Kingdom to about 53,574*l.*

These figures do not seem very striking. They show a magnificent and well-watered country practically unutilised, with some, but faint, signs of modern progress. There is no general agriculture, by which is meant grain crops, except a little rice. There is little dairy and cattle farming. There is nothing but cocoa, balata, sugar, and coffee, the latter being a rapidly increasing production. What, then, remains? Some people say gold! And it must be confessed that in British, Venezuelan, and Dutch Guiana this article may be the foundation of very important industries. To a certain class of mind—not perhaps the least thoughtful and refined—digging for gold does not appear the best and most grateful occupation for the people of purely agricultural countries.

CHAPTER IX.

CAYENNE.

STILL eastward lies Cayenne, the portion of Guiana belonging to France. The name is known in Europe, because it formed for many years an extensive French convict settlement, and neither Surinam nor Demerara has been particularly happy in having such a neighbour. Napoleon III sent many political prisoners during twenty years after 1851 to this distant province.

The French from the beginning of its history have been connected with Cayenne. In 1626 and in 1635 they attempted to form settlements. In 1664 it was granted to the Compagnie des Indes Occidentales. In this century (seventeenth) both the English and Dutch troubled it, but with short intermissions it remained in the hands of the French. There were the usual troubles and often disastrous conflicts with the Indians. The Jesuits were active in founding missions, but their efforts do not appear to have had a sustained success. After the French conquest of Alsace and Lorraine, a large number of Germans were sent to the colony, but all these soon died from misery and disease. It has been a convict settlement since 1797. The general feature of the country is flat, rising into a moderately high mountainous region. Neither the physical, sanitary, nor social aspects of Cayenne are attractive to visitors in search of health or pleasure. Besides several thousands of convicts and their guardians, the population is small, numbering altogether, including some 18,000 Creoles, not more than 28,000.

The country is well wooded, and many of the finest of the Guiana timbers are to be found. The productions of sugar, cocoa, and coffee have been reduced to a very unimportant value. At the same time this country, like all the Guiana territories, is endowed with the presence of gold. When this idea becomes firmly fixed in the minds of European or South American adventurers, and when sufficient labour is available, miners will be attracted. In 1895 about 100,000 ounces of gold were exported. A number of coolies from India were at one time introduced, but the Indian Government, finding the labour of these people diverted to the mines, where they suffered great hardship and were subject to a heavy mortality, and finding too that her Majesty's Consul had no influence in securing the good treatment of the labourers, prohibited the emigration from British India. It is possible, however, that an occasional ship may still be despatched to Cayenne from Pondicherry or Karikal.

Here, then, is a great country, of a size that would make a European State shrink into insignificance, with boundless possibility of agricultural and commercial wealth, known only as a station for convicts, and its inhabited portion as an abode of fever. There is no British Consul's report of sufficiently recent date to be useful; in any case, little interest would probably be taken in the statistics. The real importance of the Colony lies in the gold workings, and the more gold is found and worked, naturally the greater amount of the import trade from France. These appear to be the two main conditions which govern the future of this Colony and its value to the Mother Country

CHAPTER X.

TRINIDAD.

TRINIDAD is an island, situated between 10° 3' and 10° 50' latitude N., and between 61° 1' and 62° 4' longitude W. of Greenwich. Its length is 65 miles on the southern and 53 miles on the northern side, and its breadth on the eastern and western sides respectively is 48 and 49 miles. It is separated from the continent of South America by the Gulf of Paria, into which fall the waters of the northern mouths of the Orinoco. The Dragon's and Serpent's Mouths, the Bocas forming the entrance to the harbour, convey the most picturesque impression of the approaches to Trinidad. Trinidad is bounded on the north by the Caribbean Sea ; on the south by the channel which separates it from the Delta and Caños of the Orinoco ; on the east by the Atlantic Ocean ; and on the west by the Gulf of Paria. The superficial extent or area is 1,754 square miles, or nearly 1,287,600 square acres. There are three ranges of mountains running in a parallel line from east to west, clothed with forest. The central and southern ranges are accessible on all sides. The northern range rises abruptly on the sea side. There is a certain unreclaimed air about Trinidad caused by the woodland ; and where this is broken by cacao plantations, the bois immortel from its height and size preserves the appearance of forest.

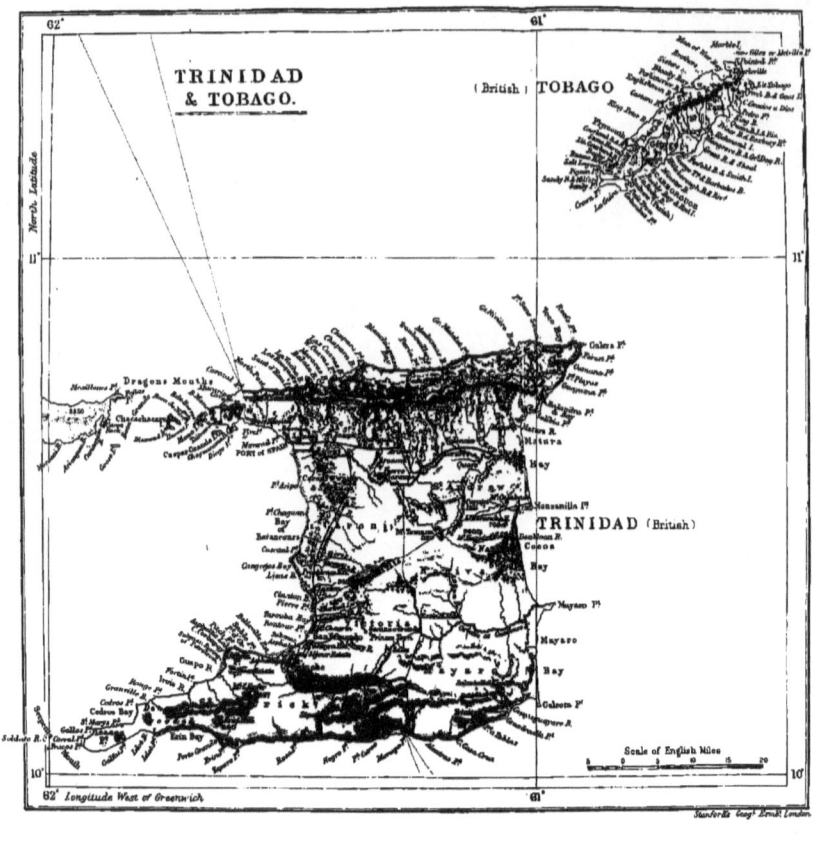

The Princes in the 'Bacchante' entered the Gulf of Paria through the Boca de los Monos, one of the Dragon's Mouths. The green hills at once attracted attention. But the green appearance was caused by high trees, not by grass and shrubs. There were, however, clearings to be noticed, fishermen's huts, and patches of white sandy beach. The currents are strong here, and ships under sail find some difficulty in making the passage. On the western shore of the bay the first glimpse of the Spanish Main is seen, the mountains of Venezuela being in sight. 'We ran through the channel,' says Kingsley, in the account of his visit, 'then amid more low wooded islands, it may be for a mile, and then saw before us a vast plain of muddy water. No shore was visible to the westward. To the eastward the northern hills of Trinidad, forest-clad, sank to the water; to the south lay a long line of coast, generally level with the water's edge, and green with mangroves, or dotted with coco-palms. That was the Gulf of Paria and Trinidad beyond.' The foregoing is a recognisable account of the approach to Trinidad. All travellers notice the curious change in the colour of the water as the Bocas are neared. This is produced by the waters of the Orinoco rushing down and bringing alluvial deposits from the mountains hundreds of miles away. The waters of the Gulf of Paria are, in consequence, muddy. The entrance to the Gulf is, as stated above, somewhat difficult of navigation. The channel which lies between the southern shores of Trinidad and the mainland is the Boca del Serpiente, or Serpent's Mouth. The northern entrance to the Gulf, the Dragon's Mouth, is divided into four channels, the Boca de los Monos or monkeys' passage, the Boca de los Huevos, or egg passage, the Boca de los Navios, or ship passage, and the Boca Grande. Vessels may anchor in the Gulf from 3 to 20 fathoms on a bottom of gravel and mud. The tides being checked, there is an accumulation of mud to such an extent that some one predicted a long time ago that Port of Spain would eventually become an inland town. There is no doubt that near Port of Spain the water is very shallow, requiring large boats to lie out some miles in the Gulf, which is a large salt lake shut in on all sides, with the exception of the passages above mentioned, where the ebb and flow of the tide produces strong currents, but makes little impression on the wide expanse of the Gulf.

Port of Spain can just be seen through the masts and rigging of the coasters and merchant ships. The street from the landing place is broad and straight. The Marine Square, with its fountain in the centre, and the business houses shaded with palm trees, next attract attention, as well as the two towers of the Roman Catholic Cathedral, the square-towered English Church, and other noticeable buildings. Bright purple flowers brighten the aspect of the brick buildings. The houses stand on pillars of two or three feet above the ground, as is the custom in the West Indies. The stores or large shops of Port of Spain, with their porticoes and high doorways, seem solidly built, especially the older ones, recalling probably the days of the Spanish occupation. The number of idlers in the streets does not give a very favourable first impression to the visitor. But the negroes and negresses of the seaport afford no standard by which to judge the whole black population. Some Indian and Chinese coolies in the streets suggest (the East Indian especially), as in Demerara, a very important and indeed indispensable part of the labouring population.

The large black vultures, 'Johnny Crows,' who act as natural scavengers in the town, and are extremely useful in

this respect, constitute a peculiar and noticeable feature of the place. Going up the street into the suburbs, pleasant little villas are to be seen, and then a large expanse, the Savannah, which makes an admirable public park and racecourse. The Botanic Gardens are well kept up, and are useful for the information which they are the means of providing for planters of sugar, coffee, cocoa, and other products. The Botanic Gardens in the West Indies are in communication with the Royal Gardens at Kew, and specimens of plants and seeds are often usefully exchanged. In the Botanic Gardens, Government House is situated, a residence with peculiarly lovely surroundings. The house itself is large and handsome. On the lawn is a vast ceiba, or silk-cotton tree, with great limbs and branches forming a thick roof of green. The beauties of the gardens hardly lend themselves to a cold and halting description by written words. The palms and flowers, the spice trees and orange trees, the wonderful creepers, or 'vines' as they are locally called, attract the eye with their exquisite forms. The 'Cottage' just outside the Gardens, which was the Governor's residence before the present house was built, and in which Kingsley wrote his 'At Last,' is now amongst the things of the past, having been demolished. Kingsley's vivid account of the sights and scenes of the 'Cottage' and its surroundings will be found in his well-known work. He was particularly interested 'in the great arches of the bamboo clumps,' which are still called Mr. Kingsley's cane brake. These canes grow very high, and add much to the picturesqueness of the scenery of which they form the foreground. The horseback rides that are available from Government House are extremely beautiful and varied; one, in particular (if any selection is indeed possible), up the Maravilla valley, over the Saddle, a peculiar formation at the top of the hill, and thence to cacao plantations, the young trees having their umbrellas or shade trees to protect them from the sun.

But before noticing the sights of the country a few more particulars respecting the town might be acceptable. Port of Spain (with a population of 33,782) is situated (says De Verteuil) at the angle formed by the junction of the north-west prolongation of the island with its main land, and about two miles northward of the River Caroni, from which once upon a time Sir Walter Raleigh landed on the soil of Trinidad. Two spurs running from the northern range towards the sea encircle a small plain, from one to two miles broad and about four miles in length along the seashore. The St. Ann's and Maravilla valleys open on this plain. The streets of Port of Spain are wide, with footways and open gutters down which the rain rushes. The detached houses standing in their own grounds in the upper part of the town give a pleasant rural aspect to the place. Port of Spain, owing to its being only 25 to 30 feet above the sea level, does not present an imposing aspect seaward. Goods are landed in flats from ships lying from one and a half to two miles out. A plan now receiving attention is to build a pier for that distance, so as to allow big ships to discharge their goods alongside into a line of trucks that would be in connection with the railways on land. Whether this can be successfully carried out is at present a subject of experiment, but the idea shows an enterprising spirit. The lower or southern part of the town, known as Marine Square, consists of land formerly recovered from the sea. The retiring sea has also allowed a new quay to be built for the landing and despatch of goods in lighters and the smaller-sized boats. Port of Spain became the capital of the island in 1783. In March 1808 it was almost destroyed by fire, whilst in 1896 a disastrous fire occurred, completely destroying the business part of the town, and doing damage to the extent of half a million sterling. The premises destroyed have, however, been replaced by better buildings, and the principal business thoroughfare of the city has been much improved. The electric light has been introduced into many of the streets and houses of Port of Spain, including the Governor's residence.

The Government or official buildings in Brunswick Square are worthy of a visit. They are in two blocks connected by an archway. Lord Harris, one of the most respected of the English governors, whose administration was in the very crisis of the disastrous times succeeding 1846, officially opened these buildings in 1848. They contain the departmental offices, and the council chamber, with its ceiling of native woods. A new stained glass window in commemoration of the long services of a former Colonial Secretary, Mr. Scott Bushe, makes a handsome addition to the chamber. It has for its subject the Landing of Columbus in Trinidad, and at the bottom of the window a portrait of Mr. Bushe is inserted. A statue of Lord Harris, by Behnes, adds artistic dignity to the room. The great discoverer is also remembered by a bronze statue erected above a fountain in Columbus Square. The Town Hall, the centre of the municipal interests of the town, should be visited, especially for its fine portraits of several of the most distinguished governors. The police barracks, an extensive and costly pile of buildings, are situated close by. There is a public library in Chacon Street. The town is traversed by tram-cars.

In mentioning the present capital, the small town of

St. Joseph, founded about the year 1577, and for a long time the chief town of Trinidad, deserves remembrance. It stands on a narrow eminence at the entrance of the Maraccas valley. It is mainly inhabited by some Spanish families, descendants of the former possessors of the island. In 1595 Sir Walter Raleigh, having entered the Gulf of Paria, sent some boats up the River Caroni, and thence up a tributary, and captured the town.

With regard to the physical features of the island, Messrs. Wall and Sawkins, who made the Geological Survey, may be taken as the best authorities.

'One of the first objects arresting the attention of the observer is the distribution of the elevations in particular lines, forming three systems or ranges :

 1st. Parallel and adjacent to the northern coast.
 2nd. Traversing the central districts of the island.
 3rd. Parallel and adjacent to the southern coast.
' These will be distinguished as—
 The northern littoral range.
 The central range.
 The southern littoral range.

' The directions of the axes, or the dynamical lines in which the agents of elevation have acted, are nearly E. and W. for the 1st and 3rd, but inclined about 20° N. of E. and S. of W. for the 2nd; but the latter does not maintain a perfectly parallel course throughout its whole extent.

'The northern littoral range traverses the entire length of the island, and possesses an average breadth of nearly seven miles, occupying an area (including small islands) of 358 square miles. There are generally two ridges, the subordinate one rising immediately from the sea, and attaining

TRINIDAD: WHARF, NOW BEING RECONSTRUCTED, AT PORT OF SPAIN.

an average elevation of 800 feet, and the main ridge (locally termed Cordillera), which varies from 1,600 to 2,200 feet. There are several high peaks rising out of this ridge ; the culminating summit in the western section is the three-peaked mountain of Tucutche, rising to 3,012 feet, and in the eastern section the height of Aripo, attaining 2,740 feet. Towards either extremity the ridges fuse together, and form on the east a gradual incline to the sea ; on the west descending towards the lower hills of the islands of the Bocas, where the chain is interrupted, to rise again, and attain a greater elevation on the adjacent mainland.

'The valleys are entirely transverse, and of some breadth in the western division, becoming merely deep ravines for the passage of the waters to the eastward ; they are often contracted near their mouths, expanding in the upper parts into somewhat basin-shaped cavities. The small islands dotting the gulf, or placed at its entrance, are detached portions of this hilly system, and present the same features, but on a smaller scale. The declivities are invariably steep, often 35° with the horizon, rising almost precipitously from the sea on the north, and descending at high angles to the low land on the south.

' The whole district is richly clothed with tropical vegetation, frequently characterised by magnificent timber. The purity of the waters, the coolness of the nights, and the beauty of the scenery, often grand and majestic, combine to render this the most agreeable portion of the island.

'The central range extends from Point à Pierre on the west to near the southern bank of the L'Ebranche on the east, a length of about 35 miles, and as the average breadth may be 3½ miles, the area occupied is 122 square miles. When seen from a distance the aspect is that of a low ridge, with occasional elevated peaks ; but when examined from some central eminence in the district itself, the appearance is that of a hilly country, with an irregular distribution of the elevations. This seeming irregularity is produced by the number of ridges which emanate from the hill of Montserrat ; one series curving round Tamana, and connecting with Mounts Harris and Carata, whilst another runs north of the central line to Tamana and L'Ebranche.

'Portions of the district are very abrupt and precipitous, but in the western division there is some gently undulating and rather elevated land, which, from its fertility, is admirably adapted for cultivation. The ridges and higher parts are characterised by fine open woods, with many noble specimens of the cedar (*Cedrela*), but the valleys or ravines are often crowded with such an excess of bushes and creepers as to render progress irksome in the extreme.

'The view from Tamana possesses a peculiar charm ; it is by far the most comprehensive in the island. The eye luxuriates in every shade of the richest greens ; a vast extent of woodland, from eastern to western sea, from northern to southern hills, without the slightest perceptible trace of cultivation, save where the scarlet flowers of the 'madre del cacao' mark the winding course of the Caroni, testifies the supremacy of nature. Scenery more sublime may be readily obtainable, but for loveliness of hues, for exuberance of vegetation, this is a prospect which can scarcely be surpassed.

'The highest summits, proceeding towards the east, are :

Montserrat	952 feet.
Tamana	1,025 ,,
Mount Harris	903 ,,
Mount l'Ebranche	718 ,,

'The southern littoral range is not so continuous as the two preceding, and may be considered as commencing at the Point Gran Calle, Guayguayare, and running to Canary, whence the elevation diminishes to the depression of the Moruga, rising again beyond that river, and graduating finally towards the gently swelling land of Siparia.'

The maximum elevation is noticeable in the eastern part, where there are three peaks termed the Three Sisters. When Columbus saw them they suggested to him the name of the island.

The slates, sandstones, limestones, and shales forming the strata of the northern littoral range present a continuation of the littoral range of Venezuela, affording one, among several proofs, that Trinidad was once part of the mainland, but separated in the course of centuries by the action of the sea, assisted perhaps by volcanic agency.

Caverns exist in the limestone. They contain stalactitic lime, with crystallised spar. One of these caverns, that in Diego Martin district on the north-west coast, is full of numberless bats. But a much more remarkable cavern is to be found at the bottom of Oropouche Hill. This hill rises to over 2,000 feet, and consists of fissured calcareous rocks. There is the accumulation of a considerable body of water in the upper part of the cave, which flows in a constant stream and forms the origin of the River Oropouche. This cavern is the habitation of the Guacharo, the original description of which was given by Humboldt.

A list of some of the principal excursions from Port of Spain to places of interest in the island might be useful. Mr. J. H. Collens' 'Guide to Trinidad' may be consulted with advantage. There is a pleasant railway ride to Arima. On the hill is the Roman Catholic church of Our Lady of

Laventille and an old fort called Fort Picton. Many sugar estates are noticed in passing. In the residence on Plantation Valsayn the capitulation treaty was signed by Chacon, giving the possession of the island to the British. Sir Ralph Abercromby and Admiral Harvey were present on behalf of England. St. Joseph, the old Spanish capital, is seen at the foot of the northern hills. Arima is a busy, thriving place, with many streets, shops, and a racecourse.

In the railway journey from Port of Spain to San Fernando the visitor cannot help noticing the principal sugar districts of the Colony—the large cultivated estates, interspersed with forest land. San Fernando lies at the foot of the Naparima Hill. It is about thirty-two miles by water and forty-two by road from Port of Spain. Besides the railway there is an excellent coastal steam communication between these two principal ports. San Fernando dates from 1792, and was established by Governor Chacon. Like most West Indian towns, it had its ordeal by fire in 1818, and was afterwards rebuilt. So recently as 1883 it experienced another serious conflagration, which destroyed many of the shops and stores. This caused no hindrance to the business of the town, for the buildings were soon renewed. A number of public institutions, hospital, churches, barracks, town hall &c. will be found on Harris Parade.

From High Street, San Fernando, Princes Town can be reached either by the Cipero tramway or by the Guaracara line, which runs up into the interior by the same way as and at some little distance from the Cipero. Princes Town derives its name from the visit of the two sons of the Prince of Wales. It was previously known as the Mission. It is now a large and attractive-looking village. A few miles from Princes Town is a mud volcano. There was rather a serious eruption in 1887 which considerably raised and enlarged the surface of the mud. The inhabitants are thankful these eruptions are not frequent.

To explore Montserrat and notice the beauties of the district, the best way, no doubt, is that recommended by experienced travellers—to proceed to Couva on the Government line and then take to horseback. In this district great quantities of cacao are grown.

After taking the train to Arima, a ride on horseback along the east coast presents many natural objects of interest. One of these is the Cocal, a large cocoa-nut plantation, belonging to the borough council of Port of Spain. It is close to the seashore, and was originally formed by the wreck of a vessel laden with cocoa-nuts. With 50,000 trees it is not surprising to hear that there is a large factory attached to the estate, turning out 30,000 gallons of oil and 1,000 bales of fibre annually.

Diego Martin is seven miles from Port of Spain, and the famous piece of scenery, the Blue Basin, is a short distance farther. A river falls through a mountain gorge into a pool below, the water of which, from some reflection of the sky through the foliage, appears to be blue.

The three principal objects of greatest interest in the island are the cascades, the high woods, and the Pitch Lake.

The greatest cascade is the Maraccas, falling perpendicularly 340 feet from an elevation 1,100 feet above the sea. This is extremely beautiful, and after heavy rains is really grand in its force and volume. The falls are within an easy distance of Port of Spain. They are graphically described by Mr. Krüger, and referred to later on. The high woods may first be discussed.

Kingsley in the early morning came to Port of Spain. He was rowed in a southerly direction upon the Gulf. The party viewed the high tree which marks the entrance of the Chaguana Creek, and were depressed by the aspect of the mangrove swamps. They rowed on, disturbing the stargazing fish with his prominent eyes : of these eyes some curious stories are told. The fish appears at first to possess four distinct eyes, each of its two organs being divided across the middle, and apparently separated into two distinct portions. Folk believe that the fish with the lower halves of his eyes sees in the water, and with the upper halves sees in the air, and this produces the condition of being equally at home in water and on land. The proceedings of these 'four-eyes' made Kingsley laugh. But the creek at last ended at a wharf. A sudden thunder shower emphasised the importance of being well provided with waterproofs and wraps. A chill might lead to ague and fever. Taking passage in a tramway truck, they came to a house with a palmiste, or cabbage palm, on each side of the garden gate, columns a hundred feet high with a crown of dark leaves. A walk to the depôt, where the timber belonging to the Government was being felled, brought the party to the high woods. The darkness pierced by rays of sunlight, the green ferns, the strange colossal shapes towering up, the apparent confusion of forms, the terror lest one's way should be lost, and a lifetime should be lived in the presence of these fantastic forms and in this green night. Dreams of Comus and his rabble would come upon one, and the enchanter's wand be feared. But the rapidly ascending sap in the trees, such as the 'water vine,' reminded Kingsley of Jack and the Bean Stalk, an equally poetical story, to many minds, with that told in verse by Milton. The lofty stems, like cathedral pillars, losing themselves at the top in a green cloud, give an idea of distance and of beauty. Beautiful distances may indeed be said to be the prevailing character of the scene, with difference of colour and endless variety of form. The smell of the vanille orchis comes gratefully to the senses. The mighty trees and the parasitical growths that cover them—the great balata tree with its milk that congeals into gum and gutta-percha, the orchids which are to be found on every bough and stem—the quick destruction and the hasty revival of vegetation—all these are to be observed, and in such profusion and multiplicity, the forces of nature appearing so silent and yet so sure, that the mind finds it difficult to take the whole in, and perhaps falls back upon the conclusion that it is but an appearance after all, and not a true and tangible reality.

Trinidad has a number of asphaltic deposits. There are petroleum springs, beds or veins of asphaltum, and accumulations of mineral pitch. Three principal varieties of asphaltum are to be found in this island, viz. asphaltum glance, ordinary asphaltum, and asphaltic oil. The first is hard and brittle, and, containing very little earthy impurity and water, is valuable but scarce. The second, ordinary asphaltum of a brownish black colour, contains a larger portion of earthy admixture and water, and is flexible or plastic. The third is very largely diluted with water. The Pitch Lake is subject to all the conditions favourable to a large accumulation. The surface of the lake, 99 acres, is not an unbroken plain of asphalt, but there are numerous depressions which hold the rain water. When it first rises to the surface, the asphalt is mixed with an oily substance, which causes it to be in a somewhat fluid state. Evaporation leaves it more solid, so that it can be walked upon. The most remarkable feature of this natural wonder is the constant movement which must be going on, the power of the gaseous influences being especially noticeable. The expanse is broken in a few places by trees and bushes growing out of sand and bituminous matter. The afternoon sun strikes with full force on this coast, and, as little wind is felt, the atmosphere becomes very hot.

Visitors at first sight do not quite understand the Pitch Lake. It is a curiosity, a wonder, a something that is not explainable at the instant. They poke their sticks into it, and find that the pitch does not adhere. They entertain themselves a little as to its origin, whether by a convulsion of nature or by the growth of centuries. The same forces have produced it that have made the coal fields of England and Wales. We should have pitch lakes in England if we had the fierce tropical sun to act as a dominant power.

Kingsley went by steamer some thirty miles from Port of Spain, along a flat mangrove shore. The 'beach was black with pitch,' and the smell was pungent. The La Brea pine apples attracted attention. After going along various pitch roads, the lake opens into view. Poetical minds are at once filled with suggestions as to the Stygian pool and Dante's Inferno ; but the carts taking the pitch down to the wharf, for the purpose of paving the streets of New York and London, represent the more modern and business aspect of the scene. For many years the question was how to utilise the pitch. The well-known Admiral Lord Dundonald took a keen interest in it. He

PITCH LAKE, TRINIDAD.

wrote a pamphlet upon the subject. The Cochrane family are still connected with the district. The exclusive working of the pitch is granted to a company, who pay to the Government a very considerable sum annually for the privilege.

The late Lady Brassey joins in the chorus of horror at the Pitch Lake. It is a 'hideous-looking place ; a lake of thick pitch, very like solid black mud, intersected by channels, holes, and crevices filled with water.' The asphalt was being dug out in huge blocks and placed on barrows for conveyance to the boiling house. The inevitable quotation from Dante follows. The party, armed with long sticks, and crossing the crevices on planks, ventured on the 'black Stygian area.' The children were amused at finding they could make little balls of the pitch without its defiling their hands. The grove of Moriche palms is noticed by every visitor. The Princes, after landing at La Brea, and driving through the Pitch Road in a cart, noticing the flowers and vegetation at the roadside, came upon the lake, which they liken to a large marsh of black mud hardened at the surface, but intersected by pools and lines of stagnant water. The constant movement of this originally vegetable mass, transformed into coaly and asphaltic matter, is one of the most striking aspects of this scene. Whatever is taken away, the vacant space is soon filled up.

A former Colonial Botanist of Trinidad, Mr. H. Krüger, in discussing the flora of the island, gives the following description, which may be read in connection with previous references to the same points : 'The northern chain of mountains, covered nearly everywhere with dense forests, is intersected at various angles by numbers of valleys presenting the most lovely character. Generally each valley is watered by a silvery stream, tumbling here and there over rocks and natural dams, ministering in a continuous rain to the strange-looking river-canes, dumb-canes, and balisiers, that voluptuously bend their heads to the drizzly shower which plays incessantly on their glistening leaves, off which the globules roll in a thousand pearls, as from the glossy plumage of the stately swan.

'One of these falls deserves particular notice—the Cascade of Maraccas—in the valley of that name. The high road leads up the valley a few miles, over hills, and along the windings of the river, exhibiting the varying scenery of our mountain district in the fairest style. There, on the river side, you may admire gigantic pepper trees, or the silvery leaves of the calathea, the lofty bamboo, or the fragrant pothos, the curious cyclanthus, or frowning nettles, some of the latter from ten to twelve feet high. But how describe the numberless treasures which everywhere strike the eye of the wandering naturalist?' After describing the botanical appearances on the path to the cascade, the colonial botanist says: 'From a perpendicular wall of solid rock, of more than 300 feet, down rushes a stream of water splitting in the air and producing a constant shower, which renders this lovely spot singularly and deliciously cool. Nearly the whole extent of this natural wall is covered with plants, among which you can easily discern numbers of ferns and mosses, two species of Pitcairnia, with beautiful red flowers, some aroids, various nettles, and, here and there, a begonia. How different such a spot would look in cold Europe! Below, in the midst of a never-failing drizzle, grow luxuriant ardisias, aroids, and, it may be added, ferns and other varieties.'

From a position near this spot the Tucutche, the highest mountain in Trinidad—upwards of 3,000 feet—may be ascended. The savannahs, covered with grass and scrubs, are a characteristic feature of the island scenery. Of the 'forms of vegetation' in the island, palms are perhaps the most conspicuous. There is a good show of the plantain and banana. The silk-cotton trees are also in evidence; also the mimosa, with its elegant form. In the forests the orchids are plentifully found, with their gracefully formed and richly coloured aspect. There are all imaginable varieties of the pothos and aroids. Of lianes the forests are full. They assume all possible forms, sometimes appearing like ropes or as having been flattened into tapes. They creep up the highest trees and hang down in festoons; they run along the ground; they provide (the water vine especially) grateful drinks for the thirsty traveller. Many of them bear beautiful flowers, among these being the begonias, dolichos, norantea, the passion-flowers, and the Securidaca. Of the tall grasses the sugar cane and the bamboo are noticeable in a Trinidad landscape. Lilies are represented, but not to any extent.

After the description of the varied scenery, the hill and dale, the multiform tropical vegetation, it might be desirable to mention the rainfall and the temperature. Formerly Trinidad was reputed to be unhealthy, but this is not the case. A rate of mortality of 1 in 30 is surely not excessive, and the general health of Trinidad is equal to many large towns in Europe. The climate is intertropical tempered by insular influences. There are no hurricanes—the periodical seasons occur at regular intervals, although a drought occurs occasionally. The dry season commences with January—when the weather is reported to be fine for harvesting—and ends in May. During this period, indeed, it may be said that the weather is good for sugar making, that is, reaping and manufacture. From June to December is the rainy season. The driest months of the year are February, March, and April, when the heat of the sun is greatest. About 80° is the mean annual temperature of Trinidad. In some years the maximum has reached above 90° in particular months, but from 80° to 84° is generally observed. About 80 inches of rain falls in the year, or say about 71 or 72 on the average of a series of years. The Colonial Office List gives the rainfall at 65½ inches on an average of 25 years. The atmosphere is warm and slightly damp, but with the care that visitors would naturally exercise in coming fresh to a tropical country there can only be an increase of health, stimulated by the forests which employ the mind, the waterfalls which satisfy the imagination, the savannah expanses which induce a feeling of largeness and of rest, and the Pitch Lake which suggests not only the Inferno, but the possibility of walking up Broadway and Regent Street in a state of comparative comfort. Trinidad, therefore, is undoubtedly warm, but fairly equable in temperature. Its healthiness is apparent from the men who have lived there ; some English families have lived there a long time. The late Hon. Frederick Warner had occupied a leading position for many years. He was one of the best representatives of Trinidad, in its climate (if it may be permitted to say so) and in its mind. Dr. De Verteuil, too, the author of the standard book on Trinidad, who knows more about the Colony, in a literary and practical sense, than anybody else, will stand up for the climate of Trinidad. The range of temperature is really from 71° to 84°. In December and

TRINIDAD.

January the temperature has been as low as 68°. It is quite clear, therefore, that for Europeans with a desire for work in a tropical climate there cannot be any objection. The best water from Maraval and St. Ann's is available in the town.

The population of the island according to the last census is as follows: with an area of 1,754 square miles, 200,028 people, including an Indian coolie population of probably 70,000 people, after deducting the number of return immigrants. The estimated population at the present time is 237,934.

The acreage of Trinidad is estimated at 1,123,000 acres, of which about 150,000 are believed to be suitable for sugar, 240,000 for cacao, 200,000 for rice, ground provisions, cocoa-nuts, tobacco, &c., and 500,000 fitted for pasturage, fibres, and other plants of that description.

The total imports and exports in 1895 were, including bullion and specie:

Imports	£2,276,864
Exports	2,065,104
	£4,341,968

But as Trinidad is an emporium for bullion, it should be stated that, on the average, 300,000/. is received as imports, and about the same amount is exported.

The export of sugar (Colony produce and manufacture) in 1895 was 1,092,444 cwts., of the value of 596,415/.; rum, 178,167 galls., 10,455/.; molasses, 1,498,215 galls., 42,551/.; cocoa, 29,458,813 lbs., 620,634/.; and asphalt, 86,148 tons, of the value of 97,318/.

The Trinidad hard woods might also be utilised for

shipment to other countries ; but these, of course, require preparation for the cabinet-maker and the ship-builder.

The Public Revenue for 1895 was 598,884*l.*, and the expenditure 605,514*l.*

There is a very good railway system in Trinidad ; it runs from Port of Spain to Arima, a little way into the interior, 16 miles from Port of Spain, and then along the coast to Couva, the Couva line, 18 miles from the junction at St. Joseph (24 miles in all from Port of Spain). Then an extension has been made to Claxton's Bay, another 4½ miles, as well as to Prince's Town. Further activity has recently taken place in the Railway Department, a line from Arima to Sangre Grande (12 miles) being nearly completed, whilst construction work is advancing on a line from Chaguanas to Tabaquite (about 15 miles). Claxton Pier, on the coast, is a well-known station. The railway runs here through a flat marshy country. The names of the stations coming back from San Fernando to Port of Spain are Claxton Bay, California, Couva, Carapichaima, Chaguanas, Cunupia, St. Joseph, Caroni, and San Juan. These names indicate the line of route. The total length of line opened is 54¼ miles, all constructed and worked by the Government. The total cost of the railways has been 628,018*l.*, of which the sum of 563,507*l.* constitutes the public debt of the Colony, the loans being raised at 4 and 5 per cent., 250,000*l.* of the total being at the former rate. San Fernando (mentioned at page 186) is a busy port, with a population of 6,633 people. It is the shipping place of the large sugar district of Naparima and the contiguous country.

The vegetable fossils of Trinidad have always been a subject of interest to the scientific explorer. What is the cause of the fossilisation of organic bodies? Has it been brought about by revolution, cataclysm, or other violent agency? Such questions would require too much space to discuss here; but the process of decay and chemical transformation must have been accelerated by much moisture and high temperature. In the fossil vegetable substances, woods are largely found; in the animal fossils, mollusca and zoophyta.

The flora of Trinidad shows the characteristics of a tropical American country. The most striking feature of the Trinidad scenery is caused by the forest growths. These show a great variety of families, the most important being the palm. The different kinds of palm indicate the richness or otherwise in the soil. The cabbage palm grows in rich soils, whereas light sandy soils are good for other palms and trees of the myrtle tribe.

To see sugar making in connection with the most advanced processes, a visit should be made to the Colonial Company's famous usine of St. Madeleine. The canes are brought by tramways from the contiguous estates: they are crushed in the mill, the boiling and filtration processes of the juice are carried out, until, having passed through turbines, the fine crystals are produced. This usine of St. Madeleine can be easily reached by carriage from San Fernando, or by the Cipero tram which goes up from the coast. It is only about four miles from San Fernando. It is by far the best appointed institution of the kind in the West Indies. The usine is in the centre of some of the Colonial Company's best estates, for a constant supply of canes is necessary to keep the elaborate machinery going. The estates are connected with the usine by a system of railways or tramways. Engines and trucks are always at work upon these lines, carrying canes to be worked up, or sugar to the nearest point of the Cipero tramway to be transported to the coast at San Fernando. Altogether there are about thirty miles of railway serving the purposes of this usine. The shops, too, for repairs are a sight to see. The factory when started was designed to make 5,000 tons of sugar annually; it now makes 7,000 tons, with a prospect of increase in good crop seasons to 8,000 tons. This means a daily supply of 900 tons of canes for 100 consecutive working days. The great mills, made by Fletcher, of Derby, the megass-burning boilers, the lifting apparatus, the vacuum pans and *triple effet* vessels, the electric light, all make up a wonderful picture of the practicalities of sugar making in the present year of grace. All the elements of successful competition with the beet are here, and the work turned out is on the largest scale, the usine being probably one of the largest in the world. Every year sees the cost of production less. That cost has been reduced nearly 50 per cent. during the last fifteen years.

The different productions in the Colony are represented in the Botanic Gardens. Mr. J. H. Hart, F.L.S., the Superintendent of the Botanical and Agricultural Department of Trinidad, spoke as follows in a lecture delivered before the Governor in 1888: 'The sugar cane is an introduction of Asiatic origin. The bread fruit, the ackee, the jujube, and the camphor tree are also strangers. Coffee found its way to us from Abyssinia through the French colonists. Logwood was introduced to Jamaica by Barham, and probably into Trinidad by Lockhart. The Mango was captured from the French while their botanists were transporting it to the French West India Islands.

Jamaica ginger, so called, had its origin in the East Indies. Cinnamon, clove, nutmeg, Brazil nut, and the Saman tree are comparatively old introductions to Trinidad, while the mangosteen, the litchee, the butter nut, the durian, the loquat, the eucalyptus, Liberian coffee, Chinese ginger, and the various rubber plants belong to a more recent date. Ramie was introduced into the West Indies over thirty years ago, while sisal hemp, a most promising article of culture, is of recent introduction. Turning to vegetables, the French bean is Indian, the artichoke Brazilian, while cucumbers, melons, lettuce, celery, parsley, carrot, turnip, and numerous others, are all exotics.'

Besides the above, cinchona has been introduced from the South American continent, and rubber trees from Central and South America and other places.

But a word may be said here about fruit. The natural market for fruit is of course the United States. A line of fine steamers has been organised to ply between Trinidad and New York, and a supplementary coast service calling at all the Trinidad ports for produce, as a feeder to the main line, is also an important part of the scheme. A regular communication between Trinidad and New York in eight days will afford a long-desired opportunity for fruit growers. Light railways are proposed to be constructed in the interior of the island to bring the fruit rapidly down to the ports. Up to the present, however, but a very small quantity of fruit has been shipped from the island, and the United States tariff may have a deterrent effect. The production of fruit for export will be quite a new thing. The fruit will be purchased for cash in the very garden of the grower, the risk and cost of transport being undertaken by the purchasers. There is no question of competition here with any other Colony, because the market for fruit in the United States is practically unlimited unless shut out by protective duties. The touch of frost upon the orange trees of Florida has introduced an element of uncertainty into that great American industry. Trinidad palms, properly grown, at a cost of half a dollar, sell at three to four dollars each in New York. Trinidad tobacco has been seen and smoked in London, in the form of cigars. The secret of its proper preparation, however, has not yet been understood. The cigars tasted recently will require much improvement to command a European market.

After the above description of the remarkably attractive natural features of the island, an historical sketch may here properly be introduced; and here again there is no lack of interest. The discovery of Trinidad was made at one of the most critical moments of the career of Christopher Columbus. The date was July 31, 1498. There was but one cask of water remaining in each ship, when the man at the mast-head saw three mountain tops, and the joyful cry of 'Land!' rang out. As the ships approached, it was seen that the three summits sprang from a common base. Columbus had already decided to call the next country he discovered by the name of the Trinity, and, true man and loyal Churchman as he was, he religiously kept his word, being confirmed in his intention by the remarkable coincidence of the three mountain tops. 'La Trinidad' the island was called, and it remains so to this day.

Columbus approached the south-eastern point of the island, which he called 'Punta de la Galera,' from a rock resembling a galley under sail; this name, however, was afterwards changed to 'Punta de la Galeota,' the meaning being the same, while 'Punta de la Galera' was given to the north-eastern point. A glance at the map will show that these names are still in existence, Galeota Point being at the south-eastern extremity, and Galera Point at the north-eastern. He sailed along the southern coast, rounded the point through a dangerous passage, which he called the Serpent's Mouth, and up through the Gulf of Paria to the northern pass, which he called the 'Dragon's Mouth.' He was surprised at the greenness and apparent fertility of the country. The groves of palm trees, the forests coming down to the coast, the abundance of water, the wooded hills. 'In a word,' says Washington Irving, 'the softness and purity of the climate, and the verdure, freshness, and sweetness of the country, appeared to him to equal the delights of early spring in the beautiful province of Valencia.' He took possession of the island on behalf of the Crown of Spain. For some time it was neglected. A few Spanish families established themselves on the banks of the River St. Joseph and formed a small town or village, but the difficulties of this early colonisation were great. The Indians whom Columbus saw had fairer complexions than any he had hitherto seen. They were of good stature and bearing, and had a considerable quantity of smooth hair. The history of the cruel treatment by the Spaniards of the Indians throughout the West Indies is well known, and the details need not be recapitulated here. Trinidad was no exception to this policy, the Spaniards thinking that the island contained gold. In 1595 Sir Robert Duddeley, with one large and three smaller boats, came from Africa, anchored in Cedros Bay at the south-western corner of the island (where Columbus a century before had entered the gulf), and explored a portion of the island, going through the woods and lodging in the Indian villages. The next distinguished English visitor was Raleigh, who in March 1595 sailed into the gulf through the same passage between Los Gallos and Point Icacque. He saw the Pitch Lake (the commercial importance of which he noticed at once); he saw the oysters growing on the mangrove trees, where the branches of the trees touched the water; he listened to the tales told him by the Spaniards of the fabulous wealth of Guiana; he heard from the Indians bitter complaints of the Spanish Governor's bad treatment of them; he at once attacked the Spaniards, sailed up the gulf, passed through the River Caroni, and captured the town of St. Joseph, which was then the capital of the island. But Raleigh, after inflicting as much punishment as possible upon the Spaniards, sailed away to find his El Dorado. The possession by Spain continued. Spanish Don succeeded Spanish Don in the government, a regular governor being first appointed in 1730. A better class of Spanish settlers began to arrive. Serious troubles with the Indians were not unknown. Some Dutchmen landed and made a raid upon St. Joseph as the seventeenth century was drawing to its close; negro slaves began to be imported from Africa; cacao plantations were formed. But the Colony made little progress until 1783, when a M. de St.-Laurent, a French planter of Grenada, went to the Spanish representatives at Caraccas and made statements which roused the Government at Madrid to take measures for utilising the resources and fertility of Trinidad. Accordingly a royal cedula, or proclamation, was issued, offering inducements to foreigners of all nations to come and settle there. Each white person, of either sex, being a Roman Catholic, was promised a free grant of thirty-two acres, and half that quantity in addition for every slave he should possess. Free coloured people were also offered half the advantages given to the whites. Exemption from various taxes for ten years was also a feature of the scheme. The total population in 1783 was 2,763, composed as follows: 126 whites, 295 free coloured, 310 slaves, and 2,032 Indians. But the attention which had been called to the island by the Spanish Government attracted a considerable number of people (mostly French) from other parts of the West Indies. In 1798 the population was 17,718; or 2,151 whites, 4,476 free coloured people, 10,009 slaves, and 1,082 Indians. The last Spanish Governor, who was appointed in 1783, Don J. M. de Chacon, acquired much confidence and respect for his just, firm, yet conciliatory rule, and his desire to bring about a better state of things, to improve the administration, and to reform abuses. The French revolutionary excitement spread to the island and rendered government difficult. At last the end of the Spanish possession came. In February 1797, England being then at war with Spain, a British expedition sailed from Martinique for the reduction of Trinidad. The admiral was Henry Harvey, and Sir Ralph Abercrombie was the military commander. The fleet was a particularly powerful one. The flag-ship carried 98 guns. There were a number of seventy-fours and others of lesser armament. The military force consisted of 6,750 men. Governor Chacon had only four large battle ships manned by 1,600 seamen and marines, and 500 soldiers on land, though some accounts give the number as considerably larger. On the morning of February 16 the alarm reached town that the English fleet had arrived. In the night the Spanish Admiral Apodaca called a council of war, composed of his captains, who agreed that the Spanish ships could not be defended, nor could they escape, and it was therefore resolved to burn the ships rather than allow them to fall into the hands of the enemy. The ships burnt briskly towards the morning. The burning of these ships took place at the east end of the island of Gasparillo, where they had been at anchor. The little fort on this island was taken possession of on the morning of February 17. The drums beat, and the Spanish troops were mustered. A detachment of Spaniards, under the command of Captain Tornos, was sent to prevent the English from landing, but found themselves unable to cope with the overwhelming force of the British; they consequently retreated as fast as they could to town. Some British guns were planted on the hills above the town, which rendered resistance of no avail. Governor Chacon then sent his aide-de-camp with a flag of truce. Suspension of hostilities was agreed on, and the next day a long conference took place between Abercromby, Harvey, Chacon, and Apodaca. It ended in the surrender of the island to his Majesty's arms; and on February 18, 1797, the articles of capitulation were signed by Abercromby, Harvey, and Chacon. On that day the Spanish troops laid down their arms, and the island of Trinidad, after having been a Spanish possession for nearly three centuries, and a real Spanish Colony a part of the time, beheld the British standard hoisted on her forts. The centenary of the island as a British Colony was celebrated in Trinidad during February 1897 amidst great rejoicings. Don J. M. de Chacon left the island a few days after the capitulation. He and Admiral Apodaca were, on their arrival in Spain, tried by a council of war. The accused were honourably acquitted. Abercrombie, after making the best arrangements that the confused state of the Colony allowed, departed two months after, leaving his aide-de-camp, Lieutenant-Colonel Thomas Picton, as Governor, whose first act was to institute a council—a council of advice. On March 27, 1802, the definitive Treaty of Peace between England and France and her allies, viz. Spain and the Batavian Republic, was signed at Amiens. By the third article all places taken during the war by Great Britain were to be restored, except Trinidad and Ceylon; and in the fourth article his Catholic Majesty cedes and guarantees in full property and sovereignty the island of Trinidad to his Britannic Majesty.

Thus Trinidad became a British Colony. How Picton ruled, what complaints were made against him, how his proceedings became the subject of much debate in England, are matters the interest of which has largely passed away. For nearly a century now British rule and laws have existed there. The island has certainly made great progress in population, production, and institutions for the welfare of the people. It still contains a French element of considerable proportions, and a Spanish one of less extent. It has been subject, like all the West India Colonies, to the legislation of the Mother Country, beginning with the stoppage of the slave trade, the subsequent abolition of slavery, the protective system of the first part of the century, and the disastrous (as it was then thought to be, and certainly was in its immediate effects) legislation of 1846. It is now unquestionably a prosperous Colony, and with the increase of its sugar and cocoa production, and the development of its other industries, it may look forward to a great future.

As a conquered possession it has always been governed,

from the time of Picton's first council, as a Crown Colony; that is, all the members of the Legislature—unofficial as well, of course, as official—are appointed by the Crown. The Governor presides over this body (the Legislative Council) and has a vote, and a casting vote when numbers are equal. There are nine official members, including the Governor and the Commissioner of Tobago, and eleven unofficial members, including one for Tobago, but the occasions are extremely rare when the whole of the unofficial members vote against a Government measure, and practically the whole control of affairs is exercised by the Governor under instructions from the Secretary of State, with whom he is able to communicate by telegraph, an obvious lessening of the Governor's responsibility since the time when despatches took six weeks or two months in course of post. Besides the Legislative there is an Executive Council, composed of the Governor and seven members, viz. the Colonial Secretary, the Attorney-General, the Auditor-General, and the Commandant of the Local Forces, together with three nominated members. The Governor's salary is 5,000*l.* a year.

The Education question, in a Colony where difference of religion is so marked, has been settled after many years of discussion, and progress in this direction is certainly noticeable. Kingsley found himself on his arrival in the middle of a controversy in which he took part. It was the old subject of the mixture of secular and religious education. It seems, however, to have been settled in a manner satisfactory to the Roman Catholics, whose numbers preponderate, and also agreeable to the majority of the Protestants of the island. The secular schools are now supported entirely by the Government, while denominational schools are only aided by the Government. Upon the extent of the assistance given by Government to the respective denominations it is, perhaps, only natural that some feeling should occasionally show itself, especially on the part of the Roman Catholics, who think that the proportion of the population which they represent entitles them to a larger grant. The Queen's Royal College is a secular establishment for higher education, while St. Mary's College is the analogous Roman Catholic institution. Several exhibitions and scholarships of considerable value are attached to these establishments. In the Government schools there are upwards of 7,000 children, and in the assisted or denominational schools upwards of 14,000. Including private schools, the coolie mission, and other educational agencies, there are about 21,000 children at school, out of a total island population of all ages of about 238,000.

CHAPTER XI.

TOBAGO.

TOBAGO has been supposed to be Robinson Crusoe's Island, and the idea is entertained by recent writers. But where Man Friday came from, whether from Trinidad or elsewhere, is not decided. Tobago is within sight of Trinidad, and is now incorporated in the government of that island, with an official and an unofficial representative upon its Legislative Council; its geology suggests a connection with Trinidad and the Spanish Main, and its political congruity with the former has now been recognised. The estates are in the hands of one or two people, and many negroes live on their own small plots, without much incentive to exertion. Tobago is a comparatively flat country, and there are no high mountain trees to intercept the rain, but in parts there is rich land suited for sugar. Bamboo groves are to be noticed, which suggest paper-making; and ground suitable for cocoa, spices, and coffee is awaiting cultivation. Tobago is volcanic in its origin. It has a central range of hills nearly 2,000 feet high, and the ridges are broken in their descent to the seashore. The scenery is picturesque, the climate thoroughly tropical, or what is sometimes called intertropical. There is very little sugar made now; formerly indigo and cotton used to be grown, but on the sandy parts of the island by the seashore many thousands of cocoa-nuts are annually produced.

Its principal town is Scarborough, on the south, looking to the higher ground on which Fort King George, now innocent of soldiers, stands as a relic of the past. Scarborough and Courland Bay have good shipping accommodation. The political history of the Colony has been very diversified. It had formerly a legislative council, appointed by the Crown, and an Assembly elected by voters in the different parishes. In 1874 the two legislative bodies were abolished, and a single Chamber constituted, partly nominated and partly elected. During the last twelve years it has been to all intents and purposes a Crown Colony with a small legislative council, and in 1889 its incorporation into Trinidad was proclaimed.

When Columbus discovered Tobago in 1498, the only inhabitants were the Carib Indians. The British landed there in 1580, and James I. claimed the sovereignty in 1608. The island received a charter or grant for a settlement in the same way as many other islands in the West Indies, and places in South and North America. In the Colonial State Papers there is an entry under date February 1628 of a grant to Philip, Earl of Montgomery, Lord Chamberlain, of certain islands, between eight and thirteen degrees of N. latitude, called Trinidado, Tabago, Barbudos, and Fonseca, with the islets belonging to them within ten leagues of their shores, and all customary royalties and immunities, reserving a rent of a wedge of gold of a pound weight when the King, his heirs or successors, should come into those parts. Whether Charles I., or any of his heirs and successors, ever visited the islands to receive the wedge of gold (or what was at one time the mode of payment to governors, viz. some hogsheads of sugar) is not known in history. At all events, the grant

P

was made, and the sovereignty confirmed. But until 1632 Tobago remained unoccupied by Europeans. A company of Dutch merchants then sent out a party of colonists, calling the island New Walcheren, but the scheme failed owing to attacks by Indians and Spaniards. Another grant was made in 1645 to James, Duke of Courland, which brought about a further settlement. Then the Dutch in 1654 again appeared in the island, and practically retained possession of it until 1662. Then Louis XIV. of France created Cornelius Lampsis Baron of Tobago, and constituted him proprietor under the Crown of France. The historical suggestion that arises from these proceedings is that the French and Dutch (and of course the Spaniards) were the first colonising powers in the seventeenth century. The English Royal Family had, however, some ideas of profit and influence in connection with these Colonies, and Charles II. confirmed the grant of the island to the Duke of Courland. There was, of course, trouble with the Dutch; but in 1667 the Dutch had to give up possession to the French after a naval fight in Scarborough Bay between the French Admiral Estrées and the Dutch Admiral Binks. The island, however, was restored by the French to the Duke of Courland, whose property was taken over by London merchants in 1681. But still no particular right of sovereignty was generally recognised. It seemed to be a place for the settlement of the representatives of all nations. The Spaniards from Trinidad, the Dutch, the French, all had a hand in determining the fortunes of this small island. It was declared neutral by the Treaty of Aix-la-Chapelle in 1684. The Treaty of Paris of 1763, by which France resigned her rights to England, was apparently only a temporary settlement, for in 1781 the island was captured by the French under the Duke of Bouillie, and in 1783 it was again formally transferred to the French. In 1793 it was taken by a British force, but restored again to the French in 1802. In the following year Commodore Hood and General Greenfield recaptured it, and in 1814 it came formally into British possession, and has remained in British possession ever since. What have we done with this historic island, the scene of so many conflicts during successive centuries? We tried to colonise it, we fought for it, we expended blood and treasure to keep it, and again it may be asked, what have we done with it? Its present condition seems to show that the true colonising spirit of Englishmen has died out in the nineteenth century. Or else the faculty of government has been lost. We can only destroy its individuality and annex it as a kind of appendage to Trinidad.

It was formerly reckoned one of the Windward Islands, of which it was the last to the south. It is situated in N. lat. 11° 9′, W. long. 60° 12′. It is about nineteen miles N.E. of Trinidad. It is twenty-six miles long, and seven and a half at its greatest breadth. It is officially stated to have an area of 114 square miles, or about 73,313 acres.

In 1792 Sir William Young visited Tobago. He went to Riseland or Sandy Point, in the S.W. part of the island, a country almost flat, but beautifully spotted with mountain cabbages and various trees, Trinidad, at nineteen miles distance, appearing plain to the eye. On riding five miles across the island from Riseland to the Courland Bay division, he had opportunities of noticing its capabilities, and he was much struck with its beauty from the flat of Sandy Point gently breaking into hills, till at the N.E. end it becomes a scene of mountains and woods. The healthy negroes, with their provision grounds, contributed to the animated aspect of the scene. 'Twenty-two miles from Port Louis, from the very point of the town of Port Louis, the country becomes hilly; and as you farther advance, the hills rise into mountains, not broken and rugged, as the convulsed country of St. Vincent's, but regular though steep, and on a large scale of regular ascent and descent. The scene of nature is on an extensive scale, and gives the idea of a continent rather than an island. It is not alone its vicinity to the Spanish Main that suggests this idea. The appearance of the island fully warrants the assumption, and the contiguity of South America only more fully marks its being torn therefrom, and of its being, in old times, the southern point or bold promontory of the vast bay of Mexico.'

At the end of the last century, then, whatever may be thought of Sir W. Young's geographical details, the island was cultivated, and proprietors enjoyed the visit to their estates. In 1805 Tobago shipped 15,327 hogsheads of sugar. The cotton and indigo industries, formerly of considerable account in the productions of the island, have disappeared, and sugar, rum, molasses, cocoanuts, and live-stock now form the principal articles of export. The total population in 1891 was returned at 18,387, and the estimated population in 1896 at 20,039. The revenue of 1895 was stated at 8,803*l*., and the expenditure at 8,218*l*. The value of imports in 1895 was 13,643*l*., and exports 10,517*l*., but it is difficult to furnish the true figures of the imports as goods purchased in Trinidad are brought into Tobago without report, owing to the two islands being one for trade purposes. With regard to exports, the large apparent decrease of recent years is due to the fact that specie sent out of the island is treated as an export. In 1894 specie amounting to 4,963*l.* was sent to England, while in 1895 only 563*l.* was exported. Exports of cocoa, sugar, &c., to Trinidad are also omitted from the return. These amounted in 1895 to 11,626*l.* In 1875 the exports were 92,015*l.* An average of 70,000*l.* was observed up to 1879. An average of 60,000*l.* was maintained to 1884, and the average figure for 1891 and the immediately preceding years was about 31,000*l.* It will thus be seen that this historic Colony has been allowed to dwindle, and the utilisation of its productive qualities, which formerly attracted the attention of foreign countries, has practically been abandoned. At the same time it is not too late to awaken a fresh interest in the Colony, which is well adapted for the cultivation of coffee. Land is cheap and fertile, and grants of Crown land would be made to persons possessed of the necessary capital on the easiest of terms. The land-tax is the smallest in the West Indies, being only fivepence per acre.

CHAPTER XII.

GRENADA.

GOING yet north from Trinidad and Tobago to Grenada, there is a N.E. trade wind, which is a pleasant change from the still atmosphere of the Gulf of Paria. Grenada is situated between 12° 30' and 11° 58' north latitude, and 61° 20' and 61° 35' west longitude. Its length is 21 miles and its greatest breadth 12 miles. It contains 76,500 acres, or 133 square miles. The north-west coast of Grenada is a series of conical hills, of rounded outline, and covered with forest trees and brushwood. From north to south there is a line of hills, rising in various places to 3,000 feet. This chain, especially from one particular spot, called the Grand Etang, an almost perfectly circular fresh-water lake, 2½ miles in circumference, 14 feet deep, and 1,740 feet above the sea level, is the source of numerous small rivers and streamlets which serve to irrigate the country. Mount St. Catherine or Morne Michel is very picturesque, rising to a height of 2,749 feet. There are numerous valleys extending to the south-east side. Several chalybeate and sulphurous springs exist, one of which is very remarkable for its heat and strong metallic constituents. A hot spring in St. Andrew's parish emits carbonic acid gas, and contains iron and lime. Some of the sulphurous streams are hot enough to boil an egg. Lake Antoine, with its subterraneous com-

GRAND ETANG, GRENADA.

munications with different streams in the island, is also a very interesting natural feature. This lake was considerably agitated, throwing up lava and sulphur, during the great outbreak of the Soufrière in St. Vincent.

St. George's, the capital, is on a peninsula a mile in length, forming one side of the harbour; it is situated within an amphitheatre of hills. The hills were formerly used for strong fortifications, commanding the harbour, which is entirely landlocked and could now be easily defended as a coaling station. Père Labat said that Grenada, with its natural advantages, ought to be a rich and powerful Colony. He found his countrymen engaged in producing tobacco, indigo, and other articles. On three sides of the harbour green hills are seen rising. The other side is commanded by the site of the deserted batteries on the hill, and the crumbling castle is hardly strong enough now to sustain the British flag, according to the latest visitor's description. After landing, it is observed that the houses are irregularly built, and not all of them in the best repair. But nature covers all defects. Banana and orange trees afford beauty to the scene, and the groves of mangoes, almond and cedar trees add to its picturesqueness. A good view of the town of St. George's can be obtained from the hill. Seen from the bay the town, with its red-brick houses, its cocoa-nut and bread-fruit trees, its broad street up the hill side, its Roman Catholic and its English church, with their towers, is a pleasant place to look upon.

It might be interesting here to give the impressions of a visitor to Grenada in 1792, already referred to in connection with Tobago. Sir William Young in 1792 anchored in the carenage (or, as he writes the word, careenage) and immediately landed. On the following Sunday he went to church, where he found the Governor, the Speaker of the Assembly, and a respectable congregation of people of all colours. In the gallery the girls and boys sang the psalms very well. Altogether he enjoyed the service. He describes St. George's as a handsome town, built chiefly of brick ; 'it is divided by a ridge which, running into the sea, forms on one side the carenage, and on the other the bay. In the bay town there was a handsome square and market-place, and the carenage town contained the chief mercantile houses, the ships lying landlocked and in deep water close to the wharf. On the ridge, just above the road of communication between the towns, stood the church, and on the promontory or bluff head of the ridge stood a large old fort built by the Spaniards.'

The above picture of Grenada drawn 100 years ago suggests liveliness and business, but that drawn by Mr. Froude, is particularly depressing. While he no doubt correctly noted what he saw—the place where the old forts stood, the solitary gun, the deserted harbour, the worm-eaten piles and broken platforms of the former wharves, the un-roofed warehouses, and the general appearance of desolation —the impression thus produced is not a justifiable one, for Grenada now bids fair to become a very prosperous island, not with sugar, but with cocoa and spices.

St. George's has recently been much improved by the building of a tunnel, named the Sendall Tunnel after a former Governor, which connects the carenage or inner harbour with that part of the town in which the market square and the principal shops are situated. This improvement has necessitated the making of a new street, which is protected from the sea by a massive stone wall.

The geology of the island is very complicated and irre-

ST. GEORGE'S, GRENADA.

GRENADA.

gular; the mountains and different parts of the lowlands consist of mingled portions of red and grey sandstone, irregular alternations of hornblende, hard argillaceous schist, and a variety of gneiss. Immediately behind Richmond Hill limestone was found, and was used at one time for agricultural purposes. Basaltic rocks are met with on the N.W. coast, and probably magnesian limestone. At Point Salines, at the extremity of the island, fuller's earth of the finest quality is abundant. In St. Patrick parish, specimens of the natural magnet, and sulphur in its native state but not crystallised, are largely met with. The curious suggestion of an original whole, afterwards rent asunder by some violent agency, is a fascinating one to the earnest student of Nature and her ways of acting. One cliff, a short distance from St. George's, is stated on good authority to be of volcanic origin; immediately under the soil is a stratum of 'pudding' stone, then appears one of iron pyrites (exhibiting regular prisms), then one of alluvial formation, and lastly one of brown sandstone. In other cliffs grey and brown sandstone with loose sand and gravel are found mixed with alluvial soil; but apparently no shells have been found. The red sandstone found in the parish of St. George, which is much used for building, is thickly studded with beautiful crystals of carburet of iron, and in some sandstone districts there are vegetable remains.

Grenada has its lively monkeys and its harmless snakes, its scorpions and its centipedes, and its formidable ants, which at one time caused great havoc. These ants were in such myriads that they formed bridges with their bodies across the widest streams, and they even extinguished the fires kindled in the fields for their destruction. A reward of 20,000*l.* was vainly offered for a remedy, but Nature, in one of her grand compensatory moods, sent the hurricane of 1780 and effected that which human ingenuity was powerless to bring about.

The climate is good, with a variable heat according to height. In the low country 82° F. may be taken as an annual average, but in the higher parts 10° lower may be experienced. In January 1880 the temperature of five days, taken at noon, was from 78° on one day to 82° on another, and at 6 P.M. the variation was from 79° to 80°, showing an equable temperature. Rain falls to the extent of 70 to 80 inches a year, and the frequently recurring showers throughout the year are very grateful.

Grenada was discovered by Columbus during his adventurous voyage in 1498. He found it occupied by a race of warlike Caribs. These, however, were left in possession for another century, for the Spaniards did not attempt to form a settlement. In 1650 the French Governor of Martinique, Du Parquet, determined to seize the island, which was thought to be a dangerous undertaking, because of the fierceness and courage of its Indian inhabitants. The proceedings exhibit a curious mixture of fanaticism and cruelty. The commanders administered the Holy Sacrament in the most solemn manner to the soldiers upon their embarkation and arrival; a cross was erected, before which the soldiers knelt and prayed for success. At first, things went smoothly. The natives seemed disposed to treat the French cordially. But the French opened so-called treaty negotiations with the chiefs, which the latter did not understand. After giving the Indians some knives, hatchets, beads, and brandy, it was stated that the French had purchased the island. A few months went by, and a policy of extermination was ruthlessly begun. The Caribs were massacred and their houses burnt. A story is told that a

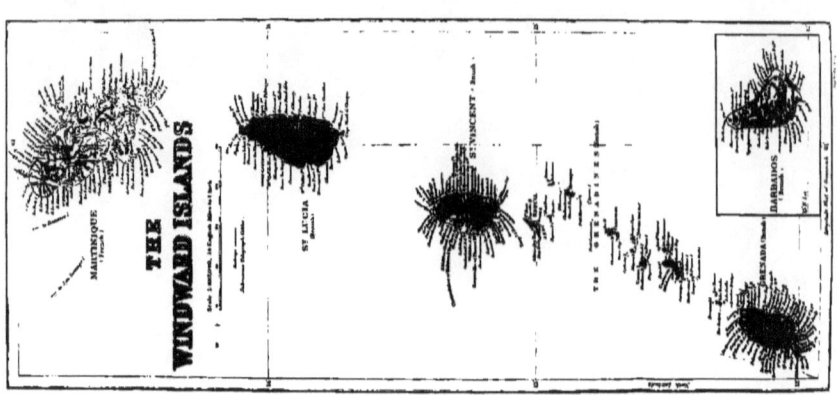

party of Caribs, escaping from the sword, ran towards a precipice and threw themselves into the sea, the place afterwards being known as Le Morne des Sauteurs, or Leapers' Hill. In 1657 Du Parquet, to avoid the cost of maintaining a military force there, sold the island to the Comte de Cerrillac for 30,000 crowns. But little progress was made. The Governor, sent by the new proprietor, so disgusted the Colonists by his conduct that many of them left the island. Those who remained seized the Governor, tried and executed him. The island was officially annexed to France in 1674, the proprietary interest receiving compensation. In 1700 the island contained only 251 whites and 525 blacks, who occupied themselves on three sugar and fifty-two indigo plantations. In 1762 the English, under Commodore Swanton, captured it, and it was regularly ceded to Great Britain by the definitive Treaty of Paris in February 1763, St. Lucia at the same time being restored to France. The inhabitants were declared to be British subjects liable to taxation in the same manner as the rest of his Majesty's subjects in the other British islands of the group. This gave rise to a famous controversy between the Colonists and the Crown, in which the former were victorious. The other islands were subject to the duty of 4½ per cent. upon their produce, to pay for the expenses of Government and to enable the King to pay a large number of pensions to Court favourites in England, and other persons who were entirely unconnected with the Colonies. This imposition the Grenadians resisted, and the case came before the Court of King's Bench in 1774, resulting in a judgment being given by Lord Chief Justice Mansfield against the claim of the Crown. The effect of this judgment was not confined to Grenada, for the duty had to be abandoned in Dominica,

St. Vincent, and Tobago as well. In 1779 Grenada was retaken by the French. Count D'Estaing appeared off the harbour and town of St. George's with a powerful fleet and 5,000 troops. The Governor, Lord Macartney, had but a small defensive force available. But a most gallant defence was made. An entrenchment was thrown up round the summit of Hospital Hill; this was invested by the French, and carried after a stubborn resistance. The Governor and his little force retired into the old fort at the mouth of the harbour; but this being covered by the Hospital Hill battery, the guns, left unspiked, being turned against the English, there was nothing to do but to make an unconditional surrender, and the French resumed their possession of the island. In 1783, however, it was restored to the English by the Versailles Treaty of Peace. In 1795 an insurrection broke out, supposed to have been connected with the French revolutionary tendencies of the period. But whatever the origin, the greatest distress was experienced during the eighteen months the disturbance lasted, and it took many years for the island to recover from the troubles of that unhappy time. Its history during the present century, under British rule, is analogous to that of the other West Indian Colonies. Like them it passed through all the various stages of emancipation, the apprenticeship system being finally brought to a close, and full freedom effected in 1838.

The island at one time had a Legislative Council and House of Assembly, but it finally drifted into Crown government. An Imperial Act was passed in 1876 authorising the Queen to comply with a petition from the then Legislature, and to set up a government according to her wisdom. This blank sheet of paper was naturally filled up with the institution of Crown government, the Legislature now consisting of six official members, and seven unofficial members nominated by the Crown. The Governor, who sits at the head of the table, has a vote which would make the numbers equal, and a casting vote which necessarily places the whole legislative power in his hands. Up to quite recently the governorship of the Windward Islands was vested in the Governor of Barbados, but Grenada, the Grenadines, St. Vincent, and St. Lucia now form officially the Windward Islands, the Governor of this group usually residing in Grenada, the official headquarters of the group, but making frequent official visits to the other Colonies. Each island in the group has its own Legislature, laws, and financial arrangements. Each has its own Chief Justice, its own resident Administrator of the government and body of officials, but there is a single Court of Appeal, and in one or two other matters there is a common arrangement. The Windward federation, therefore, has not made much progress up to the present, and perhaps is not likely to be carried any farther. Old historic countries, with the seas between them, present insuperable difficulties to the application of an arbitrary plan which could take no account of their individual interests and tendencies, and of the wide differences that exist in the origin and character of their populations.

The island of Grenada is divided into six parishes, most of them named after patron or national saints, such as St. George, St. David, St. Andrew, St. Patrick, St. Mark, and St. John. The first, St. George, contains the seat of government, the post office, the law courts, the public library, and all the official institutions. It is situated on the S. and W. part of the island, and is 26 square miles in size. St.

David's lies towards the S.E. St. Andrew's is on the E. and includes the town and port of Grenville St. Patrick is on the N.E. side and includes a town called Sauteurs. St Mark is a small district on the N.W. St. John is on the W. side and includes Charlotte Town.

The above parishes of Grenada contain much rich sugar land. Sixty years ago there were 119 sugar estates and 47 coffee and cocoa plantations and settlements, a striking contrast to the present condition of the Colony, for sugar has practically disappeared from its list of productions. In earlier years of the century the sugar produced, say for ten years ending in 1831, ranged from 12,000 to 20,000 tons, with a proportionate quantity of rum. In 1873 this had dropped to 3,600 tons, in 1883 to 1,840 tons, in 1887 to less than 200 tons, and the present time almost nil. A fine sugar island, therefore, in regard to this special article of production, has gone entirely out of cultivation. What are the causes of this need not be lengthily discussed. Want of steady and continuous labour, necessitating an expensive system of coolie immigration, and the low prices of sugar, owing to the European bounties, are no doubt the primary reasons for this decadence. The extinction of sugar means, of course, the loss of all the capital originally employed in the industry, and an abandoned estate is valueless. Cocoa, spices, and nutmegs are now, however, being increasingly cultivated, and are the present mainstay of the island. Notwithstanding decreased cultivation, taxation has increased, the revenue being in 1895, 58,468*l*., a large portion of this amount being raised by customs duties, whilst the expenditure for the same year was 63,675*l.* There is a public debt of 113,000*l.*, which represents a little less than twice the revenue of the year, and an indebtedness of a little less

GOVERNMENT HOUSE, GRENADA.

than 2*l.* per head of the population. The total value of imports in 1895 was 175,712*l.*—78,079*l.* coming from the United Kingdom, and the total value of exports in 1895 was 172,020*l.*, nearly the whole coming to the United Kingdom, as the European market is the best for cocoa and spices. The value of cocoa exported in 1895 was 138,519*l.*, and spices 20,983*l.* The planters of Grenada are fully alive to the importance of increasing the agricultural capabilities of the Colony, and quite recently, at the request of the Government, Professor Harrison, the Government Analyst of British Guiana, visited Grenada to select and report on sample soils from different districts of the Colony, with reference to the products for which they are best suited and the manures necessary to correct their deficiencies. A Commission was also appointed to report on the measures which it might be advisable to take in consequence of the serious fall in the price of cocoa, and its recommendations were all in favour of adding new agricultural industries to the resources of the island, such as the cultivation of coffee, the kola nut, tobacco, &c. Under proper care, and provided no single staple is allowed to reign where sugar has been deposed, there is no reason why Grenada should not again occupy the highly prosperous condition it did in years gone by. There is very little trade between Grenada and the United States, which is the great and indispensable market for the sugar Colonies. The population of Grenada is now estimated at 59,101. The attention of the Government is being directed to the necessary improvements of the roads, for which new loans, on the security of the general revenue, would be raised. The *ad-valorem* import duty is now $7\frac{1}{2}$ per cent.

With regard to education, there are ten Government

elementary schools and twenty-seven aided schools of a similar character conducted by the various religious bodies. About 3,569 children are in daily attendance, the number on the rolls being 7,025. The public revenue partly supports also a grammar school and two secondary schools for girls. Fees are charged in all schools, and the duty of parents to provide elementary education for their children is made by ordinance a legal obligation.

The island of Carriacou and a number of the Grenadines are dependencies of Grenada. St. Vincent has the government of those nearest to her. The Grenadines are small islands lying between Carriacou and Grenada. Carriacou was once a prosperous place. It is about nineteen miles in circumference, and has 6,913 acres of land, and grew cotton and sugar. Its population is 6,031. Owing to the dearth of timber it is subject to drought. It has a town called Hillsborough. Several of the Grenadines, such as Becquia and others, were also cultivated. From the anchorage off Carriacou, Grenada is visible. The little rocky islands which are seen on all sides are said to be the result of volcanic action. The principal industry now carried on is the raising of stock and provision growing. For a quiet life Carriacou may be recommended, and cultured people have found acceptable work and placid enjoyment in this island washed by the Caribbean Sea.

ST. VINCENT: LANDING PLACE AT KINGSTOWN.

CHAPTER XIII.

ST. VINCENT.

THE next island that claims attention going northward to Barbados is St. Vincent. It is situated in 13° 10' N. lat. and 60° 57' W. long., between Grenada and Barbados. It is twenty-one miles to the S.W. of St. Lucia, and 100 miles W. of Barbados. It is eighteen and a half miles long and eleven broad, and contains 84,286 acres. Some of the small Grenadines are included, as before stated, in the government of this island. The aspect of St. Vincent is mountainous, the bold, abrupt peaks being very striking, and the intervening glens of a beautiful and romantic character. The connected range goes from north to south, and is splendidly wooded. The ravines of the interior, as they approach the north-west shore, form valleys, where cultivation may be carried on. On the north-east the surface is more level, and a large plain is available for produce. The soil in the valleys is very fertile. The island is distinctly volcanic; traces of strata which have been subject to fire are numerous, and the fantastic appearance of the rocks shows that, by some extremely forcible action, they have been moved from their original positions. In short, St. Vincent is a country of sharp peaks, gradually opening into valleys towards the coast. Kingstown, the capital, is situated in the S.W. of the island, along the shore, for about a mile, of a deep and beautiful bay. The town is in an amphitheatre of hills rising gradually behind it until the highest peak is reached in Mount St. Andrew. There are three principal streets in the town.

Behind the town, sugar estates were once in existence. In the town itself the public buildings are substantial but not particularly elegant. The church is a brick building, and of rather imposing appearance. On going up the road behind the town, and proceeding thence to the south coast of the island, some of the Grenadines are visible. The Government House is built of wood, and stands in a circle of palm trees. It has one of the best views in the West Indies. The Botanic Garden, about a mile from Kingstown, was the earliest of the gardens established in the West Indies, and formerly had a great reputation for its extent and beauty. From the upper part of the garden a beautiful view of the sea and some of the Grenadines can be obtained. Three miles from Kingstown is the small town of Calliaqua, which has a convenient beach for shipping. Eastward is the extensive valley of Maniqua, which is said to be an exhausted crater. Altogether the island is interesting, beautiful because of its verdure, peculiar because of its peaks, wonderful because of its Soufrière.

The Soufrière is, indeed, the natural marvel of St. Vincent. It is a mountain in the north of the island ; it lies about 3,000 feet above the sea. Its volcanic character is amply demonstrated, not only by a great outbreak, but by constantly recurring mild demonstrations. This mountain has been described as presenting the grandest scene in the West Indies. Visitors going up to the Soufrière even now see the two craters with their sulphurous steam. Many years ago a graphic description was given by a visitor

ST. VINCENT. VIEW OF KINGSTOWN.

(Captain Sir J. E. Alexander) of this mountain, the points of which will probably be recognised now. The crater, he said, is three miles in circumference, and 500 feet in depth ; it contains within it a conical hill beautifully streaked with sulphur, and covered with shrubs and flowers. The road to the Soufrière passes through cornfields and a thicket of long grass and ferns, which reach over a horse's back ; the path then can hardly be seen, and seems to be on a narrow ridge, on each side of which is a precipice, that to the west being most terrific. For some distance beyond the resting place the path continues intricate as before, and then the crater ridge is reached. This is more thinly sprinkled with trees ; towards the summit it is quite bare, and furrowed with the traces of the mountain torrents and of lava, while sand and ashes are under foot. To the south is a mountain which seems to overhang the traveller ; it is richly covered to the top with tufted foliage, which forms a contrast to the scene on the north ; the destructive agency of fire has annihilated the vegetation. A mighty cloud of vapour fills occasionally the crater to the brim, gradually clears off, and then the awful majesty of the scene is unfolded. The eastern top of the crater is about 3,500 feet above the level of the sea, and there also the depth from the top to the surface of the lake is 300 feet, the circumference of the caldron at the top is about three miles ; a cold mist commonly rests on the surface of the green, slimy, and unfathomable water at the bottom ; and so horrible is the scene, that one almost expects to see the fluid rise from the surface of the dreary lake. The three peaks to the north of the crater are nearly all of the same height—that is, 4,000 feet above the sea. In walking along the brink of the crater, it is necessary to clamber over ridges covered with slippery moss, on a loose soil, without a shrub to hold by, and one false step will send the adventurer rolling down into the Soufrière. After a mile and a half is accomplished, the new crater is seen : it lies to the S.E. of the other ; and if the mist is thick, and a breeze blowing, as is often the case, it is necessary to crawl forward on hands and knees, otherwise it is impossible to avoid a fatal accident whilst looking into the lesser crater. The two craters are separated only by a narrow ridge or saddle, which, though apparently impassable, a sailor once succeeded in crossing. The new crater is more of an abyss than its neighbour : its sides are more rugged and frightful, but it is much smaller at bottom, where there is a mass of black ashes and sand, and a little water of a red clayey hue ; sometimes it is quite dry. It is possible, but it is a perilous enterprise, to descend to the surface of the lake in the great crater. It is necessary to slip down rocks and gulleys, having only small projecting stones, roots of grass, and shrubs to hold by and stand upon. The rapid descent occupies about twenty minutes, and then there is a small promontory, which juts out a few yards into the water.

The great historic eruption of the Soufrière was in 1812. Smoke and blue flame were seen. An earthquake, felt severely in Caraccas, on the continent of South America, took place on April 27, following earth disturbances in the region of the Mississippi. About the above date a severe concussion of the earth was noticed, and the Soufrière began to show signs of agitation, which continued for three days. A great body of smoke arose, of a sulphurous nature. Sounds like thunder filled the inhabitants with terror. The Caribs and the negroes fled to the town in the extremity of their fear at the trembling of the mountain. Birds fell to the ground. All leaves and grass were hidden, and the cattle found no food. The sea was much discoloured by the fine shower, but remained calm. As darkness came on, the flames burst through the curtain of smoke. Thunderous sounds deafened the ear and electric flashes blinded the eye. The caldron boiled and the lava burst forth on the north-west side. A great stream of fire was formed into two parts by a contiguous height, and fell into a ravine. The bushes were set on fire by globular balls projected from the crater. The fiery lava reached the sea. Another lava torrent descended to the eastward. The roar of the mountain and the noise of the moving lava carried dismay to every heart. In the middle of the night a shock of earthquake added to the terrors of the situation. Then for two hours showers of cinders fell. Earthquakes continued, and the island trembled in every part. The time of daybreak was terrible. It was dark as night. Black clouds overhung land and sea. The island was covered with the cinders and dust from the mountain. The volcanic sounds gradually sank away, and men's hearts came to them again. Fifty people were killed in these extraordinary manifestations of natural power. Beds of rivers were levelled.

But perhaps the most extraordinary result of this eruption was seen in Barbados, 100 miles away. Barbados, as is well known, has a shallow soil above the coral. It will hardly be believed that the outbreak in St. Vincent increased the soil of Barbados and actually fertilised it. Across the sea for all these miles came this wonderful shower, probably the most novel way in which one Colony could assist another. But Barbados was much alarmed at first and could not understand the phenomenon. The strange and unparalleled appearance caused the greatest anguish.

In the minds of the people, the Day of Judgment was come. From half-past twelve in the night or rather early morning of May 1, 1812, to six o'clock in the evening of the same day, Barbados went through one of the most extraordinary times any population could experience. At half-past twelve A.M. a great cloud came over Barbados—a cloud that seemed to touch the ground; then a sandy grit began to fall. At two o'clock sharp explosions were heard, resembling the cannonade of war ships. Then ashes fell, and sounds like distant thunder came upon the ear. There was a small glimmering of daylight about half-past five, after which the darkness became blacker than ever. Ashes in heavy showers continued to fall. Globes of fire occasionally were seen through the darkness. At nine o'clock in the morning the sky assumed a fearful purple colour. Up to noon light breezes and constant falls of ashes were observed. Large birds, loaded with fine ashes, fell to the ground. Soon after noon daylight partially struggled through, and the dim outline of the sun was seen. For twelve hours the island had been visited with darkness and ashes, the latter falling in a fine powder. It was then a dull twilight for some hours, and in the afternoon the abnormal darkness again set in, and did not lift until the following morning. The cause of this strange phenomenon was not an action at sea, as at first supposed. Days passed, and still the matter remained unexplained. At length news came to Barbados of the eruption of the Soufrière in St. Vincent, and the explanation became as obvious as the daylight and as palpable as the darkness. The ashes were brought to Barbados by the upper currents of the air. Nor, after all, was this a perfectly singular phenomenon, although at the time thought to be unprecedented. In 1835 Central America was shaken by the eruption of a volcano. Its violence was felt at Bogotá, 900 miles away, and even Jamaica heard the sounds and felt the ashes. And it might be interesting to recall that in England, some few years ago, the strangely beautiful and heavy-coloured sunsets were attributed to the dust of a volcano in active operation in a distant part of the world.

St. Vincent was discovered by Columbus during his third voyage, which was so full of interest and so full of results, on January 22, 1498. It was St. Vincent's Day in the Spanish calendar, and the island therefore received an appropriate designation, consistent with the general practice of the great discoverer. No settlement was, however, effected at the time, the Caribs being warlike and numerous. This tribe, or family of tribes, continued in possession until 1627, when a grant of the island was made by Charles I. to the Earl of Carlisle, whose name so often occurs in the history of the acquisition of property in the Caribbee Islands. This grant was included in a general one of all the Caribbee Islands by letters patent under the Great Seal of England. The Earl of Carlisle became by this patent the sole proprietor of the Caribbee Islands, comprising St. Christopher, Grenada, St. Vincent, St. Lucia, Barbados, Martinique, Dominica, Marie Galante, Deseada, Todos Santos, Guadeloupe, Antigua, Montserrat, Redonda, Barbuda, Nevis, Eustatius, St. Bartholomew, St. Martin, Anguilla, Sombrero, and Anegada, and many other islands. It is quite clear that statesmen, and other political persons in the time of the Stuarts, took a great interest in geography. Everything was fresh. Dreams of wealth, possibilities of adventure, were in the minds of Englishmen. But what they achieved has not been taken advantage of to the full, in respect of the Colonies in the above list that still own allegiance to the British Crown. It is curious to notice the changing circumstances which they have undergone. Take only, in illustration, the island now under consideration, St. Vincent. In the years between 1660 and 1670 the proprietary interest in the Caribbee Islands was still in existence under the general government of Lord Willoughby of Parham. Although in 1672 St. Vincent was incorporated in one government with Barbados and other places, still no attempt was made to colonise it. An understanding was indeed arrived at between the English and French that St. Vincent and Dominica should be left to the Caribs, upon the supposition that the latter would agree to give up their claims in the other islands. For three years—that is, to 1675—the Caribs remained undisturbed in their possession of St. Vincent. In that year a ship from Guinea was wrecked near the coast. A number of the negro slaves escaped into the woods, and a race called the black Caribs sprang into existence. In 1719 some French settlers from Martinique arrived, but the numbers were few and the effort at colonisation feeble. The system of royal grants to individuals still apparently continued, for George I. in 1723 made a grant of this island and St. Lucia to the Duke of Montague. This adventure was a failure, and in 1748 the island, by the Treaty of Aix-la-Chapelle, was again declared neutral, and the original inhabitants remained in possession. Nevertheless, the French persevered in their settlements, until it became a sufficiently French possession to justify General Monckton and Admiral Rodney capturing it by force of arms in 1762. In 1763, by the Treaty of Paris, it was ceded in perpetuity to Great Britain, the rights of the native proprietors being practically ignored.

ST. VINCENT. 233

This Carib question, which was quite as important in its time as the Maori question of later days, put to the test the English policy in regard to native races. In 1772 hostilities arose with the Caribs. These were inevitable, sooner or later, owing to disputed possession of lands. A treaty was, however, made early in 1773, by which an extensive district was set apart for occupation by the Caribs, upon their acknowledgment of the British sovereignty. The chances and changes, however, of this mortal life were not over for St. Vincent; nor indeed could any Colony feel secure of a permanent nationality so long as ships of war were in the seas and the thunder of their cannon reverberated through the West Indian hills and valleys. In 1779 the island was attacked by a small body of French from Martinique. The Caribs were still discontented with their treatment by the British, and with their co-operation the island was taken without any effective resistance. In 1780 the great hurricane took place, which destroyed the church, laid many buildings low, and ruined crops. In 1783, at the general peace brought about by the Treaty of Versailles, Great Britain resumed possession of the island. It then contained sixty-one sugar estates, and plantations of coffee, cotton, and cocoa. In 1795 it felt the influence of the revolutionary tendencies of France. The Caribs even became excited with these doctrines, and, assisted by some of the French inhabitants, an insurrection broke out. The island was much disturbed for two years. Disastrous conflicts took place; buildings and estates were plundered, and many English lost their lives. But Sir Ralph Abercrombie in 1796, assisted by General Hunter, after considerable fighting, succeeded in subduing the outbreak, and measures were taken to remove the Caribs to the island of Ruatan, in the Bay of Honduras. Upwards of 5,000 Caribs were thus transported in 1797. Owing to these disturbances property was destroyed and depreciated to one-third of its value. But the very fine part of the island which had been occupied by the Caribs, and called the Carib country, was taken over and put in cultivation. At this point what might be called the political history, so far as it related to different nationalities, ends. The fortunes of the island, in the same way as other Colonies, were afterwards determined by the course of philanthropic and commercial legislation in England.

In its constitutional arrangements St. Vincent is another instance of representative institutions being wiped off the slate and a more arbitrary writing substituted. It formerly had a Council and Assembly, but there is now a single Chamber, composed of four official members and four unofficial members, nominated by the Crown. The island is under the general government of the Windward Islands.

From 1800 to 1829 the production of sugar was from 18,000 to 20,000 hogsheads, with of course proportionate quantities of rum and molasses, but the present position of the industry may be conveniently illustrated by the following figures, showing the collective value of the export of sugar, rum, and molasses in 1895 compared with the export in a series of years from 1880 to 1894. The value of the export in 1880 was 128,603*l.* ; 1885, 86,341*l.* ; 1890, 63,621*l.* ; 1894, 30,482*l.* ; and 1895, 21,581*l.* This decline is of course mainly due to the causes which have depressed the industry in other West Indian Colonies, but the Colony has suffered more severely than other Colonies, owing to the absence of such improved machinery as has elsewhere met reduced prices by turning out a superior quality of sugar at a reduced cost of production. Professor Harrison of British Guiana, who recently visited the island to report upon its soil, &c., was of opinion that if the natural fertility of the soil were aided by scientific methods of cultivation and improved machinery, St. Vincent might successfully compete with the most favoured of the sugar-producing Colonies. Considerable quantities of coffee and cotton were at one time produced, but these industries have also declined. Even the cultivation of arrowroot, which had a good reputation in the market, has decreased, owing, it is officially reported, to over-production and the substitution of other farinaceous products, especially flour of rice, for the uses to which arrowroot has hitherto been applied. It is quoted now, according to quality, from $1\tfrac{1}{2}d.$ to $5d.$ per pound, as against Bermuda arrowroot $1s.$ $2d.$ to $1s.$ $7d.$ Cocoa is a rapidly increasing export, the value having risen steadily from 640*l.* in 1880 to 3,246*l.* in 1895.

The total value of exports in 1895 was 68,690*l.*, of which 25,876*l.* came to the United Kingdom. This is a very much reduced value as compared with previous years, and only about half the value shown in some years during the last decade. The total value of imports in 1895 was 64,842*l.*, of which 27,687*l.* were from the United Kingdom.

The revenue of the island, about half of which is raised by import duties, in 1895 was 25,459*l.* The expenditure for the same year was 28,911*l.* The public debt, raised entirely by the issue of 5 per cent. debentures redeemable within short periods, amounts to 17,170*l.*

As above indicated, the population of St. Vincent has been subject to several fluctuations. The present population is about 44,970, principally African. The aborigines of the island were the yellow (as distinguished from the black) Caribs. Where these yellow Caribs came from is not quite determined. They might have come from Guiana, or from some other part of the mainland of South America. But in St. Vincent they differentiated, apart from their own tribal divisions, into two tribes. The black Caribs have already been accounted for in the mixture of the African and the pure yellow in the Colony. The yellow Caribs were of a small stature; the black were tall and stout, and spoke with a rapidity that seemed to denote energy and recklessness. The black Caribs were, indeed, a powerful clan. They formed communities, erected huts, and kept together, principally near the sea coast. They had their own tribal interest and their government and their chief, and in course of time they acquired the dominant influence over the yellow Caribs. The influence of the Carib population in this and other islands has been great. If they had not resisted, we might not have had sufficient incentive to persevere. But civilisation has elbowed them outside the boundary, and they are no longer a factor in the village and town life of the island.

Education is progressing in St. Vincent, not perhaps by leaps and bounds. The Church of England organisation has been doing its best. Other religious bodies have been endeavouring, with equal earnestness and self-sacrifice, to take hold of the impressionable mind of the negro. But while the negro in his own community has been enjoying himself (why shouldn't he? asks the humanitarian), the general interests of the Colony have not, perhaps, been so well supported as they might have been. No one knows what is the absolute right in these things, and in course of time, which smooths all the rough edges of this world, no

ST. VINCENT: MARKET SCENE AT KINGSTOWN.

doubt a proper adjustment will take place. With regard to the efforts of native races, of people of African origin, of Englishmen and Frenchmen, the full resources of the Colony have certainly not been utilised. What remains for it in the future?

CHAPTER XIV.

ST. LUCIA.

ST. LUCIA (this wildly beautiful island, as it is called by Montgomery Martin) was discovered by Columbus on his fourth voyage, on St. Lucia's Day, June 15, 1502. It is 13° 50′ N. lat. and 60° 58′ W. long. It is within 24 miles of Martinique, and 21 miles, in a north-easterly direction, of St. Vincent. It has an area of about 160,000 acres. The island is divided by a ridge of hills. The approach from the south is very remarkable. Two rocks rise from the sea; the gods call them Pitons, mortals recognise them as sugar loaves. They shoot to a great height in parallel cones, tapering like church spires. They are surrounded on three sides with verdure. They have been compared to the Pillars of Hercules, guarding the entrance to a beautiful bay, that of Soufrière. A sandy beach, and cane fields on the rising ground, complete the picture. These Pitons are two pyramids of solid rock, and their remarkable and picturesque character attracts the immediate attention of the visitor. One of them is computed to be 3,300 feet above the level of the sea, and the other about 3,000 feet. No connection has been traced between them and the other mountains. Their western side is washed by the sea. When Breen published his description of St. Lucia in 1844 they were virgin peaks. Their proximity to the *Soufrière*, or

THE PITONS, ST. LUCIA.

half-extinct volcano, suggests that their present form is due to an eruption at some very early period, before the political history of the island began. Not a great distance from these Soufrière Pitons there is a mountain, about 3,000 feet high, called the Piton des Canaries. It is surrounded by dense forests and deep ravines. The mountains run south and north through the island. They present themselves in most fantastic shapes. There is always a wonderful array of clouds upon the summits of the hills, forming either a silky veil or an impenetrable shroud. The beautiful coves and bays are also a feature in the landscape. To the student of Nature, who wishes to understand her workings, St. Lucia offers an exhaustless source of interest. A cultured and literary imagination (if such a thing is possible in these commercial days) might find much enjoyment in contemplating the varied natural scenery of this island. Dense forests and fertile valleys, smiling plains and frowning precipices, lively rivers and deep ravines, make up a wonderfully attractive picture. The valleys are situated transversely on either side of the central chain of mountains. St. Lucia has its natural curiosity in the Soufrière or sulphurous mountain. It is about half an hour's ride from the town of Soufrière, and two miles to the east of the Pitons. The crater is about 1,000 feet above the sea level. Its size is about three acres, and it is covered with sulphur, cinders, and other remains of former activity. Some boiling fountains are to be seen, and there is always some sign to be observed of the volcanic agencies comprised within. The hot springs and mineral waters of the Soufrière were formerly considered of medicinal value. Louis XVI., acting upon the advice of a committee of doctors who analysed the waters, caused baths and buildings to be erected on an extensive scale between the volcano and the town of Soufrière, and many invalids resorted to them from other places in the West Indies. Fifty years ago these baths were claimed as belonging to a private owner of estates, and no efforts have been made to repair them or to continue their use for the public benefit.

The rivers of St. Lucia are numerous. They take their rise in the mountains, and flow down to supply the plains. During the rainy season these streams become rushing torrents, and the rivers on the lower levels overflow their banks.

The port of Castries, the principal shipping place of the island, has an excellent harbour and affords safe anchorage and plenty of room. Large vessels can anchor close to the wharf. The centre of business and the seat of government is the town of Castries. It was formerly called by the general name, so common in the West Indies, of Carenage. It was christened Castries in 1785, when the marshal of that name was the French Minister for the Colonies. The town is in some parts below the sea level, and indeed stands upon land won from the sea. The streets are wide and well devised, running in parallel lines from east to west and north to south. There is a large square planted with trees. Government House is situated on a terrace, and commands extensive views over the harbour. Pigeon Island can be seen in the distance, and the mountains of Martinique descried across the channel. The town of Soufrière also offers some lovely views. From a hill a striking view of the Pitons is obtained. From Morne Fortuné, a hill 800 feet high, once a strong military post, some splendid scenes may be contemplated, though the picture may be saddened by the sight of the ruined fortifications. Pigeon Island, lying slightly westward of the northern extremity of St. Lucia, was a most important point of defence, being a convenient and healthy location for troops.

The three principal roads in the island are : 1, from Castries to Vieux Fort, through the leeward districts, about sixty miles, including Morne Fortuné, Roseau, Soufrière, and the Etangs or lakes ; 2, from Castries through the windward districts, about forty-five miles ; and, 3, the road from Castries to the town of Gros-ilet at the northern end of the island, about nine miles.

St. Lucia was originally inhabited by Caribs, and no English settlers appear to have arrived until 1639 ; difficulties arose with these natives ; many of the English were killed, and a number were driven from the island. In 1642 the King of France granted it to the French West India Company. But their efforts were of little result. Subsequently it was sold for a small amount to Messrs. Houel and Du Parquet, the latter assuming the government under the authority of the Crown of France. After the death of Du Parquet in 1657, several French governors succeeded. But troubles continued with the Caribs, and both France and England claimed the right to St. Lucia. In 1663 some English from Barbados took possession of the island, and it was governed by the British until 1667. It was then voluntarily ceded to the French, and it became a dependency of Martinique. In 1686 an attempt to retake it was made by an English man-of-war, but this failed. In 1718 Marshal Count d'Estrées received a grant of the island. He was a business man. He sent out troops and cultivators. In 1723 the British King, George I., made a similar grant to the Duke of Montague. He likewise sent out stores and artillery. The French, however, sent a

R

force from Martinique, and the result of negotiations was that both the English and French troops should withdraw, and that the island should remain neutral until the two Crowns should give their decision. St. Lucia then began to make progress, notwithstanding the absence of a properly constituted government. Coffee and cocoa plantations were established. The French were still anxious to assert their possession. A very unsettled state continued until 1762, the French under Governor de Longueville maintaining the upper hand in the administration. In that year, Martinique having been taken by Admiral Rodney and General Monckton, an expedition was sent to St. Lucia, to which the island surrendered. The Treaty of Paris in 1763 concluded the British occupation, and in the general division of territory St. Lucia was assigned to France. In 1778 the war was renewed between France and England. Among English statesmen, and naval and military leaders, a strong idea was entertained of the importance of St. Lucia. Secure in British possession, it would be an effective check upon the French in those seas. In the Little Carenage the largest ships of war could be careened. Adjacent British islands could be defended at short notice, and altogether as a military and naval station it was, in that time of conflict, particularly appropriate. In December 1778 the English fleet from New York arrived. The French defensive force was weak, and all the strong points were taken by the English. But D'Estaing was coming with his fleet to reduce Grenada and St. Vincent. He was informed of the state of matters in St. Lucia, and proceeded to its relief. He came towards the harbour of Carenage, where Admiral Barrington was waiting for him. For a day the cannon thundered from the hostile fleets, and the French retired discomfited. Nothing daunted, however, D'Estaing anchored in Gros-ilet Bay, and proceeded to disembark troops, but the heights were held by General Grant with a strong force and the struggle was a desperate one. With great bravery the French conducted the assault, being finally received at the point of the bayonet, and repulsed with great loss of life. Terms were agreed to, and the British commanders were left in possession. Whether the island was worth all this expenditure of military and naval force, is a question which has been asked many times. But when these seas were the theatre of the conflicts of European Powers, a strong position was essential, and a victory was of more importance than cocoa trees and sugar canes. The bays—Cul-de-sac, Castries, Choc, and Gros-ilet—were particularly convenient for ships of war, protected by the batteries of Morne Fortuné, the Vigie, and Pigeon Island. The French, in May 1781, determined to attempt again the conquest of the island. Count de Grasse invested it, and the French troops under the Marquis de Bouillé made a landing at Gros-ilet. But Admiral Rodney was soon on the alert. Defensive measures were taken, and the French retired. Tired out with these exciting troubles, the colonists lost heart for the moment, but the prices of produce raised their spirits, cultivation was extended, and good profits made. Sir George Rodney, when he resumed his command in February 1782, after a visit to England, was a proud man as he reviewed his fleet in Gros-ilet Bay. The French fleet, under Count de Grasse, was watching him from Fort Royal Bay, Martinique. On April 12, 1782, the inevitable fight took place. The great victory over the Count de Grasse was accomplished, by which Jamaica was saved, the strength of the allied Powers was broken, and the British flag was made supreme in these seas. It was from a rock on Pigeon Island that Rodney watched, through his glass, the movements of De Grasse's fleet as the stately ships came out of the harbour at Martinique. De Grasse was full of the anticipations of victory. When he came out from Martinique that April morning in 1782, he felt himself in a position to sweep the seas. The story of that wondrous fight has been often told. It was one of the decisive events in the history of the world. We, as well as our then enemies, may be proud of it, for a grander fight was never fought. It was not for the possession of an island or two, but for a dominating influence in Europe and the world that the struggle was intended. The fleets were fairly matched, the French perhaps having the superiority in the number of men. On the morning of April 12, 1782, Rodney bore down and came to close quarters off Dominica. His flagship, the 'Formidable,' was in the thick of the combat, and when he exchanged close broadsides with the 'Ville de Paris,' the ship which carried De Grasse's flag and fortunes, England, France, and Spain might be imagined as waiting (if they could have known of what was happening) with breathless anxiety the issue of that cannonade. The French fleet was broken up, many thousands of men were killed, and Rodney received the sword of De Grasse on board the 'Formidable.' At the present time, just over a hundred years since that great event, some people may ask, what good came of it at last? But then, the very existence of England, with the American Colonies being torn away from her, depended upon her naval power and its effective exercise, by which means alone her influence among the great European nations could be secured. St. Lucia seems a little place to be the scene of this great stroke for empire; yet her name must ever be remembered in history, at all events, so long as a British ship rides through the seas and the British flag denotes undiminished Imperial power.

What, then, is our present position with our neighbours? We are on the best of terms with them. Without French intelligence, industry, and enterprise, many of these island Colonies would be among the waste places, or rather the tropical wildernesses, of the earth. St. Lucia would be in a very backward state but for its contiguity to Martinique and Guadeloupe. In commercial alertness, engineering methods, agricultural economy, the French have taught us some valuable lessons, and side by side with them in the West Indies we are acting the part of cordial friends, instead of, as before, assuming the character, and we did that very cordially too, of national foes.

The sound of the cannon was followed by the softer notes of peace. Diplomatists over a table estimated the results of blood-stained decks, sinking ships, and dying men. Conditions for a general peace were arranged at Versailles in January 1783. In these, St. Lucia was discussed prominently, because of its central and strategic importance in connection with naval operations. It had been so often fought for, the nationalities of its population were so evenly divided, that neither side was willing to give it up. But in the general arrangement as to the possession of these Colonies, it was decided to surrender St. Lucia to the French. On January 3, 1784, it was accordingly given up to Viscount de Damas, the French Governor-General. Under the good administration of the Baron de Laborie, who was an engineer officer and made excellent roads, the island enjoyed five years of peace and progress. After his death, in 1789, the revolutionary influence in this, as in other Colonies, caused disturbance and bloodshed. The name of the island was mentioned with praise in the National Convention. The tricolour was hoisted on Morne Fortuné, and the regular Governor, Colonel de Gimat, had to run away. The greatest excitement prevailed; the estates were deserted, and the negroes, with arms in their hands, were full of the rights of man. No opinion is here expressed as to the French Revolution. To the historical student it might seem to have been an inevitable protest against tyranny and corruption; but in the Colonies its ideas came like strong wine to a people unprepared to receive them. The war broke out. Again a British fleet, with hostile intentions, was seen in West Indian seas, this time under the command of Admiral Jervis, afterwards Earl St. Vincent. Admiral Jervis and General Grey attacked St. Lucia, and on April 4 Prince Edward, the Duke of Kent and father of Queen Victoria, at the close of a long march from the landing-place, planted the British colours on Morne Fortuné. St. Lucia thus became again a British possession. Disturbances arose. Citoyen Victor Hugues kept things lively. He got together all the forces of discontent. He recovered the whole of the island except the military post at Castries and Morne Fortuné. The British troops were few and without heart. They nevertheless not only maintained their position for some time, but sallied forth and defeated the enemy in several engagements. An attack upon Soufrière, which was the stronghold of the Republican forces, failed, with heavy loss to the British; and some time after, the latter withdrew to the ships, not being powerful enough to stand a desperate attack upon Morne Fortuné, which was in pre-

ST. LUCIA.

paration. St. Lucia then became the headquarters of Republican attacks upon other islands, and the position of Great Britain was seriously menaced in almost every quarter. In 1796 Sir Ralph Abercromby appeared upon the scene with 12,000 soldiers, and some ships under the command of Admiral Sir Hugh Christian. In the operations which succeeded, Brigadier-General John Moore, afterwards Lieut.-General Sir John Moore, took part. The Republican forces were driven, after much hard fighting, from their positions on the hills. At last the fortunes of the British expedition depended upon dislodging the enemy from Morne Fortuné. Roads had to be made ; guns had to be dragged across ravines and up hills. In the desperate fighting which ensued many British officers and men fell. The fort was at last carried ; its defenders, principally black men, marched away as prisoners of war. The British colours were again placed on the ramparts, this time by General Moore, who was appointed Governor ; and Abercromby went away to look after affairs in St. Vincent and Grenada. Disaffected bands were roaming about St. Lucia, and the task of restoring order was a difficult one. General Moore had to use stringent measures, and his troops were being wasted by disease. The general himself was very nearly captured as he was being rowed along the coast. His exertions so prostrated him that he was carried on board a vessel while in an insensible condition, and returned soon after to England, and lived to be the hero of Corunna. This guerilla war, or bush fighting, lasted in St. Lucia until 1797, when tranquillity was finally secured by General Prevost. A system of judicial administration was established in the year 1800, subject to the French laws which had been in force before 1789, and worked by officials with French names. The game of shuttlecock, however, was not yet ended. By the Treaty of Amiens St. Lucia was again restored to France, and possession was taken in the name of First Consul Bonaparte. Soon afterwards the West Indies were again the theatre of war. Naturally St. Lucia was to the front. The French Governor awaited the British attack at Morne Fortuné, which was delivered on June 22, 1803. The works were carried at the point of the bayonet, and the long struggle, lasting for more than a century and a half, for the possession of the island, was over when at Midsummer 1803 the British flag was again run up on Morne Fortuné.

From historic struggles to snakes may seem a wide divergence. St. Lucia has a great snake, the Fer de Lance. It catches rats in the sugar-cane fields. Government premiums have been offered for its extirpation, but it still seems to preserve a vigorous existence. Its rat-catching propensities, which might be considered a point in its favour, do not diminish the objection to it.

The climate is not unhealthy, the temperature ranging from 75° to 90°. There are heavy falls of rain, and the swamps produce a miasma which might be prejudicial unless care be taken. Excessive perspiration, which brings on prickly heat, is to be avoided. Soufrière is particularly healthy, owing to the dryness of the soil. In the valleys the health-giving qualities of the climate are not quite so good. Castries is healthy. There is a dry and wet season. During the hurricane months anxiety is felt. The Barbados hurricane of August 1831 extended to St. Lucia. A breeze and then a storm of wind frightened the inhabitants. Houses were laid flat, some lives were lost, and some ships foundered in the harbour. An earthquake shook the island in 1842, and a still more dreadful one occurred in February 1843. The vibration was felt in all the islands of the archipelago; the sea rose and precipitated itself upon the land; the ground opened and water was projected in fountains. Fire is not an infrequent visitor to St. Lucia, but in this respect it only shares the liabilities of every other island.

The soil of St. Lucia is noted for its depth and richness, the valleys being especially fertile. Sugar, coffee, cocoa, and maize are adapted to it, spices, dyeing materials, and medicinal plants are grown, whilst European vegetables are prolific, and the fruits are delicious. One great feature of St. Lucia is its forest trees, and much timber for building is obtainable. The rivers teem with fish, and in the shooting season, from August to November, the sportsman can find game. The turtle and shell fish are not to be despised. The yellow serpent, or the Fer de Lance, has been above mentioned. This is supposed to have an enemy in the cribo, or black snake. The cribo is a kind of boa constrictor, and often takes hours and sometimes days to swallow its victim. A cribo was once taking a 'square' meal of this description, when the bystanders killed him, and he and his partially swallowed victim were put into spirits and preserved. The insect life of St. Lucia is also varied, and much of it 'urgent,' but perhaps not more so than in other tropical countries.

St. Lucia is under the general Government of the Windward Islands. It has a Legislative Council with six official members (including the Administrator), and six unofficial members nominated by the Crown. It is, therefore, after the strictest pattern of a Crown Colony. The population is about 45,906; public revenue in 1895 was 48,564*l.*, and expenditure 57,579*l.* Nearly half the revenue is raised by customs duties. The public debt of St. Lucia on 31 December, 1895, was 185,380*l*. The interest ranges from 6 to 3½ per cent., and the charge for interest and sinking fund absorbed more than one-sixth of the revenue of the year. The total value of imports in 1895 was 154,945*l*., and exports 102,155*l*. A large quantity of pimento sticks was shipped during the year, and the cultivation of cocoa is being successfully carried on, the value of the export for the year 1895 amounting to 16,637*l*. The trade (imports and exports) with the United Kingdom is about half the total.

The island is particularly adapted for the establishment of usines after the style of those which have been so successful in Martinique and Guadeloupe. One of these central sugar factories was in existence for some years, and the island Government had a large interest in it. Recently, however, the Central Sugar Factory Company has ceased working the factory and estates, owing to want of funds, but a local syndicate has taken over, under an agreement with the Government, the working of the estates, with such good results as to justify the belief that the cultivation of the property will be permanently maintained and extended, with profit to the syndicate and every advantage to the Colony. Another usine is being built entirely by private enterprise, and it is said that one or two more are being planned. The labour supply is being increased by coolie immigration from India.

At the time the Panama Canal works were in progress a considerable number of labourers left St. Lucia, attracted by the prospect of high wages. No less a sum than 1,405*l*. was paid for the repatriation of St. Lucians who had emigrated to Colon and were left destitute there when work was stopped on the canal.

ST. LUCIA.

There are in St. Lucia thirty-seven primary schools receiving assistance from public funds, and there is also the Castries Grammar School, known as St. Mary's College, for higher instruction, to which the Government contributes 200*l.* a year. A great drawback to educational progress is the patois, a corruption of the French language, which is so largely used by persons of all classes.

St. Lucia has been selected as the chief coaling station for the fleet in the West Indies, and is being strongly fortified.

Its strategic importance was recognised by the Colonial Defence Committee in 1890, as the following extracts from the Report of the Royal Commissioners will show :—

'1. The withdrawal of the Imperial troops from some of the islands with a view to concentration at others, and the preparation of local schemes of defence, requiring that local funds should be voted, appear to render it essential that the general question of defence should be more widely understood than at present.

'2. Until the appointment of the Royal Commission of 1879 the defences of the Empire had never been considered as a whole, and the fortifications which existed at various points, as well as the garrisons there maintained, were in many cases legacies of a period when political and military conditions widely differed from those of the present day. This was especially the case with regard to the West India Islands, which had been the scene of much fighting during the French wars, and which had been fortified to a great extent to meet the exigencies of the times.

'3. These islands were then direct sources of wealth to the Power which held them, and were fought for on account of their own intrinsic worth as the spoils of the victor.

Conditions are now greatly changed. The islands are no longer likely to be fought for as sources of wealth. Mere territorial aggrandisement in this portion of the world is not likely to be the aim of any European Power, and an enemy's probable objectives would be strategic points calculated to give him present and future advantages in naval warfare, or by their loss to injure the naval and military prestige of the Empire.

'4. Under these circumstances, the general policy recommended by the Royal Commission was that strategic points should be definitely decided upon in order to meet the requirements of the British Navy; that the available troops should be concentrated at these points, and that scattered garrisons of Imperial troops should no longer be maintained.

'In the words of the Commission, it is "essential to reduce if possible the number of garrisons scattered throughout the Colonies, and to concentrate the troops in those positions which are of vital importance.

'"It is evident also that small detachments in isolated positions, without defences or artillery, afford no protection whatever against attack which may be brought against them from seaward; their presence, on the contrary, by inviting attack only tends to court disaster.

'"From these considerations it results that, in the event of war with a maritime Power, it would become imperatively necessary to withdraw the small detachments which, mainly for the maintenance of peace and order within their borders, are now kept in some of the less important Colonies.

'"We, however, observe that the Colonies in which these detachments are stationed having been led to depend upon them for securing internal peace and order, their sudden withdrawal in the absence of any organised means in substitution for them would be attended with serious risks. It is very desirable, therefore, that the Colonies so situated should take prompt measures to organise their own police."

'In accordance with the recommendations of the Royal Commission, it was decided to fortify and maintain Imperial coaling stations at Jamaica and St. Lucia, these points being selected on account of their strategic importance in relation to the operations of her Majesty's Navy in these waters, and to concentrate there all the Imperial troops in the West Indies.

CHAPTER XV.

MARTINIQUE.

WHILE it is not within the scope of this book to give lengthy details of the possessions of foreign countries in the West Indies, a few words may be said regarding them, especially as several have been at one time or another British Colonies. The important part which Martinique has played in the wars has been already indicated. It was from Fort Royal Bay that the Count de Grasse and his fleet sailed out on that memorable day in 1782. Martinique was captured by the English in 1762, but we only retained it for a year. We recaptured it in 1794, and once more gave it up at the Peace of Amiens. We were again in possession in 1810; since the Treaty of Paris (1814) it has been, undisturbed, in the hands of the French. St. Pierre is described as a pretty town of an essentially French appearance, with water running down each side of the street. The negro labourer is industrious and well looked after, the plantations are carefully cultivated, the usines are busy centres of work. The labour supply of the island has been supplemented by coolie immigration. The population consisted a few years ago of 150,000 negroes, 17,000 coolies, and 20,000 whites, a very much larger number of the latter than in any neighbouring British colony. The total population was returned in 1895 at 187,692. To Morne Rouge, in

MARTINIQUE. 255

the centre of the island, is a favourite excursion. From the summit a most extensive view is gained, especially of the peak of Morne Pelée in the north, 4,400 feet high; and of Morne Carbet in the south. The general character of the scenery is mountainous, certainly volcanic, and there are the usual picturesque accessories of ravines and rushing streams.

Martinique was discovered by Columbus in his second voyage, but the Carib population was not disturbed until 1635, and it was later in the century before steps were taken for its extensive cultivation. The usual troubles arose with the Indians, who were gradually thinned out. Slaves were introduced from Africa and large estates were formed. Mr. Bonwick, in his excellent little book on 'The French Colonies and their resources,' gives the following particulars. Martinique is over fifty miles to the south-east of Guadeloupe. One of the Windward Islands, or Lesser Antilles, it contains 200,000 acres (or 380 square miles), of which above a third is in regular cultivation. The three Pitons, or peaks, are near the shore, the highest being 3,500 feet. A long chain, fifty miles, crosses from north-west to south-east. There is an abundant rainfall, and several rivers are navigable to a very small extent. The climate shows three seasons, cool in spring, hot and dry in summer, hot and wet in autumn and part of winter. Though in about 14° and 15° N latitude, the tropical heat is mitigated by the sea breezes and the fresh winds from the mountains. The trade winds blow strongly in the cool season from the eastward and north-eastward. Afterwards the breezes are east-north-east to west, and even to south. The island is subject to hurricanes and earthquakes. So late as 1851 two new craters opened.

The fertile soil is supposed to be the result of ancient lava. The government is carried on by a Governor, Privy Council, and Council-General, the thirty-six members of which are elected by universal suffrage, the island being divided into thirty-two communes. The island, like Guadeloupe and other French possessions, sends representatives to the Assembly at Paris, consisting of a senator and two deputies. The local budget for 1896 was 5,078,400 francs, and there is a contribution from the French budget, and in the French tariff the Colonial produce receives certain advantages. The policy of the Mother Country in severing religion from education has been carried out in the Colony. There are primary schools and lyceums, as well as a law school at Fort de France.

Fort de France is the capital, but St. Pierre is the principal place of business. This town is on cliffs overlooking the Bay of St. Pierre. It consists of two long and narrow streets running parallel to the sea. It looks well from the water, and has a handsome cathedral. The former name of Fort de France was Fort Royal, under which designation it was frequently mentioned as a place of importance in the military operations. The mail steamers of the Compagnie Générale Transatlantique make it a port of call. Morne Rouge is the holy city where is situated a grotto associated with the Virgin. The Stations of the Cross are set up on the hill. Many ships visit the island, and much business is transacted. There are seventeen large central usines, and upwards of 500 ordinary sugar works. The value of the sugar exported annually comes to a large amount, 29,330 tons having been exported during 1895. Coffee, cacao, cotton, tobacco (but now in very small quantities), manioc flour, yams, and roots, beans, bread-fruit, and bananas, and rum, are also produced, making a total trade (internal and export) of between 40,000,000 and 50,000,000 francs. The value of total exports varies, but the average may be put at 20,000,000 francs, the majority going to France. The imports are valued at about 22,000,000 francs, about half coming from France.

Mr. Bonwick thus tells the romance of Martinique. 'The beautiful Empress Josephine was born here on July 23, 1763. Her home, now partly in ruins, was called La Pagerie, after her father, Lieutenant La Pagerie. Here is the tomb of her mother, who died in 1807 at the age of seventy-one. Here an old negress told her she would marry a king, but die in the hospital. Napoleon raised her to the throne, and she died at Malmaison. At sixteen she married M. Beauharnais' (also born in the island), 'who died in Paris in 1794. It was no happy union, and a separation took place in 1788, when she returned with her daughter Hortense to the old island home, where she resided for three years. In one of her letters from Martinique, she showed how much happiness could be enjoyed in that lovely country, saying, "I love to hide myself in the green woods that skirt our dwelling. There I tread on flowers which exhale a perfume as rich as that of the orange grove, and more grateful to the senses. How many charms has this retreat for one in my situation." A white marble statue in St. Pierre keeps her memory alive in the place of her birth.'

Another story connected with Martinique is that of H.M. ship 'Diamond Rock.' The story has been told in many ways and with varying details, but in its main facts it is a romance full of truth. In 1803 Sir Samuel Hood saw that French ships escaped him by running past a rock which rises 600 feet out of the water. It is about a mile round. Hood laid his seventy-four, the 'Centaur,' close alongside this Diamond Rock. He made a hawser, with a traveller on it, fast to the ship and to the top of the rock. Guns and ammunition and provisions were hauled up. In this fortress, so cleverly improvised, Lieutenant James Wilkie Maurice, with 120 men and boys, was established; they had a grand time of it, sweeping the sea with their guns, and doing much damage to the enemy. The rock was borne on the books of the Admiralty as his Majesty's ship 'Diamond Rock.' From January 1804 to June 1805 the position was maintained. It was only at last surrendered for want of powder and water, and even then it took a French squadron of two seventy-fours, a frigate, a corvette, a schooner, and eleven gunboats, to make the garrison—or rather 'crew'—give up their ship. Kingsley saw its pink and yellow sides shining in the sun above the sparkling seas. In shape it is like one of the great Pyramids, but double the size. Kingsley took off his hat to this memorial of British pluck—to this strange ship which once domineered over the seas.

CHAPTER XVI.

DOMINICA.

DOMINICA stands between the two French Colonies, showing, in its internal condition, a lamentable contrast to their prosperity. And yet Englishmen have always taken a great interest in this island; its 'lonely roadstead,' where Rodney caught up the French, and the magnificence of the approach, excite the enthusiasm of visitors. Dominica has all the features of a volcanic island, although in a larger form, showing that there Nature had exerted her greatest force. The situation of Roseau, the capital, is particularly attractive, with the clear air, the sparkling sea, and the bright hues of the verdure with which the hills are robed.

Dominica is situated in 15° 25′ N. lat. and 61° 15′ W. long. It is 29 miles in length and 16 in breadth, and has an area of 304 square miles. Its lofty, rugged mountains are particularly striking. Morne Diabloten, where Labat tried to catch some of the black devil birds, now so rarely seen, is the highest, being 5,314 feet above the sea. From the top of this mountain Diabloten the scene is terrible in its grandeur, yet enchanting in its beauty, when the eye takes in the valleys, with their shining rivers fed by cascades from the mountains. Tennyson's description of Enoch Arden's island (apart, of course, from its details connected with the story) has often been quoted as fitting exactly the general physical aspect of Dominica. It might not be out of place to give the perfect word-picture again:

> No want was there of human sustenance,
> Soft fruitage, mighty nuts, and nourishing roots;
> Nor save for pity was it hard to take
> The helpless life so wild that it was tame.
> There in a seaward-gazing mountain-gorge
> They built, and thatched with leaves of palm, a hut,
> Half hut, half native cavern. So the three,
> Set in this Eden of all plenteousness,
> Dwelt with eternal summer, ill content.
>   The mountain wooded to the peak, the lawns
> And winding glades high up like ways to Heaven,
> The slender coco's drooping crown of plumes,
> The lightning flash of insect and of bird,
> The lustre of the long convolvuluses
> That coiled around the stately stems, and ran
> Ev'n to the limit of the land, the glows
> And glories of the broad belt of the world,
> All these he saw; but what he fain had seen
> He could not see, the kindly human face,
> Nor ever hear a kindly voice, but heard
> The myriad shriek of wheeling ocean-fowl,
> The league-long roller thundering on the reef
> The moving whisper of huge trees that branch'd
> And blossom'd in the zenith, or the sweep
> Of some precipitous rivulet to the wave,
> As down the shore he ranged, or all day long
> Sat often in the seaward-gazing gorge,
> A shipwrecked sailor, waiting for a sail:
> No sail from day to day, but every day
> The sunrise broken into scarlet shafts
> Among the palms and ferns and precipices;
> The blaze upon the waters to the east;
> The blaze upon his island overhead;
> The blaze upon the waters to the west;
> Then the great stars that globed themselves in Heaven,
> The hollower-bellowing ocean, and again
> The scarlet shafts of sunrise—but no sail.

The town of Roseau is on a point of land on the southwest side of the island, which point forms two bays, Wood-

DOMINICA : GOVERNMENT HOUSE.

ville to the north, and Charlotteville to the south. The following is the impression made on a visitor (H. N. Coleridge) some fifty odd years ago : 'The landscape behind the town is beautifully grand ; indeed the whole prospect from the edge of Morne Bruce, a lofty table-rock occupied by the garrison, is one of the very finest in the West Indies. The valley runs up for many miles in a gently inclined plane, between mountains of irregular heights and shapes, most of which are clothed up to their cloudy canopies with rich parterres of green coffee, which perfumes the whole atmosphere, even to some distance over the sea; the river rolls a deep and roaring stream down the middle of the vale, and is joined at the outlet of each side ravine by a mountain torrent, whilst at the top, where the rocks converge into an acute angle, a cascade falls from the apex in a long sheet of silvery foam. Beneath, the town presents a very different appearance from what it does at sea ; the streets are long and spacious, regularly paved, and intersecting each other at right angles ; there is one large square, or promenade ground, and the shingled roofs of the houses, tinged with the intense blue of the heaven above them, seem like the newest slates, and remind one of that clear and distinct look which the good towns of France have when viewed from an eminence.

'The Grand Savanna, nine miles from Prince Rupert's Bay, and twelve from Roseau, is a fine fertile elevated plain, upwards of a mile in extent, and at a good distance from the neighbouring mountains, whose terraces jut out from their breasts ; around whose declivities flourishes the richest verdure, while murmuring cascades of babbling brooks burst through the luxuriant vegetation, or roll along the hilly avenues, surrounded by magnificent piles of rocks, sometimes black and bare, sometimes green, with countless traceries of lovely creepers, interspersed with ferns and palms.'

Dominica was discovered by Columbus, on Sunday, November 3, 1493. It was the first land seen on his second voyage, after having been twenty days at sea from the Canaries. The island was included in the grant made to the Earl of Carlisle in 1627. The right of possession, however, remained undecided, and it was agreed that Dominica should be considered neutral, and that the Caribs should be left in possession. In 1756, the island was captured by the English, notwithstanding that a large number of French planters had established themselves in the Colony. It was assigned to the English by the Treaty of Paris in February 1763. Commissioners were then appointed under the Great Seal, with authority to sell and dispose of the lands by public sale, to English subjects, in allotments, under grants from the Crown. The French inhabitants also obtained leases on certain conditions. Half of the island was thus apportioned, producing, under the terms of occupancy, 312,090*l.* sterling. A force from Martinique in 1771, according to the Colonial Office List, under the Marquis de Bouillé, attacked and captured the island. The new French Governor by his tyranny and brutality incurred great unpopularity. Under this Governor, the Marquis Duchilleau, great confusion and distress occurred. The island was restored to England at the peace of 1783, Sir John Ord, Bart., being appointed Governor. During the war of 1805 a French squadron attacked the island; the capital, Roseau, was burned, but, by the brave behaviour of the colonists, and the skill of Sir George Prevost, the island was saved, and it has been in

British possession ever since. This year 1805 was a very remarkable time for the Colony. The name of the invading General was La Grange. Roseau was attacked on both flanks, but it was burnt (as above stated); some accounts say accidentally. Roseau had to pay an indemnity of 12,000*l.*; if this were so or not (the chances are it was never paid), the island, as the result of these proceedings, continued in British possession. What we have done with it since no one knows, except those who are directly interested, and to these the last half-century has been disastrous. Some people say, Restore it to the French, and allow them to raise it to the level of their own contiguous Colonies; but such a course could not be advocated in these pages.

Dominica, as before observed, is volcanic; the soil in some places is a light brown coloured mould, that appears to have been washed down from the mountains, mixed with decayed vegetable matter. In the level country, towards the sea coast, and in many districts of the interior, it is a fine, deep, black mould, peculiarly adapted to the cultivation of the sugar cane, coffee, cocoa, and all other articles of tropical produce. The under stratum is a yellow or brick clay in some parts; in others it is a stiff terrace, and frequently very stony. Large quantities of excellent freestone have been quarried in the Savanna, and at one time this formed an article of export to Guadeloupe and elsewhere. Several of the mountains of this island are continually burning with sulphur, of which they emit vast quantities. From these mountains issue various springs of mineral waters (whose virtues are extolled for the cure of many disorders), which in some places are hot enough to cook an egg in less time than ordinary boiling water. The sulphureous exhalations from these springs are very strong, often too intensely penetrating for continued respiration, while the soil, or sulphur and sand, around them in the Soufrières is too hot for the feet, and scarcely firm enough to tread upon.

With Dominica begins the most northerly group of the Lesser Antilles. Those belonging to the English Crown were federated by an Imperial Act in 1871. The total area of the federated Colony, which includes Antigua, Montserrat, St. Kitts, Nevis, Dominica, Anguilla, and the Virgin Islands, is 704 square miles, and its population, according to the Census of 1891, was 127,723, being an increase of 74,958 compared with that of 1881. The present estimated population is 133,000. This federation, although it is not usually considered a success in securing better government and greater economy of expenditure, received some justification from the fact that in the reign of William and Mary these islands had a common Legislature. This, indeed, was one of the arguments which had weight with the Imperial Parliament in agreeing to the later federation. This old General Legislature met for the last time in 1798, and the wonder is that having apparently been so successful (although the most important of its laws were disallowed by the Home Government—especially the repeal of the $4\frac{1}{2}$ per cent. duty) it was not retained, instead of being allowed to fall to pieces.

The general Government of the Leeward Islands Federation may more fitly be described, and the results of that measure be better discussed, when Antigua, the principal island, is reached.

Dominica is a Presidency within the above general Government. There is a President, with an Executive Council of seven members. Traces of old constitutional

SEA WALL AND JETTY AT ROSEAU, DOMINICA.

rights still exist in the fact that there is a Legislative Assembly existing, but as it consists of seven members nominated by the Crown, and seven elected members, with the President in the chair, possessed of a casting vote, there is not much room for any action independent of the Government. The franchise which governs the elected portion of the Legislature is the possession of land or houses rented at 4*l.* per annum, or the voter must be an occupier of premises worth 8*l.* per annum, or have an income of 25*l.*, or pay taxes amounting to 15*s.* per annum.

There are some signs of the ancient vigour and prosperity still in the aspect of Roseau, although the grass is growing in the streets, and the houses are in need of repair. The former agricultural prosperity of the island was not a dream of sanguine colonists, for Dr. Nicholls has shown what can be done again, by his profitable cultivation of limes and Liberian coffee.

The white population is mainly French, and Roman Catholic. The blacks speak a French *patois*. At the peace of 1763 the island contained 600 whites and 2,000 blacks. In 1788 there were 1,236 whites, 445 free negroes, and 14,967 slaves—total 16,648. In 1831 the total population had risen, principally by the increase of the slave and free black people, to 18,970. Its population in 1891 is stated at 26,841, including about 300 Caribs.

With this increase of population, however, there has been a decrease of prosperity. Formerly the slopes were covered with coffee trees, but this industry has practically disappeared. In 1777 its exports were 1,302 hogsheads of sugar, 63,000 gallons of rum, 16,803 gallons of molasses, 1,194 cwt. of cocoa, 18,149 cwt. of coffee, 11,250 lbs. of indigo, 971,000 lbs. of cotton, besides hides, dyewoods &c. to the value of 12,000*l*. From this time forward the resources of the island were still further developed, until in 1830 there were 4,071 hogsheads (of nearly a ton each) of sugar exported, and 1,311,473 lbs. of coffee, besides rum and molasses. The biggest year for coffee, upon a first glance at the statistics, was apparently 1828, when 2,546,635 lbs. were exported. Now nearly the whole of the sugar industry has disappeared, owing to the abandonment of estates to avoid continued annual loss, the quantity exported in 1895 being only 844 tons. One principal reason alleged for this state of things is the want of steady and continuous labour. The imports in 1895 from the United Kingdom were 30,062*l*., from Colonies 13,461*l*., from foreign countries 23,733*l*.— or a total with other small items of 69,789*l*., To the economist, who judges of the progress of a country by its buying and exchanging power, the figures tell a discouraging tale. The same conclusions are to be drawn from the exports. From an average of 60,000*l*. (in 1878 it was 84,703*l*.) the amount for 1895 had fallen to 39,471*l*., comprising 19,680*l*. to the United Kingdom, 4,501*l*. to Colonies, and 15,290*l*. to foreign countries. Very nearly half the island is eminently adapted for agricultural purposes, but scores of thousands of acres are awaiting the hand of the cultivator. Sugar, perhaps, is impossible in the future, principally owing to the want of capital necessary to establish or renew estates. There might be room for a central factory, the canes to be grown by the occupiers of small holdings, if such persons could be depended upon to grow sufficient produce to keep the factory going. But cocoa, coffee (for which the island is admirably adapted), limes, and lime juice, spices, and oils could be more extensively cultivated, and the old timber trade (once so flourishing) could be again renewed with

DOMINICA : LABOURER'S HUT.

something of its pristine success. There is much to do in Dominica with willing hands and a moderate capital. There is plenty of fish in the rivers, as well as abundance of game. The revenue in 1895 was 22,859*l.*, and the expenditure 27,102*l.*

CHAPTER XVII.

GUADELOUPE.

BREAKING for the moment the discussion of the British Leeward Islands, in going northward we arrive at the next important French Colony, Guadeloupe. This island, like others in the chain of the Lesser Antilles, is volcanic, but although subject now to occasional disturbance, smoke in the day and flashes of fire in the night, the forces of nature are quieter than they were at one time, the last great earthquake being in 1843. The violence of the original eruptions may be gathered from the fact that the island contains a volcano of a very great height. The rainfall on the hills contributes to the rivers, which are numerous. It is a natural feature worthy of note that Guadeloupe is divided into two parts by a small sea canal of about 30 yards wide, navigable by small vessels, and connected with good bays at both ends. Basseterre, at the base of one of the volcanic hills, is the port and principal town. Guadeloupe (or Guadalupe) was so called by Columbus from the resemblance its mountains bore to some he knew in Spain of the same name. This was also in compliment to the monks of the monastery of Guadalupe in Estremadura, to whom he had promised that he would call a newly discovered place after it. It is said that Columbus first saw the pineapple here. The Spaniards at once entered into hostile relations with the

Caribs. The island is 30 miles both in length and width. It is 13 miles N.W. of Marie Galante, and 73 miles north of Martinique. The Spaniards kept it until 1635, when it was ceded to the French. The English took and sacked it in 1691, and also obtained possession of it at three subsequent dates. But from early times it has been characteristically a French Colony. The east part of the island is called Grande Terre, which is flat, while the mountainous part is on the other side of the Salt River. The air is temperate and healthy, the water good, and the soil rich. Grande Terre contains 120,000 acres, and what is called Guadeloupe proper 180,000. It is in the former district, Grande Terre, that the principal sugar estates and works are situated. After the troubles with the Caribs, which the French for many years subsequent to their first occupation found so embarrassing, the island made way, and its real prosperity began after the Peace of Utrecht. In 1755 it contained 9,624 white colonists and 41,000 slaves. There were 334 sugar works or 'presses,' 15 indigo plantations, 46,840 cacao trees, 11,700 tobacco plants, 2,257,728 coffee trees, 12,748,447 cotton trees, besides a large number of horses, mules, cattle, and other stock for draught and food.

The usines are now principally supported by capital subscribed by shareholders in Paris, who always seem to have faith in these West Indian ventures—a faith justified by steady, and in many cases large, dividends. The present population of the island is about 167,000, composed of white, coloured, and black, and some 15,000 coolies, drawn from the French settlements of India—Pondicherry and Karikal. The Government consists of a Council-General, elected by universal suffrage (with of course a Governor and his Executive), and the island is represented in the French Parliament by a senator and two deputies.

The revenue and expenditure are respectively about six millions of francs. In the budget of France for 1897 there is an item of 1,586,759 francs for this Colony. The island is divided into arrondissements, cantons, and communes. There are 97 elementary schools with an attendance of 11,000 children. The total imports and exports amount to 44 millions of francs. The quantity of sugar exported in 1895 was 43,000 tons. A considerable variety of produce is grown besides, such as coffee, cacao, vanilla, spices, potatoes, rice, Indian corn, bananas, vegetables; also some cotton and ramie fibre, and the forests are thick with valuable timber. The island has seen its troubles, but upon the whole it presents to the world a picture of successful Colonial enteprise, characteristically French. There is necessarily a lessened value of sugar exported owing to prices being reduced by the European bounty system, and notwithstanding the share possessed by these French Colonies in the protective legislation of France.

A word must also be said of the dependencies of Guadeloupe. One of these is Marie Galante, a small island about 40 miles round, with a population of 17,000. It has taken its share in the contests of the last and preceding centuries. It was named by Columbus in 1493, when he saw it, after the vessel on which he was sailing. He took possession of it in the name of the King of Spain. The French established themselves here in 1648, and the town was twice sacked and destroyed by the Dutch. The English attacked it in 1691 and again in 1765, but since 1766 it appears to have remained in the possession of the French, with one exception, when the fortunes of war at the beginning of the nineteenth century once more placed it temporarily in our hands. The island is well timbered, the climate is healthy, and the soil good. In some parts it is mountainous. It used to produce coffee and cotton in good quantities in comparison with its size and resources. The other islands need not be particularly mentioned. The Isles of the Saints were so called because they were discovered on All Saints' Day. These islands are about 10 miles S.E. of Guadeloupe. One island, Terre de Haut, has a good harbour. Another island, Terre de Bas, is devoted to fishing. On the island of Desirado, quite near to Guadeloupe, is the Leper Asylum. St. Martin, about 100 miles to the north, belongs partly to France and partly to Holland. St. Bartholomew, about 80 miles N. of Guadeloupe, at one time belonged to Sweden. The French, however, were in possession from 1648 to 1784. An exchange again occurred with Sweden; but France, so recently as 1878, by a payment of 16,000*l.*, a transaction which aroused much interest at the time, acquired the island again from Sweden.

CHAPTER XVIII.

MONTSERRAT.

THE next island to be noticed is Montserrat, one of the British Leeward Islands, and in many respects an exceedingly attractive spot. It is situated 27 miles from Antigua, 16° 45′ N. lat. and 61° W. long. The name was given to it by Columbus in 1493, in memory of a mountain in Spain upon which the monastery was situated where Loyola planned the great Society of Jesus, a Society which for so many years dominated and perhaps civilised to some extent (although several of its methods then employed are not consistent with modern notions) many important parts of South America. The name was also suggested by the broken and mountainous appearance of the island. It has been called by grave historians the romantic isle. It has been the subject of poetry, as the following lines, written sixty years ago, will testify:

Beautiful islands, where the green which Nature wears was never seen
'Neath zone of Europe; where the hue of sea and heaven is such a
  blue
As England dreams not; where the night is all irradiate with the
  light
Of star-like moons, which, hung on high, breathe and quiver in the
  sky,
Each its silver haze divine flinging in a radiant line
O'er gorgeous flower and mighty tree, on the soft and shadowy sea!

MONTSERRAT.

Beautiful islands, brief the time I dwelt beneath your awful clime,
Yet oft I see, in noonday dream, your glorious stars with lunar beam,
And oft before my sight arise your sky-like seas, your sea-like skies,
Your green banana's giant leaves, your golden canes in arrowy sheaves,
Your palms, which never die, but stand immortal sea-marks on the strand,
Their feathery tufts like plumage rare, their stems so high, so strange and fair ;
Yea ! while the breeze of England now flings rose-scents on my aching brow,
I think a moment I inhale again the breath of tropic gale.

The above lines, perhaps, except here and there, present little of the gold of true poetry; they are nevertheless valuable in that they record the impressions of a sensitive lover of nature, and in their reproduction in words of a picture that steeps the mind in light and colour they may not be despised. Even Mr. Sturge's groves of lime trees, at the present moment, not only are a part of the picture, but, what is perhaps more to be desired, suggestive of profit. Montserrat is a small island. It is only eleven miles long, and seven in its greatest width. Its total area is only thirty-two and a half square miles. And yet, without the rugged grandeur of some of the other islands, it still shows the diversity of form that is the principal characteristic of the group. It has no elaborate history, nor has it borne the brunt, to the same extent as other islands, of Imperial wars. It is true it has been taken and retaken. The first settlement was made in 1632 under Sir Thomas Warner. In 1664 it experienced a warlike occupation by the French, who made the colonists suffer in person, and, by heavy exactions, in purse. It became English again in 1668, but had to surrender to the French in 1782. Since 1784 it has been an English Colony.

It is a series of round hills developing into a mountain

T

chain, not, however, rising beyond 3,000 feet. These mountains are richly wooded, and, their sides being precipitous, many deep gullies are formed. Montserrat is not without its Soufrière, although it is a small one. It is situated about 1,000 feet above the sea, on the south-west side of the mountain chain. It is in a dell, the surroundings of which are formed by three conical hills. The path to it has been described as presenting something like the scenery of the Devonshire lakes. The gorgeous hibiscus, the light limes, and darker orange trees form a hedge on either side. With the gentle sea breeze, the exhilaration of a May morning is produced. Then a green savannah opens to the view. Looking round, a wooded mountain is seen, descending in a long grassy slope to the edge of the sea. To the south the irregular hills of Guadeloupe catch the eye, and the great peak of Nevis rises to the north in its canopy of clouds. Descending to the Vale of the Soufrière it is found to be broken into confused masses of clay and limestone. The ground is warm enough to keep the feet moving. A constantly rising vapour meets the wind. The sides of the glen rise up with most luxuriant verdure.

This island is called the Montpellier of the West, because of the elasticity of its atmosphere, the picturesqueness of its hills, and its generally lovely scenery. The temperature varies according to height, and is generally cool and dry. In early times the island was largely populated with European colonists. In 1648 there were 1,000 white families resident upon it, with a militia of 360 Europeans. The curious part of the business is that the negroes to this day speak with an Irish brogue. This is accounted for by the fact that the early settlers were Irish. A story is told of a Connaught man who, on arriving at the island, was to his astonishment hailed in vernacular Irish by a negro from one of the boats that came alongside. 'Thunder and turf!' exclaimed the new-comer, 'how long have you been here?' 'Three months,' the black man answered. 'Three months! and so black already! By the powers! I'll not stay among ye,' and the visitor returned, a sadder and a wiser man, to his own Emerald Isle.

The capital of the island is Plymouth, on the S.W. side. It is a small town, but very well built; the houses are substantially constructed of a fine grey stone. The principal roadstead is off the town, and the landing in small boats is sometimes not very easy through the surf.

In November 1896 a terrific storm of wind and rain wrought havoc and desolation over the island, roads becoming roaring torrents, and lime-fields and cane pieces turned into lakes. The floods were attended with considerable loss of life and property. Subscriptions were, however, forthcoming from the neighbouring Colonies, as well as from the United Kingdom, which relieved the immediate distress and assisted the poorer landowners to replace to some extent their losses.

Montserrat in the early days had representative institutions. In 1668 it had a Council and Assembly. It subsequently (indeed, not many years ago) passed through all the changes leading to a Crown Colony. It has its President (or, as he is now called, Commissioner) with an Executive Council, and it has its Legislative Council of six, composed of officials, or unofficials, as the Queen may direct, the President being of course in the chair. The island is under the general Government of the Leeward Islands.

Sugar is cultivated and made, but only to a small extent, say 900 to 1,000 tons, which probably may be taken as an average for several years past. The principal industry which has sprung up is the cultivation of limes and the manufacture of lime juice of the well-known 'Montserrat' brand. This business is in the hands of a limited company, and other persons will soon, no doubt, take part in the industry, and share the profits to be derived. The supporters of the company (especially as they are connected with the honoured name of Sturge) deserve every credit for their enterprise, and every success that could attend it.

The island revenue in 1895 amounted to 7,125l., raised principally from import duties, and the expenditure to 10,702l.

The value of imports, excluding bullion and specie, in 1895 was 24,480l., viz. 9,975l. from the United Kingdom, 9,653l. from Colonies and internal trade, and 4,852l. from foreign countries. The exports were 17,189l., viz. 10,610l. to the United Kingdom, 529l. to Colonies, 2,967l. internal trade, and 3,083l. to foreign countries, showing that the sugar probably goes to the United States, and that the lime juice is distributed to the United Kingdom, the other European countries, and the United States. The island has a debt of 18,100l., and its present population is 11,762.

Upon the whole, although Montserrat cannot boast of its old importance and its large white population of former days, there is yet a good prospect before it. In itself it is a model and a compact place. It awaits the attention of more Englishmen who would cultivate its various products, and who would, at the same time, be not insensible to beautiful scenery and a perfectly healthy climate.

CHAPTER XIX.

NEVIS, ST. KITTS, AND ANGUILLA.

BETWEEN Montserrat and Nevis there is a rock rising out of the sea called Redonda. The next island of this Leeward group is Nevis. This island is not simply a part of the general federation, but has within recent years (1882) been amalgamated with St. Christopher, both now forming one presidency under the general administration of the Leeward Islands. It might be suggested that, in these circumstances, the two might be taken as one, but as Nevis is the next in the geographical order northward, and as it possesses an individuality and a history (or an absence of history, which may be still better) of its own, it might be desirable to discuss it separately in some points.

Nevis is situated in 17° 10′ N. lat. and 62° 33′ W. long. It is round in form, of an area of 50 square miles (this is the official statement, but other authorities give it less), or 32,000 acres, half of which are fit for cultivation. From a distance it has the appearance of a perfect cone rising out of the sea. Its highest point is 3,200 feet. Columbus discovered it in 1498. From the white clouds which settle on its summit the great adventurer gave it the name of 'Neives,' after the snow-capped mountain near Barcelona. The sides of the mountain are green, and at the limit of the cultivated land the ferns and evergreens grow like a collar. It was first colonised by a few Englishmen in 1628 under Sir Thomas Warner. It is in shape a single mountain, at the base of which is a border of level land, extremely fertile, and at one time well planted with sugar cane. On the north and east the cone is not so perfect as when seen from the south and west. It falls off in one direction in a long slope, broken by one or two irregular hills. It had a population in 1831 of 500 whites and about 9,000 slaves, and it used to ship 5,000 tons of sugar. Its capital is Charlestown, lying along the shore of a wide curving bay, the mountain rising immediately behind it in a long and verdant acclivity. St. Christopher (or St. Kitts) and Nevis being now one Colony and under one president, the statistics may be put forward as a whole, without differentiating between the two islands.

Although the fine mansions of the planters, on the slope of the Nevis hills, are out of repair, there are still evidences of the prosperity which has been, and may be again, enjoyed. A story is told of an American who brought, some years ago, a cargo of 'notions.' But his quick returns did not come in, and he went away dissatisfied. Trading experiences of this character necessarily give an unfavourable impression, which is probably not deserved. Complaints as to the heaviness of the taxation have been more than once put forward during the last twenty years. The island has many natural resources ; its soil is peculiarly fitted for the growth of limes, coffee, cocoa, and cinchona, and also for its historical staple, sugar. Sulphur beds are waiting to be worked, and the medicinal qualities of the sulphur springs are unsurpassed. The remains of a grand stone building show the expectations which once were formed of this sanatorium. Perhaps the building may be renewed, and a good hotel on the American plan established. Another

ST. KITTS.

incident worthy of note is that Nelson married in Nevis the 'Widow Nisbet.' She was at the time in her twenty-third year, having mourned for her husband, a medical doctor, for eighteen months. In one of the parish churches may still be seen the entry of the marriage, at which William, Duke of Clarence, afterwards King William the Fourth, was best man.

St. Kitts, Nevis, and Anguilla, and certain dependencies, form one Colony, under the Government of the Leeward Islands. Nevis is only separated from St. Kitts by a strait about two miles broad. The island of St. Kitts is in latitude 17° 18' N. and long. 62° 48' W. It is about 23 miles long, and the total area is 68 square miles. This was another of the islands that Columbus discovered in 1498. It received its name probably from the great navigator himself, or from the well-known legend of St. Christopher and the Saviour. When Columbus discovered the island it was densely populated by Caribs. It has had its fluctuations of possession by certain European Powers. In 1623 Sir Thomas Warner formed a settlement. Towards the end of the seventeenth century the number of settlers was very large. But there were struggles with the French. For many years the French and English remained in their own portions of the island, and agreed to remain neutral in the case of Imperial wars. But human nature could not stand the strain, and desperate conflicts arose, resulting in favour of the French, who assumed the mastery of the island, and successfully maintained it against an attack of British ships and troops. At the Peace of Breda the English were restored to their portion of the island, but in 1689 they were again attacked by the French, many were put to the sword, and the remainder driven out. But in 1690 General Codrington and Sir F. Thornhill, with a strong force from Barbados, retaliated by driving the French from the island, and for some years the British power was undisputed. The Treaty of Ryswick restored to the French the part they had formerly possessed, which they retained until 1702. By the Treaty of Utrecht, in 1713, it was entirely given to Great Britain. The French inhabitants transferred themselves to St. Domingo. The Government received a large sum of money by the sale of the Crown lands, 40,000*l*. of which went as a marriage portion to a daughter of George II. It seems now beyond belief that St. Kitts should have been so wealthy; however, there the fact is, showing that in the Georgian era the Colonies were not backward in their support of the Throne, for which they willingly made sacrifices. In illustration of this, note the long imposition of the 4½ per cent. duty. But St. Kitts had still some changes to experience. It rapidly prospered, notwithstanding the severe hurricane of 1722, which destroyed, it is said, half a million sterling of property.

St. Kitts is recognised as the Mother Colony of this group. It is certainly one of the oldest of the British West Indian settlements, never having been colonised by the Spaniards. Both the French and English settlements in the Caribbean Islands are indebted to St. Christopher for much encouragement and a vigorous example. The arms of St. Christopher represent the great discoverer on his quarterdeck looking through his glass. The Sir Thomas Warner above mentioned in connection with the Leeward Islands was an enthusiastic gentleman of the true enterprising spirit. He sailed from England to Virginia in 1620. Thence, in 1623, he settled in St. Kitts. After his arrival with his small party

ST. KITTS.

of Englishmen, the quarrels with the French began, as above detailed. He came back to the island, after an absence in England, in 1626 with 400 recruits. The French also, under authorisation from Cardinal Richelieu, then Minister of France, established a trading connection with the island, and out of these conflicting claims, its neutrality, as explained above, was brought about, and occasionally failed.

The general physical aspect of the island has been already indicated, but for purposes of more precise description it may be said that through the oblong configuration a regular series of mountains is seen running from north to south, and in the middle rises Mount Misery, 3,711 feet in perpendicular height. From the mountains the island slopes to the cultivable land. On the west side, Brimstone Hill rises from the sea. The eastern prospect ends in two peaks, Fort George to the north, and Fort Charlotte, or Monkey Hill, to the south. Monkey Hill is the south point of a range of mountains, the apex of which is Mount Misery, bare and black, a curtain of clouds concealing its lower part, leaving its top generally distinguishable. The Vale of Basseterre, seen from one of the mountains, is extremely rich (it is difficult to find another word so expressive) in its aspect. The plantations, with the ships in the distance, constitute a picture which could not be soon forgotten. In the earlier times the productions were tobacco, indigo, and ginger. The adaptability of the soil for sugar was also shown by the export of 12,000 tons annually. Ground provisions (yams and roots of all kinds) afford, of course, a supply of food to the population. For the sugar cane the soil is particularly adapted, being a black ferruginous pumice mixed with a pure loam. It is light and porous, and easily worked with the hoe. The friable nature of the soil makes it peculiarly susceptible to rain, which very quickly—often too quickly—disappears. In addition to artificial manures, now very largely used, the planters have what is called a system of 'green dressing.' Pigeon peas or Bengal beans are planted in those parts of an estate where the canes are not grown in a particular year. These produce in a short time a mass of foliage, which is cut down and ploughed in; it rapidly decays, and adds strength to the soil. The cultivation in St. Kitts is remarkably good. The late Lord Combermere, who owned estates in the island, said, after one of his visits, that it was like the best market gardening in England. The ploughing by teams of oxen is indeed a sight to gladden the eyes of the agriculturist. While the cultivation is good, the manufacture of the sugar inclines to the older instead of the newer method, except on Brighton Estate, where the best vacuum pan sugar is made. Expensive machinery on small estates does not pay, and no one would risk the necessary capital; and here, as in other islands, the centralisation of manufacture to use up all procurable canes within easy reach of transport seems to offer the best prospects of success in the future. The labour is good when available. The negro, when he works, does so industriously, and he lives simply; but when a man can live without work, and life is worth living with the bounties of nature on every hand, it is hard to blame a man for basking in the sun and enjoying existence in his own fashion. Sweet potatoes, bananas, and bread-fruit are, as a rule, sufficient for food. When imported meats and food stuffs are wanted, the eighteenpence a day wages for hoeing and weeding the fields, cutting the cane when ripe, and taking part in the rather warm work of the boiling-house, becomes an object of ambition, and is easily earned. The English agricultural labourer, with a much less wage, considering the difference in the cost of living and in the climatic conditions, is a poor serf in comparison. The black man only wears shoes or boots on Sunday. Why should he be cramped with the corn-producing restrictions of civilisation when he can do without those accessories? The chigoe is less formidable than the boot, and rightly so. Europeans cannot afford to try the experiment; but the black man knows what he is about, and is able to take care of himself. If he dresses simply in the week, he goes to church or chapel on Sunday in good style. He has his cloth frock-coat, his shining silk hat, his patent-leather boots, while his wife and daughters are clothed in muslin or in silk, with bright ribbons in their headgear, and parasols to match. The philosophy of clothes has been often descanted upon with very little profit, but the desire of the respectable black man in the West Indies to assert his position, and to demand consideration by means of his Sunday dress, is not the least gratifying and encouraging symptom of his general progress. Of course one great evil in these tropical as well as in European countries is that the labouring class will always gravitate to the towns, to their moral and social deterioration. A crowded lodging-room in town is preferred to a cottage and garden ground in the country. Medical attendance for the children and destitute is amply provided. There is an excellent public hospital and also a good district hospital in the town of Sandy Point.

Basseterre is the principal town of St. Kitts. It was destroyed by fire in 1867. The town has been rebuilt, with a better class of houses and wider streets. Its population is about 8,000, too large in relation to the total population of the island. Basseterre is supplied with water by pipes from the old Road River, some six miles distant, and there is a large reservoir near the town in case of need or failure of the main supply. The town is a busy place, and in the crop season is very energetic and full of life and movement. There is a good system of education at work in the island, and Sir Benjamin Pine's grammar school has done much useful work in its time.

The climate of St. Kitts is healthy, cool, and dry. The mean temperature on the coast is $75°$ to $80°$. Even in the hottest weather, the nights and mornings are refreshingly cool. The rainfall is about 50 inches. The wind is strong, and it sometimes blows a hurricane, and floods occasionally occur after an excessive rainfall. The good effect of the climate is seen in the healthy and robust appearance of the people. Altogether, with its climate and its scenery, St. Kitts presents facilities for a vigorous enjoyment of life, an enjoyment not at all inconsistent with the gentler arts by which men and women give grace and sweetness to the work they do, and to the social surroundings in which they move.

Speaking of the gentler arts reminds one that St. Kitts appears in English poetry. James Grainger published in 1764 his poem on the Sugar Cane. Dr. Grainger was an army surgeon during the Scottish rebellion of 1745. He afterwards practised as a physician in London, and became a friend of Dr. Johnson. He went to St. Kitts to settle as a physician. On the voyage he cured a lady of small-pox, and, in marrying her daughter, acquired property in the island. Residing on his sugar estate, his literary taste led him to write his poem, which does not, perhaps, reach a very exalted standard of language or ideas. He discusses soil, agricultural implements, and the best way of growing sugar. Boswell tells a good story of the 'Sugar Cane.' It was read in manuscript at the house of Sir Joshua Reynolds. The members of the Literary Club were present in full force, and after the solemn opening they burst into laughter when they heard the exhortation, ' Now, Muse ! let's sing of rats !' This line was, however, expunged, but there are many similar examples of extreme commonplace mixed up with higher but still artificial strains of poetry. He writes as follows of the island :

> O might my strain
> As far transcend the immortal songs of Greece,
> As thou the partial subject of their praise,
> Thy fame should float familiar through the world ;
> Each plant should own thy cane her lawful lord ;
> Nor should old Time—song stops the flight of Time—
> Obscure thy lustre with his shadowy wing.
> Scarce less impregnated with every power
> Of vegetation is the red brick mould
> That lies on marly beds.

This may not be poetical, but it is unquestionably practical. So is the second book, with its discourse on earthquakes and rats, hurricanes and monkeys. Here and there are touches of social life, in the description of the planter and his home. The third book is especially devoted to a description of plantation life. The fourth describes his system of managing his labourers. 'Let humanity prevail,' he says, and adds :

> Servants, not slaves; of choice, and not compelled,
> The blacks should cultivate the cane-land isles.

And so the worthy Doctor-Planter, in the curiously artificial strain of poetry common to his period, combines his imagery and his business. Nevertheless, his appreciation of life in

St. Kitts is earnest, and not less true because conventionally expressed.

The government of the combined Colony of St. Kitts-Nevis is vested in a Commissioner and Legislative Council, which is composed of the high officials of the general Government and some local members, and consists of ten official members and ten nominated unofficial. The President has an original and a casting vote. There is also an Executive Council, consisting of such persons as Her Majesty may from time to time appoint. So recently as 1866 St. Kitts enjoyed representative institutions.

The revenue of St. Kitts-Nevis, derived principally from import duties, was in 1895, 43,215*l*., with an expenditure of 55,394*l*. The imports in that year (exclusive of bullion and specie) were: From the United Kingdom, 65,538*l*.; from Colonies, 20,903*l*.; internal trade 1,988*l*.; from foreign countries, 83,852*l*., making a total import value of 172,281*l*. The exports were: To the United Kingdom, 9,354*l*.; to Colonies, 33,858*l*.; to foreign countries, 90,028*l*.; making with other small items a total export value of 140,542*l*. The small amount of export value to the United Kingdom will be noticed. The fact becomes a startling and significant one when this small amount is compared with the former export to the United Kingdom, which so recently as 1883 was 156,416*l*. The hopeless competition against bounties in Europe could not be more forcibly illustrated. The West Indian Colonies find themselves shut out of the markets of the Mother Country by the bounty-fed sugar of Germany. And a drop from 150,000*l*. to 9,000*l*., in such a short space as fourteen years, of goods supplied to England must be a detriment to British trade, for which no advantage, or supposed advantage, of cheap beetroot sugar can compensate. The tendency of the trade will of course be, that where the exports go the imports will be obtained; and the United States will inevitably take the place of the United Kingdom in supplying the wants and necessaries of these Colonies, a monopoly of trade in favourable markets which English merchants once so dearly cherished, and which English governments and parliaments did their best for centuries to conserve.

The population according to the census of 1891 was as follows: St. Kitts 30,876, Nevis 13,087, Anguilla 3,690, or a total population for the combined colony of 47,653. The Colony has a public debt of 30,000*l*. It shipped in 1895 13,095 tons of sugar (which was a very good crop as compared with some previous years), 61,530 gallons of rum, and 4,015 puncheons of molasses. Among the fruits of St. Kitts the China orange tree as well as the Seville are to be found. The flowers are odoriferous, and give their flavour to rectified spirits by infusion, and to both spirit and water by distillation. The growth of limes is an industry which might be still further extended, as well as some of the varieties of the lemon. The shaddock is of the Citrus tribe. It is supposed to have received its name from being introduced into the West Indies by a Captain Shaddock from Guinea in Africa. It belongs to the orange species, and is divided by a thin skin into quarters; its size is larger than the orange, however, and its flavour is refreshing, between sweet and acid. The fruit commonly called the alligator pear comes to great perfection here.

Anguilla, lying right north past Antigua, and situated between 18° N. lat. and 64° W. long., is between 50 and 60 miles to the N.W. of St. Kitts, and separated from St. Martin's by a narrow channel. Anguilla forms a third constituency in the Colony of St. Kitts-Nevis. It received its name from its tortuous and snake-like form. It is about sixteen miles long and from three to one and a half miles broad. In 1650 it was discovered and colonised by the English, who apparently took possession of it as an uninhabited island. Apart from incidental attacks by the French, and particularly by the famous revolutionary leader, Victor Hugues, in 1796, this narrow strip of land in the sea seems to have had a quiet time. British ships were always cruising in the neighbourhood: the commanders could not, if they would, telegraph for instructions to an official at home, who might be unable to realise the exigency of the moment; and so, by timely intervention of British ships of war, this piece of dry ocean was saved as a British possession. The islanders have always displayed the true insular qualities of bravery and independence. If they were only 100 strong, they would meet 1,000 of their foes with light hearts and good courage. No one can tell the amount of heroism which has been displayed by these small islands. The colonists were men as well as tillers of the soil. They had their virtues, passions, ambitions, fears, and hopes, and living on a little snake-like island, they tried to conduct their affairs with propriety and success, remained steadfast in their allegiance to the British flag, and behaved themselves generally as good citizens—for all these things they lived and died unnoticed, their deeds unsung by poets and unrewarded by governments. The brave deeds of colonists are now largely forgotten—if indeed they were ever borne in mind, except by such bright souls as Kingsley. The island of Anguilla is healthy. It has for its dependencies the 'Dogs' and contiguous islands. It has but a small revenue of about 550*l*. Cattle, phosphate of lime, and salt (there is a salt lake in the centre of the island) are the principal exports, the market for these being St. Thomas.

CHAPTER XX.

ANTIGUA.

ANTIGUA, the headquarters of the Leeward Islands Federation, and the seat of the Federal Council and the general Government, is the next Colony to mention. It is situated 61° 45′ W. long. and 17° 6′ N. lat. It is 40 miles N. of Guadeloupe. It is 20 miles in length, and 54 miles in circumference. It has an area of 59,838 acres, or about 108 square miles. It was discovered by Columbus in 1493, and named by him from a church in Seville, Santa Maria de la Antigua. It is one of the oldest of the British islands, having been settled by Sir Thomas Warner in 1632 with a few English families. In 1666 a French expedition from Martinique and Guadeloupe acquired the temporary possession of the island, and enforced great exactions. The Breda Treaty in 1667 confirmed it in the possession of Great Britain, and it then made a real start as a centre of production and trade. It should, however, be mentioned that Antigua was granted to Lord Willoughby of Parham (whose name is, perhaps, more closely connected with Antigua than with any other colony) in 1663. In the long list of Governors of Antigua, Lord Willoughby is the first, under the date 1668. His lordship had been in trouble with the Lord Protector, and under the Restoration he acquired the grant, and undertook his government. He

U

had been in the West Indies years before, and endeavoured to keep the Colonies against the Parliamentary forces. He did not long retain the government (if he ever personally undertook it), for in the same year (1668) Samuel Winthrope is on the official list as Deputy-Governor. In 1689 General Codrington was Governor, belonging to a family which exerted much beneficial influence upon the islands. The General was an enterprising man, of wide and liberal views. One of the finest estates in the island at the present time (Betty's Hope) is owned by his descendant, Sir Gerald Codrington, who has nothing to regret in his connection with the Colony, for the estate is well managed and produces a good income.

Antigua is said to be subject to drought, and, from all accounts, this is quite true. The seasons are the subject of much anxious thought and expectation. Antigua lies so high from the sea, there is such an unusual absence of lofty woods, that the climate is unquestionably dry, and the rainy season uncertain. The temperature is very equable, hardly ranging beyond $75°$ to $80°$, and the rainfall is stated at about 48 inches. The geological features are interesting and somewhat unusual. The island is partly calcareous and partly of trap rock formation, and there are marine and fresh-water strata, containing fossils, shells and petrified wood, capable of polish bringing out the fibres. Beautiful valleys are formed by the abrupt sides of the hills. Large ponds and stone tanks afford water for agricultural and drinking purposes, and wells on the estates are common. Between 1860 and 1870, under a popular and energetic governor, Sir Stephen Hill, an abundant supply of water for the city, St. John's, was obtained through pipes, and just above the town there is a splendid reservoir, insuring against a water famine. The general physical aspect may be shortly described. More than one half of the island on the N.E. is low, and occasionally marshy, but varied by eminences that recall English scenery. In the S. and S.W. the elevation of the land becomes more marked, and extensive valleys are formed. The greatest elevation is about 1,210 feet, on the Sheckerley range of mountains, called Boggie's Hill, about six miles to the W. of Monk's Hill.

The island is especially fortunate in its many good bays and harbours; but with the exception of St. John's, English Harbour, and Falmouth (where pilotage is necessary), the inlets are difficult of access. St. John's, the capital, is not very regular and formal in its appearance, but it is well laid out, and is of considerable size. Many fine buildings, now out of repair, tell of bygone prosperity. Government House is a good building, standing in extensive grounds, and the rooms are large and pleasant.

The following is an eloquent picture of a scene in Antigua, written many years ago : 'From some of these rocks, especially near the parsonage of St. Philip's parish, one of the finest panoramic views in the world may be obtained. The whole island, which is of a rough circular figure, is in sight. The heart of the island is verdant with an abundant pasturage or grassy down. The shores are indented in every direction with creeks and bays and coves, some of them running into the centre of the plantations like canals, some swelling into estuaries, and others forming spacious harbours. Beyond these an infinite variety of islands and islets stud the bosom of the blue sea. They are of all shapes and sizes. From the same hill, when the western sky is clear, Guadeloupe, Montserrat,

Nevis, and St. Kitts, may all be distinguished by the naked eye.'

St. John's (with a population of 9,738) is built on the N.W. side of the island at the head of a very pretty harbour, the N. side of which is partly formed by a rock called Rat Island, about halfway up the harbour, its connection with the mainland being under water at high tide. The ascent from Falmouth Bay leads to some of the most picturesque views in the island, especially from Monk's Hill, where formerly a strong fortification was maintained. The fortress has been utilised as a signal station to announce the arrival of the mails. The mail steamers call in a small bay called English Harbour, surrounded by hills, and about twelve miles from St. John's. There is a little rocky promontory projecting into the bay, with a flagstaff on it. It is reached by a flight of steps cut into the rock. There is scrub and bush on the sides of the hills, with quantities of aloes. At the sea level, at the foot of the hills, there is a sandy beach covered with shells. Besides St. John's and Falmouth, the small town of Parham (suggesting reminiscences of Lord Willoughby) may be mentioned. The following is Kingsley's account of his entrance into English Harbour. After saying that the bay is simply a group of extinct craters, 'past low cliffs of ash and volcanic boulder, sloping westward to the sea, which is eating them fast away, the steamer runs in through a deep crack, a pistol-shot in width. On the east side a strange section of grey lava and ash is graven into caves. On the right a bluff rock of black lava dips sheer into water several fathoms deep, and you anchor at once inside an irregular group of craters, having passed through a gap in one of their sides which has probably been torn out by a lava flow.' He noticed also the aloes on the cliff, the 'glaring shingle,' or rather sandy, beach, the quays and dockyard buildings, that make up the picture which the visitor, not landing, tries to take in from the steamer's deck with all his eyes, and to remember with all his might.

At this point the constitutional question comes in for discussion—or rather statement, for it would be out of place to take anything like a partisan view of a measure which has been accomplished, but which may be said to be on its trial yet, for the principle of Federation has not been carried farther than Lord Carnarvon's Act. The fact remains, that islands with distinct characters, histories, and populations, separated each from each by sea, cannot be joined together by any artificial process without some injustice, and certainly much friction. It is in vain to attempt to ignore the fact that, in the view of many responsible people, the anticipations which were formed of the Leeward Islands Federation have not been fully realised. The character of the government, the amount of expenditure, are still capable of improvement. But these are political questions, with which we have in these pages nothing to do. The only way is to make the best of institutions as they exist. Without repeating the remarks previously made as to the former common Legislature in the time of William and Mary, respecting the constitution and action of which very little has been explained, the historical record of the present form of government begins during the time of Sir Benjamin Pine, an able man, but a little excitable and imperious. A story is told in the blue books of his marching a body of marines to the Legislative Council of Nevis to assist in overcoming any opposition to the scheme. But this is a mere detail, connected with individuals rather than with principles. The Imperial Act was passed in the session of 1871, by which Antigua, Montserrat, St. Kitts, Nevis, Dominica, and the Virgin Islands were formed into a Federal Colony. The Act is 34 & 35 Vict. cap. 107. The Act professed to give one Executive and one Legislative Council for general purposes in connection with the various Presidencies. As reconstituted by the Federal Act No. 15 of 1882, this General Legislative Council consists of ten members elected by the Councils of the various islands—viz. four to represent Antigua, two on behalf of the Council of Dominica, and four from the Council of St. Kitts-Nevis. The nominated members, in addition, are three officials of Antigua, the President of St. Kitts-Nevis, one each from the five Island Councils, and a President, chosen from one of those Councils.

This General Council has powers of legislation on certain specified subjects. These powers are called concurrent with those of the Island Legislatures, but the latter are practically overridden by the provision that any island legislation on these specified subjects is void if contrary to the general legislation—or it can be repealed by the General Legislature. Among the subjects mentioned as within the cognisance of the Federal Council are questions of property and mercantile and criminal law, police, quarantine, post office and telegraph, lunatic asylum. These subjects, no doubt, are of common importance. Each island retains its own system of finance and its own taxation. The process of amalgamation stopped at the proposal of a common purse, although the Home Government have more than once wished to bring this about. The expenses of the Federal institutions are borne by the different islands in a proportion agreed upon. The Governor resides in Antigua, and pays occasional visits to the other islands.

The constitution of the Council of Antigua itself, apart from the General Government, consists of the Governor, an Executive Council, and a Legislative Council of twenty-four members—four of them officials, eight nominated by the Crown, and twelve members elected, under a suffrage, for electoral districts. The number of registered voters is not large.

From the early times of the settlement, sugar has been cultivated in Antigua. At the present time it is the one great staple. The solidly built and handsome mansion houses, embosomed in the hills, of the planters of earlier times are a substantial record of the prosperity then attained. This favourable condition of things was not, however, without its fluctuations, owing principally to drought and the absence of fresh-water streams. For instance, in 1826, 17,000 hogsheads were shipped, and in 1827 only 6,000. Such a variation has not been seen during the last twenty years, but there is always the liability of an insufficient rainfall. At the time of the American civil war an attempt was made to introduce the cultivation of cotton. This was at first partially successful; but on the termination of the war it naturally collapsed, and those planters who had given up sugar for cotton were much disappointed. So sugar remained king. Praiseworthy efforts have been made to improve the cultivation. There are more steam ploughs at work in Antigua than perhaps in any West Indian island. They are effective in the heavy clay soils, and their use is facilitated by the general flatness of the fields. The sugar is made by the ordinary process—that is, with open pans— and windmills are employed to crush the canes, as in Barbados. But attention is being given to the improvement of these methods, and, with a succession of good seasons, sufficient capital ought to be available for a more rapid application of advanced scientific processes, although an aggregation of sugar properties in this, as in other islands, would probably form the best solution of the question. It is true that one process—that known as Fryer's Concretor—was introduced some fifteen years ago; although sufficiently practical in idea, successful in working, and carried out with much skill, it has not been so generally adopted as might have been anticipated. The plan was to convert all the juice of the cane into a concrete mass, in such a way as to stand the voyage without loss, to occupy less space and consequently save freight, to preserve all that portion of the crystallisable material that would otherwise go into molasses, and thus to afford a raw material to the English or American refiner that would suit his purpose and find a ready acceptance by him. The total quantity of sugar exported in 1895 was 13,095 tons. There were 87 sugar estates in cultivation, covering some 17,900 acres.

Antigua grows vegetables and fruits in abundance, but very little of this produce is exported. Guinea corn is grown for feeding stock. Yams are largely produced. The principal fruit of Antigua is the pine apple, said to be the finest in the world. It is known in England, although the arrangements for the transport of the fruit are not yet sufficiently complete to allow it to arrive in market here in the perfect condition in which it leaves the island. From June to September a fine pine apple may be bought in the island for a penny which would do honour to any English table, and would be considered cheap if purchased for a guinea in Covent Garden. Attempts have occasionally been made to convert some of the abandoned sugar estates into sheep and cattle farms. The breed of cattle has been improved, and many useful working oxen are reared. Antigua mutton is a favourite dish, and is said to be equal to the best Welsh.

The population of Antigua in 1891 was as follows : White, 1,830 ; black, 28,584 ; coloured, 5,705 ; total, 36,119. The number of people is, on the whole, quite sufficient for the sugar estates, but the difficulty is for the planter to obtain that regular labour upon which his operations depend. If he cannot get his canes planted, weeded, or cut at the proper time, he is in danger of losing his crop. The planter cannot be blamed for being unable to pay extravagant rates of wages—and all sugar making is practically labour—that would leave his produce on the wrong side of the account when he brings it to market. This labour difficulty was the cause of the abandonment of estates in past years, signs of which are even now only too obvious. All evidence shows that there is plenty of work and wages for the Antigua labourer if he would, more largely than he does, take advantage of the opportunity. His work on the estate, supplemented by his garden or provision ground, opens a position which the Scotch crofter or the Irish peasant might regard with envy. So great was the difficulty in obtaining labour some few years ago that, at a great expense, 500 Chinese immigrants were introduced. Owing to the absence of contracts, however, the immigration was not so successful as it might have been, but it relieved the pressure for the time.

An education system in Antigua is provided for out of the general revenue. Grants are made according to results, to the schools of the different religious bodies. The Mico School, endowed many years ago by Lady Mico, is doing useful work, and turning out a supply of teachers for the Government schools.

Antigua has a Bishop, with a salary of 2,000*l.* paid by the Imperial Government. The cathedral presents an imposing appearance on nearing the harbour. The Church of England has been disestablished and disendowed, subject to rights of existing incumbents. The Moravians and Wesleyans do much good among the labourers. Some of the Moravian settlements are well chosen for their picturesque and beautiful situation. There is one event in the social history of Antigua which is always referred to with pride and remembered with satisfaction. The emancipation of every slave took place in this Colony and its dependencies by law on August 1, 1834, without any of the qualifications imposed by the British Parliament as to apprenticeship. A measure like this might be put forward as a sufficient answer to the oft-reiterated charge brought against these Colonies, that they wished to perpetuate slavery.

The revenue of Antigua, raised in the proportions common to all the West India Colonies, by import duties and internal spirit taxes, was, in 1895, 44,348*l.*; and the expenditure 70,221*l.* The public debt is 138,121*l.* The imports were— from the United Kingdom, 57,532*l.*; from Colonies, 18,798*l.*; from foreign countries, 61,226*l.*; showing with a few additional amounts a total, 144,864*l.* The export figures, as in the case of other Colonies, are very striking. Only 9,064*l.* export value to the United Kingdom; 17,085*l.* to Colonies; and 53,288*l.* to foreign countries, or, in other words, the United States. There has, therefore, been practically caused, by some means or other, not perhaps difficult to understand, the transfer of all the advantage of receiving the produce of the Colony—produce which, if

brought home, might help to stimulate the manufacturing export trade of this country, and give work and wages to many persons of our industrial population. It is only fair to say, however, that the export trade from the United Kingdom to Antigua had not decreased to any great extent, but now that the United States takes the majority of the produce of the island, a competition may spring up on the part of American manufacturers against the makers of English hardware, Manchester cotton, and sugar machinery.

Antigua has two dependencies—Barbuda and the rock Redonda. The latter has been already mentioned. Their total area is 62 square miles. Barbuda is situated 25 miles north of Antigua. It is about 20 miles broad; it formerly had 1,500 inhabitants, and the property was owned by the Codrington family. It is flat; the soil is fertile, and the air remarkable for its purity. The first settlement was made by colonists from St. Kitts, under Sir Thomas Warner, who found, as usual, Caribs in the place. The principal industry is the raising of cattle, horses, pigs, and poultry for sale in the other islands. There is a good roadstead, but the coast is dangerous.

CHAPTER XXI.

THE VIRGIN ISLANDS.

THE Virgin Islands are also within the Leeward Federation. These were named by Columbus, in 1493, after the 11,000 virgins honoured by the Roman Catholic Church. They comprise about fifty islets and rocks, many of them rising to a considerable height above the sea. The western series of the islands (including St. Thomas) belong to the Danes. The British Virgin Islands were not settled until 1648, and then only by a party of Dutch buccaneers, who established themselves at Tortola. In 1666 a party of English sea rovers took possession, and Tortola was shortly after included in the Leeward Islands Government. The best known of the British islands are Tortola, Virgin Gorda, Anegada, Salt Island, and Peter's Island.

Tortola, the largest in the group belonging to Great Britain, presents a very rugged and precipitous appearance, mountains running east and west right through the island. Waste lands and pasturage are to be noticed, and winding paths up the mountains. The soil is not good enough for sugar, but both cotton and sugar have been grown there. The chief town, Roadtown, is on the south, coming to the waterside, and looking upon a splendid harbour. In front of the town and harbour there are small islands (hereafter mentioned), and here is situated

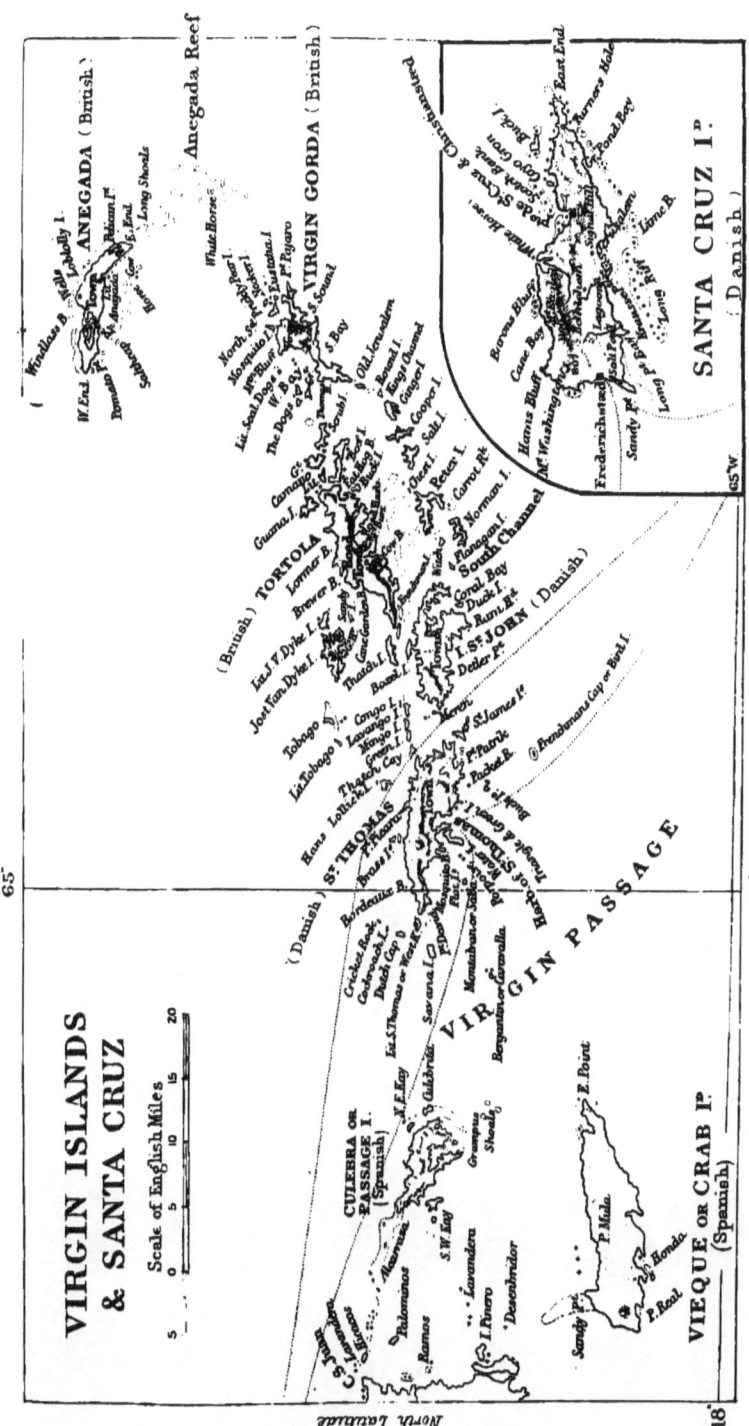

the deep-water channel, which may be generally described as between Tortola and Virgin Gorda, called still after Sir Francis Drake. This harbour is 15 miles long and 3½ broad, and is landlocked and sheltered from the wind. In time of war, hundreds of vessels have been seen here waiting for convoy. Hakluyt said it would be a safe riding for a thousand ships, the anchorage being so good, and the water deep. The absence of forests on the mountains of Tortola contributes to its hard and rugged appearance. Tortola is about 18 miles long from east to west, and 7 in its greatest breadth. It is not well watered. It used to do a total import and export trade of upwards of 20,000*l.*, exporting 1,000 hogsheads of sugar and 1,000 bales of cotton.

Virgin Gorda, or Spanish Town Island, is nearly eight miles long, of irregular shape, and very narrow at both ends. It contains 52,000 acres. It formerly had a considerable number of plantations, and exported sugar, rum, and some cotton. It has a rocky coast, and great care has to be exercised. The hill in the middle of the island is a good landmark, being seen at a great distance. Scrub Island and Beef Island form passages into Drake's Bay. Ships may enter, too, on either side of the Dogs. To the south-west of Virgin Gorda there is a cluster of rugged rocks, separated long ago by volcanic force. These are named Old Jerusalem, or the Fallen City, the Round Rock, and Ginger Island. These also form entrances into the Great Bay. Farther west are Cooper's and Salt Island. Peter's is a narrow crooked island, separated by another passage from a remarkable rocky islet, called the Dead Chest. Indeed, between all these islands passages more or less safe into the shelter of the bay are to be found. Then comes the passage between the Dead Chest and Salt Island, but this has a sunken rock. Norman's Island lies to the south-west of Peter's. It is two miles long and one broad.

There are other islands, which, with the above and Tortola, inclose Drake's Bay. There is one island, however, which deserves a passing mention. It is Anegada, or Drowned Island. It is the most north-easterly of the group. Its length is about 12 miles, and its breadth $2\frac{1}{4}$. It is surrounded by a reef called the Horseshoe. The whole island is very low, and the sea often breaks over it. Its cultivation is very small, the few inhabitants being principally engaged in raising goats, sheep, and cattle.

The position, then, of the British Virgin Islands—the position which they assume in forming the wonderful bay—will be apparent from the above description. As a great work of nature, they seem to be full of intelligent design; as cultivable lands they do not, in their present condition, show that much success, at all events of late years, has attended the hand of man, although Dr. Colquhoun, one of the old West Indian agents in England, once estimated their annual production of property at 100,000*l.* and their total aggregate of movable and immovable property at a million sterling. Through this northerly route the steamers come home, as they thus get the full benefit of the Gulf Stream.

The area of the Virgin Islands Colony is only 50 square miles. The number of the white population decreased from 52 in 1881 to 32 at the census of 1891. The coloured people have decreased from 1,546 in 1881 to 1,189 in 1891. The black population has decreased from 3,689 in 1881 to 3,418 in 1891, but this, of course, is due to

HARBOUR OF ST. THOMAS.

the constant migration between the islands. The total population, therefore, of the Virgin Islands, as ascertained by the last census, is 4,639. The revenue of the Virgin Islands is small, being in 1895 only 1,533*l.*, more than half of which is raised by customs duties and port dues. They spend about 12*l.* for their ecclesiastical establishment, 119*l.* for their educational, 219*l.* for their medical, and 91*l.* for their police and gaols. They are charged 327*l.* for their contribution towards the expenses of federation, which seems rather hard. The trade of these islands (or this Colony) is almost exclusively with the Danish West Indies—principally St. Thomas and St. Croix (or Santa Cruz). The total imports for 1895 were valued at 4,576*l.* and the exports at 3,818*l.* The Virgin Islands trade with the Mother Country only to a very small extent.

The principal island of the western division, belonging to the Danish, is, of course, St. Thomas. For many years, until quite recently, it was of much importance as a depôt for the mail steamers and an entrepôt of trade for the islands. It owed this position to its extremely convenient situation. It was like a key to the West Indies, and certainly the most convenient centre, except perhaps Jamaica, for the distribution intercolonially of passengers and goods. Many thousands of European visitors to the West Indies and South America during the last half-century have involuntarily made acquaintance with it, and while they have admired its beauty, and wondered at the activity of the negro boatmen who swarmed about the steamer on her arrival (for St. Thomas lived on the business caused by the steamers calling), yet they were not sorry to get away again, for it formerly had the reputation of being unhealthy. It is situated in 18° 20' N. lat. and 65° W. long. Its area is estimated at 37 square miles, and its population is perhaps 10,000 to 12,000. The scene presented on the entrance to the harbour, including the landlocked bay, into which the harbour widens out, is tropical in its beauty. Trollope describes the town as a Niggery-Hispano-Dano-Yankeedoodle sort of place, with a general flavour of sherry-cobblers. But then he was in a bad temper, and troubled with indigestion. It is amusing to note how industriously the pens of visitors run when they wish to record their first impression of a West Indian island. One excellent piece of advice is, not to begin writing too soon after a hearty meal, for somehow there is a subtle connection between the stomach and the brain. The tradesmen and merchants of the place, however, when imports were large and many ships were calling, risked the unhealthiness and made money. The town is built on three hills running in a parallel line at the northern or inland extremity of the bay, with higher hills, green to the top, behind. The houses and the vegetation make up a very pretty picture, and from the harbour, seen through the transparent air, it is extremely effective, especially when taking in the upper hills. The boyish joy of Kingsley, when he found himself on the beach in his first tropical island, utilising the time while the steamer waited in the harbour, and finding strange new things of a form and colour he had not dreamt of before, was very natural to anyone of his temperament. He was a little frightened when he got hold of the deadly manchineel, a flower noted for its poisonous qualities. It even impelled him to tell a story of a scientific gentleman who went raving mad after collecting toadstools from the West Indian bush and making a meal of them. Some big steamers have been wrecked in hurricanes off St.

Thomas. There is a floating dock, which cost much money, showing excellent enterprise on the part of its promoters and a real desire to be useful, as well as ship yards and repair shops. The Hamburg American Packet Company make St. Thomas their West India head-quarters and coaling station, and as the company is making important additions to their fleet, with a view to embracing a larger area of the West Indies, considerable improvement in the commercial prosperity of the island will no doubt follow.

With regard to the agricultural industry of St. Thomas, there is no doubt that, after the abolition of slavery in the Danish West Indies in 1848, the production of sugar rapidly declined. The cultivation had to be given up, labourers could not be found, plantations fell into ruin, and houses and mills were either destroyed by incendiaries or fell naturally to decay, the harsh points being covered by the quick-growing vegetation. But the losses caused by this failure were soon forgotten in the gains which followed, the island becoming an emporium for the West Indies and South America. Between 1850 and 1873 the demand for goods of every kind was very great for distribution in the above countries, and fortunes were rapidly realised. Charlotte Amalia, for this is the right name of the town, was then one of the busiest towns in the Western Tropics, and in providing amusement and spending money not at all the most backward. But soon after 1860 the great advance which steam had made in lessening the importance of entrepôts, and going straight to consuming countries, began to tell upon St. Thomas, and signs of decadence appeared. The construction of telegraph cables was also detrimental to the business of an intermediary port. Between 1870 and 1880 trade went down and the old commercial importance of the

x

island entirely disappeared. Up to 1884 the imports and exports had decreased by 75 per cent., and when in 1885 the Royal Mail Company removed their depôt, and the island ceased to be a port of call for the steamers belonging to the main line of communication, there was, of course, for a time, collapse. Barbados, at present the central station of the Royal Mail steamers, successfully competed with St. Thomas, at the time of the mail contract in 1885, in the matter of harbour dues. The removal of the depôt of the steamers was estimated to inflict a loss upon the island of St. Thomas of between 20,000*l.* and 30,000*l.* a year, but the advantage is, of course, gained by a British Colony; and for Imperial interests, not only of a sentimental but of a practical character, it is desirable that the means of communication between the Mother Country and her Colonies should be in British vessels, and by a British port as the centre of distribution. The cultivation of aloes and fibrous plants is being tried, but not with any particular prospect of success. The healthiness of the island has been apparent of late years, and there has been no epidemic of yellow fever. As has been already explained, the real cause of its former unsanitary condition lies in the fact that there was no current in the harbour to take the drainage out to sea. The decomposing matter under a tropical sun emitted gases eminently conducive to fever. But a cutting was made with complete success to endeavour to create a channel for the refuse and distribute it.

Santa Cruz, or St. Croix, near St. Thomas, and belonging also to the Danes, must be mentioned in passing. It produces sugar, average crop 12,000 hogsheads, and contains a large usine of a very elaborate character, now in the hands of the Government. The juice is conveyed to the usine from four grinding stations through a series of long pipes. Another central factory is being established at La Grange by private enterprise. At present there are about one hundred estates in cultivation, which produced in 1896 about 15,000 tons of sugar. The population of the island is about 20,000.

Saba is one of the Dutch islands, 15 miles W.N.W. from the N. point of St. Eustatius, lat. 17° 39' N. and long. 63° W. It rises 1,500 feet sheer from the sea, and is only accessible on the south side. It has no harbour and no level ground. There is a small landing-place, from which a kind of stair or narrow pathway runs up to the crater of an old volcano. In this strange island live 1,000 Dutch and about the same number of negroes. Living aloft in their volcano, the residents cultivate garden ground, the produce of which they sell to other islands. They also build good boats for sale. This quaint Dutch settlement in the middle of the ocean is composed of honest and religious folk, who are no doubt happy in their island home.

Sombrero is the most northerly of the Caribbean Islands : lat. 18° 35' 45" N. and long. 63° 27' 46" W. It has multitudes of sea fowl. Its importance consists in its being a kind of sea mark, and it is frequently sighted by ships. A lighthouse is maintained at the top by the British Government at a yearly cost of 520*l*. : a rather lonely position for the lighthouse keeper.

The island of St. Eustatius should also be mentioned. It is a crater cone rising out of the sea, and belongs to the Dutch.

CHAPTER XXII.

PORTO RICO.

PORTO RICO (or Puerto Rico) was discovered by Columbus, and is now a Spanish colony. It lies in lat. 18° 29′ N. and 66° 6′ W. long. It required many conflicts on the part of Juan Ponce de Leon, a native of Seville, to subdue it, the natives being very determined and brave, and unusually numerous. It is 95 miles long and 35 wide. It is very hot, but relieved by a breeze during the day. Hurricanes have visited the island. It is extremely fertile, possessing woods, hills, valleys, and meadows. It is known for its herds of wild cattle. Through the middle of the island from E. to W. there runs a chain of mountains, from which rivers and streams descend to water the plains below. The hills are generally covered with trees. Sugar, ginger, cotton, flax, coffee, cassia, incense, and hides were among its early productions. Mules were also exported. It produced also rice, maize, plantains, pines, oranges, citrons, lemons, calabashes, potatoes, melons, and fine salt. At first the Spaniards made little use of it except as a port of call. The capital of Porto Rico has the dedicatory title of San Juan. It is situated in a small island on the north side, united by means of a causeway to the main island. The port is large, convenient, and safe. The city was founded by Juan Ponce de Leon in 1510. Sir Francis Drake once burnt all the vessels in the port. In 1598 the

PORTO RICO.

English obtained the mastery over the island, and then abandoned it with much spoil. In 1615 there was an attack by the Dutch, and another attempt was made in 1742 by the English; but these attempts led to no practical results for the invaders.

The principal articles of export are coffee, sugar, and tobacco. The total production of sugar has sometimes reached 100,000 tons. The latest returns show that it exports 54,861 tons of sugar, 16,884 tons of coffee, and 1,807 tons of tobacco. A considerable trade is still done in the export of cattle. Cottons, woollens, jute for sugar and coffee bags, metals and rice, are the main items of the British trade. The British Colonies supply the codfish consumed in the island, the value of which is estimated at 95,000*l*. Flour is imported from the United States and Spain, estimated in value between 200,000*l*. and 300,000*l*. Other provisions are also sent by the United States and Spain to a considerable amount. Coal is almost exclusively supplied by Great Britain. Complaints are frequently made as to the excessive taxation of the industries of the island—taxation which prevents their legitimate development. A large amount of English and Spanish capital is invested in usines, collecting and working up the produce of a number of cane plantations. The population is 813,937. Slavery was abolished in 1873.

CHAPTER XXIII.

CUBA.*

CUBA, the largest Spanish possession in America, has a surface of 43,220 square miles, or equal to one-fourth of Peninsular Spain. Although only one-tenth of it is cultivated, the exports of sugar alone amount to at least eight millions sterling, without reckoning the enormous amount of tobacco, coffee, cotton, rice, and other articles. Of the old slave trade and slavery, the barracoons, and other means of keeping the people to work, nothing need be said in these freer and happier times. When the civil war in the United States closed, and the slaves in Louisiana received their freedom, Cuba was the principal slaveholding country in the world. And then came the struggle between the partisans of the different opinions. The Creoles, or native Cubans, descendants of the old Spanish, raised the cry of Cuba for the Cubans. These are called the National party, as distinguished from the old Conservatives. But, notwithstanding the political movements of this Creole or National party, the Government at Madrid managed to exercise a dominant influence. A Captain-General would be appointed, who might possibly have been an inconvenient figure in the

* *The insurrection and incendiarism in the Island of Cuba ruined the sugar and tobacco crops for* 1896. *The trade of* 1895 *is therefore that referred to in this chapter.*

Cortes, or the hero of a Pronunciamento in Madrid. In 1868, after the downfall of Queen Isabella, there was a movement which might have tended in favour of republicanism or of the monarchy, and which for the momen was conciliatory among all parties. Neither Lersundi, however, the last Captain-General of Queen Isabella, nor General Dulce, who was sent by General Prim, was authorised to settle the requirements of those who clamoured for the Creole view of local self-government. During all this time the slavery question was a bitter subject of discussion, both in the Colony and in the Cortes at Madrid. Upon this question the Peninsulars and the Insulars were at variance. General Lersundi could not control the volunteer battalions, who made themselves a great political and military power. They compelled General Dulce to quit the island. They even prevented the promulgation of the Moret Law for the gradual emancipation of slavery, principally on account of the fact that it was passed by the Spanish Parliament. Of the strength of the Peninsular and Insular parties—of the influence which they exerted (especially the latter) upon the black population—of the regiments of Spanish soldiers which were sent, and the thousands who died—no mention need be made here, except, perhaps, to call attention to the strenuous efforts made by Spain in recent years, amid all her own political disturbances, to retain a secure possession of the island, and the enjoyment of its revenues.

Cuba, the Pearl of the Antilles, as it proudly calls itself, is the most valuable relic of the once great possessions of Spain in the New World. It is still called by its old Carib name, although Columbus endeavoured to impose a designation complimentary to Ferdinand and

Isabella. The growth and expansion of this splendid country—the immense quantity of sugar and tobacco grown—the contest between the old Spanish party and the newer Creole tendencies and aims, the fluctuations in the popular opinion which have finally led to emancipation, the slave insurrections, the treatment of the Chinese coolies from Macao, which once excited so much attention on the part of the British Parliament and the Pekin authorities, the extreme fondness of the United States for the island—all these, and many other points, have continued to bring it into prominence.

Cuba was discovered by Columbus on October 28, 1492. The name first given to it was Juana, in honour of a son of Ferdinand and Isabella. It afterwards received the name of Santiago, after the patron saint of Spain. It had a still further name, Fernandina. It then had an aboriginal population. After being again twice visited by Columbus, in 1494 and 1502, an attempt was made to colonise it by Diego Columbus in 1511. The towns of Santiago and Trinidad were founded in 1514, and in the following year a town called San Cristoval de la Havana (now Batabano) was formed, the name of Havana being a few years later given to the present capital. In 1538 and 1554 it was subject to attacks by the French. In 1580 the cultivation of tobacco and sugar was commenced, the labour being supplied by slaves from Africa. Attention was given to fortifications, to make the harbour secure against the inroads of the English, French, and Dutch, by which Havana was frequently threatened during the next 150 years. An English fleet and an army under Lord Albemarle took possession of Havana after a determined resistance in 1762, the captors deriving a considerable amount of spoil. By the Treaty of Paris in 1763 Cuba (for the island retained its Carib name) was restored to the Spaniards, and its importance as a productive country became rapidly manifest. Las Casas began his successful career as Captain-General in 1790, and still further progress was made under his administration. Cuba took the side of the Royal Family of Spain in 1808 in the contest with Napoleon, and since that time the island has been governed by Captains-General appointed from Madrid. During this period, however, it has known its troubles. The feud between the native Cubans and the Spanish has been a great source of disquiet. The revolution in Spain in 1868 afforded an opportunity of protesting against the domination of Spanish officialdom, and an outbreak, which practically developed into a civil war, lasting some years, took place. Every effort was made by Spain to crush it. In eight years no less than 150,000 soldiers were sent from Spain, with, however, but little result. During recent years the island has been more tranquil, although the tension of feeling remained great between the opposing parties, which developed into a revolution in 1896 which has taxed the energies of the Spanish Government to the utmost, and even at the present time has not been quelled.

The island is long and narrow, and divides the entrance of the Gulf of Mexico into two passages. The coast is generally low and flat. The island lies between 74° and 85° W. long., and 19° and 23° N. lat. Its length, following a curved line through its centre, is 730 miles, and its average breadth is 80 miles. The highest part of the island is in the range extending in the S.E. from the Punta de Maysi to Cape Cruz. There is also a series of smaller eminences. An almost isolated mass, of which the Pico de Pontretillo is the summit, 2,990 feet above the sea, rises immediately above the harbour of Trinidad de Cuba. The rivers flow towards the N. and S. The climate is hot on the coast, and of course more temperate above. The temperature ranges from 72° to 82°. It is a country, in some parts, of impenetrable forests. The royal palm tree grows luxuriantly, and is capable of many useful purposes.

But Havana! how can it be described? The brilliant glow of sea and sky, the teeming life of this tropical vegetation. And yet it is, perhaps, rather the special town life that attracts the visitor, than the natural beauties which he sees. The harbour is pleasing, but not particularly impressive in its beauty. As the steamer enters, the renowned forts of El Moro and Cabañas appear, with their commanding cannon. These are on the left. The city on the right, lying on a level land, is gay with its houses painted in all bright colours. The numerous church domes and steeples also give one an exaggerated idea of the religious propensities of the people. Probably there is no more prominent or characteristic feature of the city of Havana than the multitude of churches. There are narrow crowded streets with uneven stones. There is the *volante*, the gig with long shafts and high wheels, waiting to carry the visitor about. There are the hotels, in one of which Mr. Froude could not stay because the young ladies from the United States kept up such continuous practising on the pianoforte. One late visitor says that the *volante* is being superseded by a one-horse fly, not of the most advanced construction. But this concerns the old city. The new town is large and, so far as its roads are concerned, somewhat unfinished. Here the best hotels are situated.

CUBA. 315

The Telegraph Hotel, for instance, is close to the railway station, the Prado, the Tacon Theatre, the Promenade, the Bull Ring and the Spanish Club, and a number of ruined bastions and half-built palaces. The shops in the town are clean and tidy, with their coloured awnings thrown across the street. Big houses and small houses are mixed up without any regard to uniformity of appearance. The stately corridor of the mansion and the humble blind of the shop front are to be seen, much in the same way as one sees a Chinese shirt-dresser plying his avocation under the shadow of the Capitol at Washington. The Partagas cigar manufactory is a sight to see, also the Honradez cigarette manufactories. The cathedral is large but not particularly imposing. It contains the mausoleum of Columbus, where his bones are now supposed to rest, after being moved from Seville to St. Domingo and thence to Cuba. The Seville monument was inscribed : ' A Castilla y á Leon, Nuevo Mundo diò Colon.' The inscription in the Havana Cathedral has been thus translated : ' O remains and image of great Colon, a thousand centuries abide guarded in the urn and in the remembrance of our nation.' The Spanish is : ' O restos e imágen del Grande Colon ! Mil siglos durad guardados en la urna, y en la remembranza de nuestra nacion.' The entrance to this vast building where lie these honoured bones is by a broad flight of stone steps. The service is conducted with impressive ceremony. On the chancel arch the royal arms of Spain are prominent, and at the side of the altar is the Colon monument. A statue of the discoverer is on the wall, with the Spanish ruff of the period. Some doubts have been expressed as to whether the remains of Columbus were really removed to this place, or whether the transfer consisted of the bones of his brother Diego, who was also buried in the St. Domingo Cathedral. But these doubts are not entertained by Spain. The memorial of Christophe is here, fitly on Spanish soil and in Spanish guardianship, and it is impossible to repress emotion upon contemplating the memorial of a man who belongs not to Spain only. Europe and America were both indebted to him for the discoveries he made, for the natural grandeur he unfolded to the Old World, and the large ideas and energies he rendered appreciable and possible.

Reverting to the earliest impressions of a visitor, the Moro Tower with its bastions is the first thing that meets the eye. It can be seen a long distance off. Batteries cover the approaches up the harbour. The old Moro is also seen, a fort which many illustrious English seamen knew too well. The inner basin receives the drainage of the city, and neither the look nor smell of the water is invigorating. The numerous churches, the palaces with their marble fronts and staircases, the narrow streets, the black costumes of the priests, all tell of a typical Spanish city. Just outside the old town many low white marble houses are seen. The Captain-General's suburban seat adjoins the Botanic Gardens, and is placed in a bower of palms, mango trees, tamarinds, China laurels, and flowering plants and bushes of all varieties. The land around the city is somewhat bare, the plantations being farther off. The Jesuit College should be visited. The monks are not so popular as they were, either in Spain or in Cuba. But still, without much public assistance, they preserve their dominant influence. In Havana they devote themselves to literature and science. The head of the Jesuit College is a liberal-minded man, interested in astronomy and hurricanes. He lives an ascetic life amid his library and scientific instruments. Attendance at clubs, where high play goes on, is a favourite amusement of the citizens of Havana. The Union Club, where the best society can be met with, is open to visitors with proper credentials, for temporary membership. With all its advantages and its beauty, Havana is still described as a city of smells and noises. Americans come to it in large numbers, either as a place of social distraction or for change of air and scene, or to buy sugar or prospect minerals, for iron and copper are both said to abound. When the wind is in a certain quarter the smell from the Bay pervades the town, and is not pleasant. But on the sea shore, away from the Bay, there is a large street, the Calle Ancha del Norte, where are the bathing establishments. Even here the houses are not by any means uniform in their appearance. The noises of Havana are as palpable as the smells, although appealing to a different sense. A literary man in search of quiet may be annoyed by the constant banging of pianos in his hotel. But the real grievance as to sound has its origin in the whistle of the railway engines in the streets, the bells of the tram-cars, and the ceaseless metal voices of the churches. Add to these, says Mr. Gallenga, the rolling of the 6,000 victorias, the omnibuses, the heavy waggons, the clatter of cafés and billiard rooms making night hideous, the jabber, the babel of voices, the twang of guitars, the squeak of fiddles, the morning gun from the guardship at daybreak, the shrill trumpets of the volunteers at drill, and the call of the waiter who mistakes you for the gentleman who wishes to catch an early train, and Havana may justly be considered a lively place.

One curious feature about the city is the small number

of white women. They are rarely to be seen about, and it is said that there are three white men to one white woman. This arises from the fact that there are so many Spanish immigrants who come for a temporary purpose, and regard themselves as residents only for a short time. The life is an hotel life and not a domestic one. One of the causes is the absence of good servants. Class prejudice between the Spaniard and the Creole, although not so great as it was fifteen or even ten years ago, prevents that amalgamation of interests and community of sentiment upon which the social prosperity of a country must immediately rest. Imported articles are very dear, owing to heavy duties, and a good deal of smuggling, no doubt, goes on. Paper money, too, is a potent weapon in the hands of the shopkeeper, who depreciates it to his customers below the level at which it should stand, and that level is low enough, for the Government of Cuba is never without its financial embarrassments, leading to the obvious but ruinous expedients for obtaining relief of the same.

The interior of the country is not particularly inviting, but to some tastes it is a pleasant change from the town. The ride by the Eastern Railway to Matanzas, about 43 miles, is pleasant, and a sugar estate or ingenio is the object of an interesting visit. The crushing and boiling house, the refining house, the negro quarters, and the proprietor's dwelling may not be poetical, but real life is going on, though the country about may be treeless and the roads bad. Upon approaching Matanzas, however, hilly ridges are seen, wooded so as to be grateful to the eye. The Pan de Matanzas, about 1,200 feet high, is conspicuous. Matanzas is situated upon a bay contributed to by the meeting of two rivers, the Yumurri and the San

Juan. The houses on the hills at the back of the city are pretty and picturesque. But along the coast to Cienfuegos the country is flat and uninteresting. The general character of the scenery, indeed, within 100 miles of Havana is flat, relieved only by bush, grass savannahs, cane fields, and chimneys of boiling-houses.

Mr. Froude, to escape from the distractions of Havana, went by railway to a place called Vedado, seven miles along the sea coast. He was there made comfortable at a lodging house, and enjoyed himself. Many people came to this place for a day's outing or a quiet dinner. The sea washed the coral rocks under the windows. There were walks beside rivers and over moors. There were farms and horses and cattle to inspect, although the numerous dogs were rather a nuisance. The baths were good, but it is dangerous to venture into the sea on account of the sharks. In this quiet retreat the politics of Cuba may be discussed *ad nauseam* with philosophic Spaniards who talk like a book. The great suburban cemetery of Havana is a place worth seeing once in a lifetime. The flowers, the vaults, the inscriptions all tend to suggest restful thoughts; much more so than the cafés, the operas and theatres, and even the churches of the town. There is thus in this great country plenty of material for reflection and amusement; much to wonder at, much to dislike, and much to find pleasure in. What about its future? Will the class feuds subside now that emancipation has come, and the island settle down, when the present revolt terminates, into the permanent possession of Spain, or will the stars and stripes replace the Spanish flag at El Moro?—a consummation which could no doubt be brought about by internal feuds, a chronic state of public bankruptcy, and a prospect of protective and differential treatment in the great Union of the West.

It is difficult to ascertain the exact particulars of the trade of Cuba. The British Consul reports that 'sporadic efforts are made from time to time to stop corruption, but no practical or permanent checks are applied to cure an evil which is hardly looked upon as an offence, but an everyday matter.' The trade of the island, although seemingly and undoubtedly very large, is in a state of depression. Money is scarce, credit has not revived, and there is a general want of confidence. At all events, this was the state of things at a very recent date. Very little sugar now comes from Cuba to the United Kingdom. The European bounties have not only frightened British but foreign cane sugar away. The rate of interest for money borrowed is so high as twelve per cent., and no advances are made even on these terms without unquestionable security. When sugar does not pay, the spending power of the country is crippled. Not that there is any less production of sugar (for it has ranged for many years between 500,000 and 700,000 tons, even emancipation making little impression upon the crop), but the profits realised are largely swallowed up in taxation and in the drain of revenues to Madrid. Up to 1887 two crops had already been grown and worked by the freed labourers, and the results were not less than in the best years of slave labour. There did not take place that rise in wages which was the ruin of the British plantations half a century ago. One unusual feature in the labour supply is that white labour can be employed in the fields. Spaniards soon become acclimatised, and although they are more expensive, yet as journeymen and labourers they are worth, each for each, two free blacks. A large amount of virgin soil still awaits cultivation, and millions of people might be usefully located. The tobacco export trade has diminished in value, although the same quantity is grown. This is caused by too great haste in preparing the tobacco for market, and the lessened price it commands. Indeed, the deterioration of Havana tobacco in recent years has been notorious. A good deal depends too upon fashion, and when there is a demand for light colours, the plant must be gathered before maturity, causing loss of quality and aroma. The best tobacco exported fetches, of course, high prices.

Consul-General Crowe gives the following particulars of the productions of Cuba in a recent report : 'Although tobacco grows well all over the island, the soil and climate of the south-west portion produce the finest. This district, "Vuelta Abajo," lies along the foot-hills of the Sierra, stretching to Cape Antonio and the northern side of the great plain, which reaches from sea to sea across the island. The most favoured lands lie near and beyond Consolacion del Sur and Pinar del Rio ; but some of the "viñales" lying in the lateral valleys of the Cayos—as the mountains are called—produce very choice plants. Consolacion is 144 kiloms. from Havana by the Western Railroad, Pinar del Rio 22 kiloms. farther. The roads on both sides are atrocious, worse than any other in the world. The oxen which bring the cargoes to the rail are very handsome, though not large. Of course transport rules very high. The very best land of the Vuelta Abajo lies near to Consolacion and the "lomas" on the eastern slope of the "cayos," which overlook the palm-covered plain. The grasses, maize, coffee, and fruits in this district are superb ; it is, moreover, the healthiest part of Cuba (yellow fever

Y

being unknown there), which becomes narrow here and is swept by a breeze from sea to sea, and abundantly supplied with small rivers, so that water is found everywhere at a depth of three feet. The planter's house-made cigars, called "vegueros" or "farmers," are celebrated at Consolacion, and possess a delicious aroma, especially when smoked immediately on being made. The leaf is of a very rich light coffee-brown, with a slight hairy down on it, soft and tender. To test the leaf the veguero always tries the strength of the material by passing it over his finger in the way one tries the skin of the glove. The "maduro" or the *ripest* is the very best; but as of late years fashion has ruled in favour of light colours, the tobacco is dried accordingly to get the required shade, but in the opinion of good judges to the detriment of the flavour, as previously stated. After the rains have well saturated the light sandy loam, the tobacco is sown in October early, and then cuttings are taken between that month and March, the second being considered better. Some vegas lying along the arroyas, which are always full of good and abundant water, never fail; others only produce the "tripa" or filling, which is worked up to form the core of the cigar, the outer leaf being of a finer brand. In this consist most of the frauds which very extensively prevail in the trade. The buyers go through the Vuelta and select, but in the "fábrica" the inferior tripa is substituted. The plant is smaller than in other countries, and the leaf never allowed to attain the size usual in Mexico, Jamaica, or the South American States, generally not more than $2\frac{1}{2}$ feet high.'

Consul Hyatt gives the following particulars of the productive forces of Cuba in a Report, dated January 1897, to the United States Government :—' Cuba stands in a geographical position which, together with her productive soil, mineral wealth, and climatic conditions, should entitle her to rank amongst the foremost communities of the world, a distinction to which I believe she will soon attain, whenever a stable government and cheerful obedience to the powers that be present to the home-seeker and investor conditions that will make home pleasant and capital secure. The soil is a marvel of richness, and fertilisers of any kind are seldom used unless in the case of tobacco, even though the same crops be grown on the same field for a hundred years, as has already happened in some of the old sugar cane fields. If all the land suitable to the growth of sugar cane were devoted to that industry it is estimated Cuba might supply the entire western hemisphere with sugar. The island has already produced in a single year for export 1,100,000 tons, while its capabilities have only been in the experimental stage. The adaptabilities of the soil for tobacco culture have long been the envy of the world, until a cigar that has not some pretension of having at least a little Cuban tobacco stands condemned without a hearing. Cuba takes great pride in the quality of her coffee, and until the rebellion of 1868 she raised a large quantity for export. It is the mountainous regions of Santiago, in the eastern part of the island, that are best adapted to this industry, but the insurrection beginning that year completely destroyed the coffee plantations. They were just getting nicely started again when the present rebellion broke out, and there will probably be but a few, if any, coffee plantations remaining when the struggle ends. . . . In mineral wealth Cuba is capable of taking high rank. Gold and silver have not been found in paying quantities. Copper mines continued in successful operation until 1867. The iron mines of Cuba, all of which are located near Santiago, overshadow in importance all other industries on the eastern end of the island, constituting the only industry that has made any pretence of standing up against the shock of the present insurrection. The ore of these mines is among the richest in the world, yielding from 62 to 67 per cent. of pure iron, and is very free from sulphur and phosphorus. There are numerous undeveloped mines of equal richness and value in this region. Railroads and other highways, improved machinery, and more modern methods of doing business are among the wants of Cuba, and with the onward march of civilisation these will be doubtless hers in the near future. Cuba, like other tropical and semi-tropical countries, is not given to manufacturing; her people would rather sell the products of the soil and mines, and buy manufactured goods. The possibilities of the island are great, while its probabilities remain an unsolved problem.'

A considerable trade in fruit has been established with the United States, and good potatoes are raised and even exported.

Cattle breeding has been successfully tried. In order to encourage general agriculture, matters have gone so far that the Spanish Government have given a premium to the best cultivators of cane, tobacco, wheat, maize, and other growths of agricultural or textile value. Prizes are also given for cattle and horse breeding, and also for the best apiary, bee keeping being very popular in the island.

There are practically no trustworthy statistics available showing the productive and commercial condition of the island. No one can tell, for instance (so the British Consul says), what is the tobacco yield, real tobacco export, or whether the income of the Colony should be placed at eleven, or sixteen, or twenty millions sterling per annum. Sixteen millions is the estimate of the British Consul. There is a Colonial debt of forty millions sterling, the annual interest of which is 1,800,000*l*. These burdens are borne by a population of 1,600,000, of whom about 65 per cent. are white, the remainder being negroes or mulattoes. Some years ago the Cuban budget reached 8,000,000*l*. (the discrepancies in the accounts cannot be accounted for), and it has decreased to its present amount because of the practical impossibility of collecting the taxes. Recently the taxes, direct and indirect, amounted to about 5,000,000*l*., to which must be added a sum of 1,600,000*l*. levied in local taxation by the 153 municipalities of the island, and there was a deficit in Governmental expenditure of more than 600,000*l*. The total value of the exports to the United Kingdom in 1895 was 131,567*l*., and the imports of British produce were of the value of 943,793*l*. A royal decree was published in July, 1888, under which vessels of nations having treaties with Spain are no longer subject to tonnage dues, but are charged 4*s*. per ton on the gross weight of all imports and exports carried by them, non-treaty vessels being required to pay this charge in addition to the tonnage dues formerly levied on all foreign shipping. The British Consul says that the sugar growers often find it impossible to furnish such security as would be accepted by the two banks still operating in Havana, but must hypothecate their crops to advance agents. The Spanish Bank ('Banco Español de la Habana') and the Commercial Bank ('Banco del Comercio') advance money on first-rate security only, and usually at high rates. There is not, however, a single Cuban bank in which money can be placed at interest, nor a savings bank in which the artisan or the labourer may deposit his earnings. Broadly speaking, banking, as it is understood in England, does not exist in Cuba, the island having no gold or silver currency of its own, the 'paper dollars' in use at Havana and other towns causing not the least of the financial difficulties. The paper dollar, however, is not a legal tender, and cannot be used in important commercial transactions or for the payment of taxes. The gold in use is mainly Spanish, the centén, the onza (value 3*l.* 8*s.*), and the doubloon (value 17*s.*). An English sovereign does not realise its full value in Cuba. With regard to exports, the abundant resources of the island, mineral and agricultural, are as yet but partially developed. Only one-tenth of the whole area—or 4,300 square miles out of 43,000—is cultivated. Forests and unexplored land make up the difference. There are, as previously stated, prosperous iron mines in Santiago de Cuba ; there is a market for Cuban woods in London and New York ; new potatoes command a good price in New York out of the American season ; there are sponge fisheries which compete with the Levant, and fibres are receiving attention. These industries, however, are only in their infancy. The production of coffee is not sufficient to supply the local demand. The value of the tobacco crop is put at 6,720,000*l.*, the export being, of course, much less. Attention is being devoted more than ever to the sugar cultivation. The Central Factory system is becoming more popular in districts where transport is easy ; but, of course, where railways are few, roads mere tracks, and there are no canals and navigable rivers, this system can only very gradually be adopted. The island was subject to a terrible cyclone in September, 1888, which destroyed over 100 plantations and caused general injury to the sugar cultivation. The production and export of honey and wax have declined. There was a fair demand for rum from Spain and South America. The import of coal from the United States is increasing largely, while diminishing from the United Kingdom.

There are many large trading steamers now regularly running between England and Cuba. There are French steamers from Havre and Bordeaux, and also a line from Bremen and Hamburg under Spanish directorship. The population of the chief cities in the island is as follows: Havana, 198,271; Matanzas, 27,000; St. Iago de Cuba, 71,307; Cienfuegos, 27,430; Puerto Principe, 46,641; Holguin, 34,767; Sancti Spiritu, 32,608; Guanabacoa, 28,789; Trinidad, 26,654; Manzanillo, 23,208; Santa Clara, 22,781; Pinar del Rio, 21,870; and Colon, 20,398. The total population is 1,631,696. The imports are estimated at eleven and a half millions sterling, and the exports at sixteen millions.

The sugar export of Cuba (principally to the United States) was in 1895 832,431 tons. In St. Iago de Cuba the cutting of mahogany is an extensive industry, principally carried on by Americans. This part of the island is also becoming a great mineral centre. One important point is the large import of codfish and lumber from Canada. There is good opportunity for the extension of this trade with Canada. A curious point is the competition of Manchester with Barcelona in the supply of cotton fabrics. In the supply of ironmongers' goods and hardware Germany is a great competitor. Although the goods may be inferior, the German commercial travellers are so enterprising and observing that they are obtaining a good slice of the trade. They are also more risky in giving credit for long periods than English firms. Steel rails are to a large extent (but not by any means wholly) imported from England. Railway rolling stock is imported from the United States. Iron bridges come from Belgium, and sugar-estate machinery comes from England, the United States, and France.

CHAPTER XXIV.

THE BAHAMAS.

ALTHOUGH perhaps not exactly in geographical order, yet there are two British Colonies still remaining shortly for review, the Bahamas and British Honduras.

The Bahamas are a group of islands, reefs, and cays termed the Lucayos (Los Cayos, or the Keys), lying between 21° 42' and 27° 34' N. lat. and 72° 40' and 79° 5' W. long. They cover a distance of about 600 miles in a crescent form, from the northern coast of St. Domingo to the eastern coast of Florida. The total area is 4,466 square miles. They are traversed by three navigable channels—first, the Florida Channel, to the north, which runs along the coast of the United States and lies to the westward of the whole Bahama group; second, the Providence Channels, passing through the group to the north and separating the Great and Little Banks; and, third, the old Bahama Channel, which passes to the south of the Great Bahama Bank, between it and Cuba. The principal islands are New Providence, with its capital, Nassau, the centre of the blockade-running during the American civil war; Abaco, Harbour Island, Eleuthera, Inagua, Mayaguana, Ragged Island, Rum Cay, Exuma, Long Island, Long Cay, and the Biminis, all being ports of entry; and Great Bahama, Crooked Island, Acklin Island, Cat Island, Watling's Island, better known by its historic title of San Salvador, the Berry Islands, and Andros Island.

The above are given in the Colonial Office List, but a more extended list is to be found in Martin's History. Turks Island and the Caicos, which are geographically part of the Bahama group, were separated politically in 1848, and are now under the Government of Jamaica. There are altogether 29 islands, 661 cays, and 2,387 rocks. They are all formed of calcareous rock of coral and shell hardened into limestone. The soil is very fertile, and there is a deal of valuable timber which might be utilised if labour were not so scarce. There are a few hills of very moderate height. San Salvador was the first land discovered by Columbus in October 1492. Columbus reported as follows to Ferdinand and Isabella upon his visit to the islands :— 'This country excels all others as far as the day surpasses the night in splendour; the natives love their neighbours as themselves; their conversation is the sweetest imaginable; their faces always smiling; and so gentle and so affectionate are they that I swear to your Highness there is not a better people in the world.' The islands were indeed then full of Indians, who met the usual fate of their race when brought into contact with Europeans. Many were destroyed; others were taken to the mines of Peru and Mexico; others, again, were transported to Hispaniola to supplement the labour of that island. Many thousands perished miserably in the mines. They were taken possession of by Sir Humphrey Gilbert in 1578, but it was not until 1629 that any real attempt was made to colonise New Providence. This settlement was destroyed by the Spaniards in 1644. The English were again in possession in 1667, and later in the century—viz., in 1680—proprietary rights were granted by Charles II. to George Duke of Albemarle, William Lord Craven, Sir George Carteret, John Lord

THE BAHAMAS. 331

Berkeley, Anthony Lord Ashley, and Sir Peter Colleton. But repeated troubles with the Spaniards and the bad management of the governors appointed prevented any profit or success arising from this act of colonisation. In 1703 the French and Spaniards attacked the English at New Providence and destroyed their properties. For a long time after this New Providence was a mere resort of wreckers and pirates. Many scenes in Marryat's novels are taken from incidents belonging to this period. Matters remained in a somewhat chaotic state until 1718, when Captain Woods Rogers was sent out as Governor. A considerable number of colonists arrived during the American War of Independence, and, with the aid of slave labour, cotton became an important article of cultivation. From natural causes, however, this cultivation became extinct in 1800. New Providence had been taken by the Americans in 1776, and in 1782 the Spaniards from Cuba obtained possession of it; but the islands were once more annexed to Great Britain, and the British possession was confirmed at the Peace of Versailles, in 1783. The proprietary interest was surrendered for a sum of 2,000*l*. in 1787, and the Crown took absolute possession. The most important event in recent years in connection with the Bahamas was that Nassau was made the headquarters of the blockade-running trade after the Southern ports were closed in 1861. During that time there was great excitement and much extravagance, and many fortunes were made. The story of that time would reveal many striking incidents and some not very creditable occurrences. However, at the conclusion of the Civil War matters settled down again, and the abnormal excitement, prosperity, and individual expenditure became things of the past. Great injury was caused by a hurricane in 1866, and subsequent droughts added to the sufferings and poverty of the inhabitants. Under the able administration of the late Governor, Sir Ambrose Shea, K.C.M.G., and the encouragement given to the fibre industry, the islands show signs of making fair progress once more, after many vicissitudes. New Providence is about 20 miles long and 7 broad. Nassau is an important city, with its public buildings, its population of 10,000, and its convenient situation as regards the harbour. The profusion of flowers and plants gives it a very attractive appearance. Its shops are good; it has a large and well-conducted American hotel, and it may be said that Nassau is principally supported by visitors from the United States. The climate of the islands is particularly agreeable and healthy, neither too hot nor subject to cold. Harbour Island, for instance, was celebrated many years ago as a resort for convalescents. In the cold season of the islands, lasting from November to May, the thermometer may vary from 60° to 75°, and in the warm season from 75° to 85°. The general flatness allows the full benefit of the sea breezes. Many fishing-boats are to be seen in the waters round the island. The principal industry is sponge, employing many people. The export of this article is valued at 50,000*l.* to 60,000*l.* a year. (In 1895 it amounted to 67,561*l.*). The sponge is brought to the surface either by men in small boats with hooked poles, or by diving. When brought up it is covered with a soft, sticky substance, and swarms with organic life. It is washed, dried, packed into bales, and exported. Some beautiful pink pearls are found in the conch shells. Fruits, fibres, and useful woods are in abundance. Both climate and soil are well adapted for the growth of orange and lemon crops, pineapples, grape fruit, tomatoes, potatoes, and other vegetable produce all of which

GOVERNMENT HOUSE, NASSAU.

might be sold at remunerative prices in the United States. During a recent visit of Dr. D. Morris, C.M.G., the Assistant Director of Kew Gardens, to the Bahamas, he placed his large experience of tropical agriculture and his botanical knowledge at the service of the Government, and pointed out the principal cultures for which the islands are suited, as well as the best methods of growing and gathering the crops and preparing for export.

Except in the island of Andros there are no streams of running water, the inhabitants using wells which have some connection with the sea, as the water in them is affected by the tides. Birds are found in numerous varieties, among them being the flamingo and the humming-bird. In the Southern Islands there are some valuable salt ponds. There is plenty of fish to be procured, and the turtle is of the best and finest sort.

The Government of the Bahamas consists of a Governor and an Executive Council. There is also a Legislative Council, presided over by the Governor, of 9 members, and a Representative Assembly of 29 members, who must possess a property qualification, and who are elected on a fairly low suffrage. A system of elementary education is maintained by the Government. In their Report to the legislature of their proceedings in 1895, the Board of Commissioners state that owing to the reduction in the funds at the Board's disposal no new responsibilities were assumed ; the number of Board Schools in operation was 41 ; they were attended during some portion of the year by 6,221 pupils ; there were 5,460 names on the rolls at the end of the year, and the average attendance was 3,418. Besides the Board Schools, there are nine schools which are privately conducted, but receive grants in aid of their local funds. The revenue is partly based upon the usual tariff, there being a long list of import duties. The revenue in 1895 was 63,232*l.* and the expenditure 62,110*l.* The imports from the United Kingdom were 36,128*l.*; from Colonies, 2,745*l.*; from foreign countries (United States chiefly), 133,708*l.*; making a total of 172,581*l.* The exports were —to the United Kingdom, 14,771*l.*; to Colonies, 1,139*l.*; to other countries, 108,101*l.*; total, 124,011*l.* So far as commerce goes the Bahamas is an American possession. The public debt is 124,126*l.*, a large amount of which was incurred in connection with the public bank, the history of which will be fresh in the reader's recollection. The population of the islands is now 51,517.

A local joint stock bank was established in 1889, which paid 10 per cent. in the first year of its working, and is now being worked with so much success and signal advantage to the Colony, that the net profits of the year 1891 were equal to 27 per cent., of which 10 per cent. was divided and 17 per cent. carried to the reserve. The stock is now not purchasable.

A steamer to convey passengers amongst the islands is at work under contract with the Government. There is regular mail communication between the Bahamas and New York, monthly in summer and fortnightly in winter, and there are several trading vessels to and from Key West. One good line of steamers makes the trip from New York to Nassau in three or four days, and from Jacksonville in Florida in less than two days. A contract has also been entered into for a steamer to run between Palm Beach, Florida, and Nassau, capable of carrying sixty first-class passengers. A subsidy of 100*l.* a week was agreed upon, but the vessel continued running, making three trips each

NEGRO HUT, EAST NASSAU.

way nearly every week between January and April, during which it carried 800 passengers. The success of the experiment justified the expectations, the passages each way being made with regularity and within the contract time, fourteen hours, and the number of passengers was even larger than was hoped for. From London the good steamers of Scrutton's line are available. With the addition of the recently opened cable the Colony is well equipped to meet the demands of its advancing trade.

The fibre cultivation is now progressing with great vigour. It reads more like a tale of romance to learn that a Colony which a few years ago was in a state of despairing depression should now be advancing with rapid strides to assured prosperity; nor is this more remarkable than the fact that the agent of this change is a plant that was heretofore regarded as an obnoxious weed which was the despair of the small farmers of the Colony. Soon after his assumption of the Government Sir Ambrose Shea detected the real properties of the 'weed,' and by his great energy and commercial knowledge he brought about a transformation in the fortunes of the place. The price of the land has increased from 5s. to 16s. 4d. an acre, and with good judgment the Governor has limited the Crown allotments to 100,000 acres for ten years, a measure that has given so great an impetus to investments that the whole quantity has been taken up by English capitalists.

The plant is apparently indestructible; it is not affected by drought; it grows in ground that would seem to make vegetation impossible; but the rocks are largely impregnated with lime, so that exhaustion from continued cultivation is impossible, the remaining elements being the same. The plant is at maturity in four years, and thereafter leaves are cut from the same plants for twelve or fifteen years, each acre yielding an annual return of half a ton of fibre. The rows are set twelve feet apart, and the continuous harvest is provided for by setting young plants between the present rows in about eight years from the first planting, so that the crop shall be ready for harvest by the time the other plants have ceased to bear. The plants for this renewal will be the suckers from the growing trees.

The process of decortisation is a very easy one, as there is no gum in the plant, and the fibre may be made ready for baling and shipment in forty-eight hours from the time the leaves are cut. Some small shipments have already been made to London and the United States, where it is pronounced to be the best of its kind yet seen in these markets, and has a value very nearly equal to that of Manilla. The allotments were judiciously distributed so that the labour advantages might be as widely diffused as possible, and cultivators assured of a supply of labourers at fair wage-rates. A great feature in the many attractions of this enterprise is that a reserve fund is unnecessary, as there is nothing in the way of repairs that may not be safely charged to current account.

An arrangement was made which goes far to safeguard the interests of capitalists as well as to conserve the natural claims of the peasantry to an adequate share in the future prosperity of the Colony. They would naturally feel discontented at seeing strangers reaping a rich return from the use of the native soil while their portion was a small daily wage, and the consequent spirit would operate injuriously in the future relations of the cultivators and their labourers. This contingency seems to be well guarded against in the policy adopted, in allotting to every head of a

A SISAL PLANTATION.

family who has not at present any land or means of purchasing, ten acres, to be paid for from their first crop at the rate of five shillings per acre—a provision which will enable all to participate in the future prosperity of the Colony, and which will not be without its effect on the moral character of the population. The work of cultivation is so easy that it can and will be done by the women, leaving the men to follow their present accustomed pursuits.

The shipments of the fibre have as yet been small, as the plantations are only now reaching the productive age, but enough has gone forward to arrest the attention of fibre dealers abroad and to bring the industry prominently before the mind of the commercial world. In future years it will be an increasing export until figures will be reached which at present would seem incredible, when the limit of cultivation now decided on shall have terminated—four years hence. It can then be considered by relation to the question of supply and demand whether the reservation should be modified or removed, and if, as some well-informed people believe, the demand will have grown beyond the production, it is difficult to place a limit on the possibilities of the future of the Bahamas.

The fibre cultivation in all the islands made considerable progress during last year, and the products were increasingly valuable. The fibres are every day increasing in value, the soil and climate being particularly suitable to their cultivation; the rope manufactured from Bahamas hemp has been tested in London with very satisfactory results. The island of Abaco is the chief seat of the industry. Two companies are there at work, each farming about 2,000 acres, in addition to all the work done by local farmers. The industry has also been established in the islands of Inagua, Andros, New Providence, and Cat Island. The number of acres under fibre cultivation is about 20,000. The islands of Abaco, Inagua, Andros, and New Providence are the best adapted for large plantations, for these islands have much level lands capable of being worked by tramways. The narrow islands, like Eleuthera, San Salvador, and Long Island, can be quite as easily worked along the seaboard by water carriage; roads, however, are everywhere needed, for without them much of the lands will be inaccessible.

CHAPTER XXV.

BRITISH HONDURAS.

BRITISH HONDURAS (the name signifying, it is said, the depth of water along the shore), the only dependency of the British Crown in Central America, is on the eastern slopes of the Peninsula, and is situated between 18° 29′ 5″ and 15° 53′ 55″ N. latitude, and 88° 10′ and 89° 9′ 22″ W. long. It is distant from England about 5,700 miles, about 900 miles south of New Orleans, and 600 miles west of Jamaica. It is bounded on the north by the Rio Hondo, the Mexican state of Yucatan being beyond this boundary line. There was a line laid down by the Convention with Guatemala in 1859, extending on the west from the rapids of Gracias á Dios on the river Sarstoon to Garbutt's Falls on the Belize river, and thence due north to the Mexican frontier. It is bounded on the east by the Caribbean Sea. Columbus in 1502, in his search for the strait which he thought would communicate with the Indian Ocean, came upon the coast of Honduras. British Honduras has a seaboard, extending almost due north and south, of about 180 miles. The length of the Colony is 174 miles, and its breadth 68 miles. It contains, with certain adjacent cays, an area of 7,562 square miles. The southern half of the Colony presents a totally different aspect from the northern. The highest peak in the Cockscomb Mountains, now known as the Victoria Peak, is 3,700 feet above the level of the sea. The country to the south of Belize is to a great extent unexplored. In 1879, the late Mr. Fowler, who was Colonial Secretary of the Colony for ten years, traversed a route hitherto practically unknown, and found a succession of valleys and hills, of undulating grassy country and pasture lands, and forests full of valuable timber. Geologically, the prevailing type of formation for the whole Colony is tertiary. The soil is a varying depth of clayey loam, overtopped with rich black mould, and a subsoil of calcareous marl, the pine ridges having a layer of sand. The two chief rivers in the north are the Hondo and the New Rivers. The former is the natural boundary to the north. The richest river valley is that of the Belize river. It rises in the Guatemala Mountains, and its course is estimated at 150 miles. The falls of Roaring Creek are small; but their beautiful surroundings make them very interesting and attractive. The country contains a number of other rivers and lagoons. The Cockscomb Mountains were explored in 1888, and the perpendicular rocks, the sources of many streams, and the picturesque vegetation, were noticed probably for the first time. The main ridge of the mountains runs from east to west, almost at right angles with the coast-line, from which they lie about 23 miles.

The earliest settlement is supposed to be that made by some persons who were wrecked on the coast in 1638. In 1671 Belize was officially reported by the Governor of Jamaica as a profitable settlement, logwood being a very valuable product. In this seventeenth century the country became the subject of negotiation between England and Spain. African slaves were introduced to cut and prepare the logwood and mahogany for export. In 1717 the Board of Trade, in a memorial to King George I., asserted the English right by treaty to cut logwood in Honduras. The wood-cutters, although frequently attacked by Spaniards, managed to hold their own. Up to 1738 the Colony was governed by magistrates elected annually. George II. in 1741 appointed two commissioners, but the system of elected magistrates continued until 1765. In 1754 the Spaniards had collected a force at Peten ; but their effort to drive out the settlers was unsuccessful. The Treaty of Paris, in 1763, between Great Britain and Spain, again recognised the rights of the British logwood cutters; and in the following year a certain amount of protection was extended to them by the Government of Jamaica. Vice-Admiral Sir William Burnaby, in 1765, made an official visit from Jamaica to Honduras. He drew up a code of laws, and endeavoured to consolidate the form of government. During 1779 and the few succeeding years the Spaniards, with considerable cruelty, attacked the settlers, and the British interest became practically extinct. The Versailles Treaty of 1783 once more confirmed the right of logwood-cutting by the British between the Belize and the Hondo, and settlements were again formed. In 1786 the name of the first superintendent, Colonel E. M. Despard, appears in the official list. His principal duty was to settle boundaries. The Spaniards, however, continued troublesome. In 1797 Colonel Thomas Barrow, with a civil and military commission, was in charge, engaged in measures of protection against the Spaniards. It was in 1798, however, that, as the result of fighting at St. George's Cay, the settlement firmly established itself against its enemies ; and from that time forth there can be no doubt of the British possession. During the present century the chief trouble has arisen from the raids of Mexican

Indians, who had overpowered the Spaniards in Yucatan. So recently as 1870 the 1st West India Regiment was engaged in this border warfare ; but since 1872 the Indians have given no trouble. It should be stated that, although nominally under the Jamaica Government, the settlement was not formally constituted a British Colony until 1862, with a lieutenant-governor subordinate to the government of Jamaica. There is a long list of superintendents before this date, but they do not appear to have possessed the full authority of Colonial Governors. In 1884 British Honduras was severed from the government of Jamaica, and created an independent government with a 'Governor and Commander-in-Chief' of its own.

The constitutional or political history of the Colony may be summed up in the remark that, having enjoyed in some form or another a representative system for 200 years, British Honduras was made a Crown colony in 1870. It now remains such, with a Legislative Council consisting of four official and five unofficial (nominated by the Crown) members, with the Governor as President ; the unofficial members thus having a majority of votes. There is an Executive or Privy Council as in other Colonies.

The chief town of British Honduras is Belize. Its appearance is bright and clean. It is built on the banks of the river for about half a mile up, and extends along the shore for over two miles. A wooden bridge, which was opened in 1859, spans the river's mouth. The wooden houses facing the sea, with their cool verandahs, are pleasant to look upon, and the scene is rendered more attractive by the cocoanut trees and cabbage palms. The court-house is in the centre of the town, and the Government house is at the south end, surrounded by gardens. The health of the

WESLEYAN MISSION HOUSE AT STANN CREEK.

town is good, notwithstanding the mangrove swamps in its vicinity (which are, however, affected by the tide), and the somewhat primitive system of drainage. The soil is sandy and loose and soon absorbs the water. The prevailing sea breeze is a great security for the health of the town. St. George's Cay is a small sandy island about eight miles north-east of Belize, and is a favourite health resort. It was formerly of importance as the headquarters of the wood-cutting industry. Corosal is a town in the extreme north of British Honduras, and was originally populated by the refugees driven out of Yucatan by the Indians. The towns of Stann Creek and Punta Gorda may also be mentioned.

The revenue is raised by import duties, liquor licences, and land and property tax, and taxes on horses, dogs, wheels and drays. The narrow belt of land on the sea coast is nearly all cultivated, and the fruit industry is extending. It is estimated that there are 2,000,000 acres of valuable Crown lands lying south of the Belize and Sibun Rivers, waiting for immigrants and settlers. To the north the Belize Estate and Produce Company own 1,000,000 acres. The public revenue of British Honduras in 1895 was 52,389*l*. During the last ten years the customs receipts have steadily increased. The expenditure was 56,535*l*. The public debt of the Colony amounts to 34,735*l*., the whole of which has been raised for improvements in the town and harbour of Belize. The import trade in 1895 amounted to 290,728*l*., the United Kingdom sending 85,560*l*., British Colonies 647*l*., and the United States and other foreign countries 204,520*l*. The export trade in 1895 was—to the United Kingdom, 117,368*l*. ; to the United States and other foreign countries, 139,428*l* ; total export value, 256,799*l.* There is also a considerable trade with Mexico, Guatemala, Honduras, and Nicaragua. Logwood and mahogany have for many years formed two of the principal exports of the Colony, but at the present time, whilst the logwood industry continues to be a remunerative one, the trade in mahogany has to some extent been abandoned, owing to the unremunerative rate at which the timber is now sold in England. A considerable quantity of bananas and plantains are exported, but the existence of this trade is seriously threatened in consequence of the low prices realised in the United States. Sugar has almost ceased to become an article of export owing to want of labour, the quantity exported during 1895 being only a few tons. Tortoise-shell, rubber, and rum also figure in the list of exports. Among the agricultural industries there should also be mentioned the Indian corn or maize, which is the principal food of the Indians and Spanish population; fruits and vegetables of numerous kinds, coffee, cocoa, india-rubber, sarsaparilla, fibre plants, such as the rhea, ramie, or china grass, plantain, banana and pine-apple fibre, and henequen or sisal hemp. Special attention has during the last two or three years been directed to the latter. Tobacco will grow luxuriantly.

The schools and religious organisations—the education system generally—the medical department, hospital accommodation, and care of the poor, all these are as efficient as the most anxious consideration can make them. The population was thus divided in the census of 1891 :— British Honduras, 22,712 ; United Kingdom, 193 ; Africa, 236 ; China, 52 ; East Indies, 291 ; other British possessions, 1,500 ; foreign countries, 6,226 ; other places, 261 ; making a total of 31,471. The 'Official Handbook' says, of the

MAIL STEAMER CALLING FOR FRUIT AT STANN CREEK.

31,000 inhabitants upwards of a third are estimated as Native Indians and the descendants of Indians and the first Spanish conquerors and settlers. Their language is Spanish, the Maya language being confined almost exclusively to the pure Indians, who are to be found principally in the northern and north-western district. The black Caribs of British Honduras are the scattered remnants of the warlike and terrible Caribs originally found on the smaller West Indian Islands. The trouble which this fierce race gave to the early Spaniards and English has already been mentioned in connection with other countries in these seas.

There is a weekly mail service, under contract, entered into during the year 1891, between Belize and New Orleans. The mail steamers await the arrival of the English mails at New Orleans, whence they proceed every Thursday to Belize and the south. The steamers, after their arrival in Belize, proceed with mails, passengers, and cargo to the southern ports of the colony. The departure from Belize for New Orleans takes place once a week. Mr. James Rankine, of New York, manager of the Honduras and Central American Steamship Company, Limited, has two steamers which perform the voyage from New York once every seventeen and eighteen days alternately. The trip from Belize to New York takes $6\frac{1}{2}$ days. The Harrison line leaves Liverpool once a month. There is no direct communication between Jamaica and Belize; but the Honduras and Central American Steamship Company have contracted that their steamers touch at a port in Jamaica on their voyage to Belize from New York. The service from London, Liverpool, and Belize, viâ New York and New Orleans, is described as follows : 'Starting from London, the train must be taken to Liverpool, thence New York is reached by one of the numerous Atlantic lines ; from New York to New Orleans the journey is by train across America, and thence by one of the contract steamers to Belize.

Here is, then, a slice of Central America, with a fine seaboard, fringing a large and wealthy country, unutilised by Great Britain, and deprived of communication with Europe except by means of a foreign country.

GENERAL STATISTICAL VIEW OF THE BRITISH WEST INDIES AND BRITISH GUIANA 1895–96.

	Area	Population (Census 1891; last census)	Imports	Exports	Revenue	Expenditure	Public Debt
	Square miles		£	£	£	£	£
British Guiana	109,000	288,328	1,443,553	1,769,500	567,749	596,493	932,704
British Honduras	7,562	31,471	151,266	244,335	52,389	56,535	34,736
West India Islands:							
Barbados	166	182,322	956,921	587,298	146,315	152,039	405,100
Jamaica	4,193	639,491	2,288,945	1,873,105	814,341	836,513	2,174,029
Turk's Islands	166	4,744	26,735	21,688	7,312	7,547	—
Trinidad	1,754	200,028	2,276,864	2,065,104	552,275	549,771	569,679
Tobago	114	18,387	13,643	10,517	8,591	8,218	5,000
Bahamas	4,466	47,565	172,581	124,011	63,232	62,110	114,126
Windward Islands:							
St. Lucia	233	42,708	154,945	137,869	48,564	57,578	185,380
St. Vincent	133	41,054	64,842	68,690	25,459	28,911	17,170
Grenada	133	54,062	175,712	174,497	58,468	63,675	113,200
Leeward Islands:							
Virgin Islands	57	4,639	4,576	3,818	1,533	1,954	—
St. Christopher	65	30,876	172,281	140,542	43,215	56,017	74,650
Nevis	50	13,087					
Antigua	170	36,119	144,864	87,125	44,348	70,221	138,121
Montserrat	32	11,762	22,728	17,389	7,125	10,702	18,100
Dominica	291	26,841	69,789	39,471	22,859	27,102	70,900

CHAPTER XXVI.

BANKS AND MONEY.

THE Colonial Bank was established in 1836 under a royal charter, which was made applicable in each of the Colonies by special local laws. The Bank has thus passed its jubilee year, and has continued sound and successful through all the good and evil times which the Colonies have seen, although in times of great depression its profits have suffered and its operations been curtailed. Its present chairman is Mr. Harry Hankey Dobree, and its headquarters are at No. 13 Bishopsgate Street Within, London, where letters of credit are granted and other financial business transacted. It has a subscribed capital of 2,000,000*l.* sterling, with a paid-up capital of 600,000*l.* Its notes are in circulation through all the Colonies, amounting in the aggregate to an issue of 433,309*l.* There are 13 branches, receiving deposits amounting to a total of 1,842,000*l.* Its reserve fund is 150,000*l.*; its dividends have been good, averaging 10 per cent. per annum, and its shares always command a premium in the market. It has also a branch in New York, the larger proportion of the produce of the West Indies now going to the United States. An institution like this plays an essential part in the Colonies. It is a truism to say that wherever produce is grown and business transacted there must be a bank with all its varied functions, and the Colonies have been very fortunate in the sound position and careful management of this indispensable organisation. It has an establishment in each of the British West India Islands and one in British Guiana. It is the only bank in the West Indies except in the latter Colony and the Bahamas, where it has competitors in the British Guiana Bank and the Bank of Nassau, which are managed locally. Many proposals have been from time to time put forward for the creation of other banks and mortgage companies (the latter on the same principle as the Crédit Foncier of Mauritius), but these schemes have come to nothing.

The British Guiana Bank was established in 1837, under a charter, with a capital of 1,400,000 dollars, 926,520 dollars paid up. It has a note circulation of 78,000*l.* The head office is in Georgetown, with a branch at New Amsterdam.

A long chapter might be written on West Indian currency, but a few words only must suffice. It is probably correct to say that the old system of keeping the public accounts in dollars and cents has been very nearly if not quite abolished, although the large trade carried on with the United States keeps this denomination of value in constant use in all mercantile transactions. For instance, the price of sugar per pound sold to America is always quoted in cents, and account sales are naturally made up according to the currency of that country, the totals for transmission to England by draft being calculated into sterling.

As above stated, all business accounts of British Guiana are kept in dollars and cents, a dollar being equal to 4*s.* 2*d.*, or at the rate of 480 dollars to the 100*l.* British sterling and American gold coin are legal tender, also Spanish and Mexican gold. Spanish, Mexican, and Columbian dollars were formerly current, but they were demonetised by a Colonial ordinance some twelve years ago, and no longer are legal tender. Some relics of the old Dutch guilders are to be met with, varying from an eighth to three guilders—a guilder being a silver token worth 1s. 4d. locally.

In Trinidad British silver and bronze are in general use. There is no limit to the tender of silver in this and other colonies. United States gold currency, gold doubloons, and British gold are all legal tender. Barbados uses British coin.

In Jamaica, British currency, United States gold, and gold doubloons are legal tender. The principal coins in use are British silver and Jamaica nickel pence. The same description may be given of the currency in the Windward and Leeward Islands.

The following extract from Mr. Goschen's report of 1878 to the Monetary Conference at Paris explains the system in force in the West Indies :—

'The coins in circulation in the West Indies (excepting in British Honduras and the Bahamas) consist chiefly of British token silver, which may be tendered to an unlimited amount. The history which has brought about this result is somewhat complicated ; but, briefly, it may be stated that in these Colonies, up to a recent date, a double standard existed—the golden doubloon, at 64s., the silver dollar, at 4s. 2d., as well as the United States gold (the eagle, at 41s.) being legal tender, concurrently with sterling coin. Gold becoming over-valued under this system, dollars entirely disappeared, and no limitation having been placed on the tender of British silver coin, it gradually became the only currency of the Colonies.'

Mr. Lesley C. Probyn, in his paper read before the Royal Colonial Institute, on February 11th, 1890, says: 'Much of the business in the West India Colonies is done by means of notes of the Colonial Bank. This bank was established by Royal Charter in 1836, which was extended by Act 19 Vic. cap. 3, under which powers were granted to issue notes of not less than 1*l.* in value; it being provided by sec. 9 that the bank should "keep in reserve at their establishments in the said Colonies, specie, or gold and silver bullion," amounting in the aggregate to one-third in value at least of the total amount of the promissory notes of the said bank for the time being in circulation in the said Colonies.'

There are four districts from which notes are issued, viz. :—

(1) Barbados, including Trinidad and all the Windward and Leeward Islands.

(2) Demerara (in British Guiana), including Berbice.

(3) Jamaica.

(4) St Thomas, including St. Croix.

The notes are redeemable at the offices of issue, and, in addition, the notes of Barbados district, issued at Trinidad, are redeemable at either place without deduction, but not necessarily so if presented at St. Vincent, or Antigua, &c.

It is not possible to give an exact account of the amount of notes outstanding in each; but the following may be taken as a tolerably good estimate of the value in sterling of the 400,000*l.* Colonial Bank notes in circulation in our West India Colonies :—

Jamaica	£150,000
British Guiana	55,000
Barbados	45,000
St. Vincent	5,700
Tobago	300
St. Lucia	8,700
Trinidad	75,300
Grenada	20,000
Leeward Islands	40,000
	£400,000

On the 1st of January 1897 the specie assets of the Bank amounted to 395,586*l*. 11*s*. 11*d*., against notes in circulation amounting to 433,309*l*. 15*s*. The Bank of British Guiana in that Colony also issues notes. An interesting feature is that while the notes of Jamaica are 1*l*. each in British money, the notes in the other Colonies are for five dollars each, which, at the rate of 4*s*. 2*d*., is equivalent to 1*l*. 0*s*. 10*d*.

In Jamaica all Government, as well as commercial, accounts are kept in sterling. In British Guiana all accounts are kept in dollars. In the other West India possessions, though the Government accounts are kept in sterling, commercial accounts are for the most part kept in dollars. It may seem questionable whether, in these circumstances, I have been right in classifying all the West India Islands as using *l. s. d.* ; but, except for some old coins still remaining in British Guiana, there are not, I believe, any coins representing fractions of a dollar in circulation. I believe I am right in saying, however, that the halfpenny and penny are generally called cents and two cents, and other coins in the same way. The fact is, except in the case of Newfoundland, there is no gold dollar in the world at 4*s*. 2*d*. It probably was adopted at that rate as an approximate to the United States gold dollar at 4*s*. 1·31*d*., and as affording with its subdivision into 50 pence and 100 half-pence a convenient decimal system. In the West Indian possessions generally the United States gold coin is either full legal tender or passes current at 4*s.* 2*d.* per dollar for the quarter-eagle and larger gold coins, and 4*s.* 1*d.* for the single dollar; and rates are still fixed for the golden doubloon, or 16-dollar piece, at 3*l.* 4*s.*, and also, though not uniformly, for gold French coins. But practically there is very little gold in circulation. In the Bahamas it is said that not only British silver, but British copper coins are unlimited legal tender; half and quarter-dollar United States silver coins, at 2*s.* and 1*s.* respectively, and French silver at the rate of five francs for 3*s.* 10½*d.* passing current. In Bermuda bronze is only legal tender up to 11*d.*, instead of 1*s.* as in England. In Jamaica and Turks Island alone, of all the British possessions, nickel pence, halfpence, and farthings are in use. The natives, it is said, object to bronze. The nickel coins are manufactured at the London Mint, and sent out at the cost of the Colony. They are legal tender to 1*s.*, 6*d.*, and 3*d.* respectively, thus disregarding the English law of all coins below the penny possessing the same legal tender property as the penny itself. British silver is unlimited legal tender.

A A

CHAPTER XXVII.

THE ROYAL COLONIAL INSTITUTE.

THIS Institute, which has, through its Council, done me the honour of allowing this book to appear under its auspices, has developed, during the twenty-nine years of its existence, into the most important and influential association connected with the Colonies. It has its thousands of members in the United Kingdom and in all parts of the British Empire. It has a handsome and convenient house and an increasingly valuable Colonial library in Northumberland Avenue. Its monthly papers and discussions are listened to by appreciative audiences, and are read in all parts of the world. It has well acted up to its motto, 'United Empire,' for the interchange of information and the cultivation of goodwill among Colonists and their brethren at home have certainly added to the ties which connect the Mother Country and her Colonies. It is incorporated by royal charter, and has for its President the Prince of Wales, who often shows his interest in the work which it is doing. In March 1889 a banquet was held to celebrate the coming of age of the Institute. An opportunity was thus given of looking back upon its history of continued progress, and of looking forward with reasonable confidence to a career of greater usefulness and prosperity. At the banquet above mentioned his Royal Highness the President delivered from the chair a lengthy address, dealing with many important points relating to the connection between England and the Colonies.

THE ROYAL COLONIAL INSTITUTE,
NORTHUMBERLAND AVENUE, LONDON, W.C

COUNCIL OF 1897-98.

President.
HIS ROYAL HIGHNESS THE PRINCE OF WALES, K.G., K.T., K.P., G.C.B., G.C.S.I., G.C.M.G., G.C.I.E.

Vice=Presidents.
HIS ROYAL HIGHNESS THE DUKE OF YORK, K.G.
HIS ROYAL HIGHNESS PRINCE CHRISTIAN, K.G.
HIS GRACE THE DUKE OF ARGYLL, K.G., K.T.
HIS GRACE THE DUKE OF DEVONSHIRE, K.G.
THE RIGHT HON. THE MARQUIS OF DUFFERIN AND AVA, K.P., G.C.B., G.C.M.G.
THE RIGHT HON. THE MARQUIS OF LORNE, K.T., G.C.M.G., M.P.
THE RIGHT HON. THE EARL OF ABERDEEN, G.C.M.G.
THE RIGHT HON. THE EARL OF CRANBROOK, G.C.S.I.
THE RIGHT HON. THE EARL OF DUNRAVEN, K.P.
THE RIGHT HON. THE EARL OF JERSEY, G.C.M.G.
THE RIGHT HON. THE EARL OF ROSEBERY, K.G., K.T.
THE RIGHT HON. LORD BRASSEY, K.C.B.
THE RIGHT HON. LORD CARLINGFORD, K.P.
SIR CHARLES NICHOLSON, BART.
SIR HENRY BARKLY, G.C.M.G., K.C.B.
SIR HENRY E. G. BULWER, G.C.M.G.
GENERAL SIR H. C. B. DAUBENEY, G.C.B.
SIR ROBERT G. W. HERBERT, G.C.B.
SIR JAMES A. YOUL, K.C.M.G.
SIR FREDERICK YOUNG, K.C.M.G.

Councillors.

W. J. ANDERSON, ESQ.
ALLAN CAMPBELL, ESQ.
F. H. DANGAR, ESQ.
FREDERICK DUTTON, ESQ.
LIEUT.-GEN. SIR J. BEVAN EDWARDS, K.C.M.G., C.B., M.P.
C. WASHINGTON EVES, ESQ., C.M.G.
W. MAYNARD FARMER, ESQ.
SIR JAMES GARRICK, K.C.M.G.
MAJOR-GENERAL SIR HENRY GREEN, K.C.S.I., C.B.
SIR ARTHUR HODGSON, K.C.M.G.
ADMIRAL SIR ANTHONY H. HOSKINS, G.C.B.

HENRY J. JOURDAIN, ESQ., C.M.G.
WILLIAM KESWICK, ESQ.
LORD LOCH, G.C.B., G.C.M.G.
LIEUT.-GENERAL R. W. LOWRY, C.B.
NEVILE LUBBOCK, ESQ.
GEORGE S. MACKENZIE, ESQ., C.B.
S. VAUGHAN MORGAN, ESQ.
SIR E. MONTAGUE NELSON, K.C.M.G.
SIR WESTBY B. PERCEVAL, K.C.M.G.
SIR SAUL SAMUEL, K.C.M.G., C.B.
SIR CECIL CLEMENTI SMITH, G.C.M.G.
SIR DONALD A. SMITH, G.C.M.G.
SIR CHARLES E. F. STIRLING, BART.

Honorary Treasurer.—SIR MONTAGU F. OMMANNEY, K.C.M.G.

Secretary.—J. S. O'HALLORAN, C.M.G.

Librarian.—JAMES R. BOOSÉ, ESQ.

Chief Clerk.—W. CHAMBERLAIN, ESQ.

There are influential Honorary Corresponding Secretaries in all the principal Colonies.

CHAPTER XXVIII.

STEAM COMMUNICATION.

THE offices of the Royal Mail Steam Packet Company are at 18 Moorgate Street, London; Secretary, J. M. Lloyd, Esq.

The Company's Transatlantic Mail Steamers are despatched from Southampton for the West Indies every alternate Wednesday. Those steamers all go direct to Barbados, whence branch steamers proceed as under :

One every two weeks from Barbados to Demerara direct.

One every two weeks from Barbados to St. Vincent, Grenada, and Trinidad, on one occasion going on from Trinidad to Tobago, and on the other occasion going on from Trinidad to La Guayra.

One every two weeks from Barbados to St. Lucia, Martinique, Dominica, Guadeloupe, Montserrat, Antigua, St. Kitts, and St. Thomas.

The Transatlantic Mail Steamers proceed from Barbados to Jacmel, Jamaica, and Colon; going on thence, once in four weeks to Savanilla, and once in four weeks to Limon.

The homeward routes are the same as outward, except that the Transatlantic Mail Steamers will return to Plymouth, thence proceeding to Cherbourg and Southampton.

As the Homeward West India packets call at Plymouth to land the mails, and then proceed to Cherbourg, passengers can be landed at those ports.

For detailed fares see the tables published by the Company. A single ticket, out or home, first class, Barbados and West Indies generally is 25*l.* on the lower deck, 35*l.* on the main deck amidships, and 43*l.* 10*s.* main deck saloon and forward. This distinction refers to the sleeping cabins—in all other respects the passengers are on an equal footing. Return first-class tickets, out and home or *vice versâ*, are 40*l.*, 52*l.* 10*s.*, and 65*l.* 5*s.* respectively. Special privileges are given to tourists. There is an abatement in the case of families, and special rates for servants. Second-class passengers are conveyed for 20*l.* between Southampton and all ports. Return tickets 30*l.*

There is a direct line of Steam Packets between London and Demerara, and Glasgow, Trinidad, and Demerara. The agents are Messrs. Scrutton, Sons, & Co., 9 Gracechurch Street, London, and Messrs. Caw, Prentice, Clapperton & Co., 173 West George Street, Glasgow. The London steamers are despatched every three weeks, and the Glasgow every month. The names of the London steamers are the Nonpareil, McGarel, and El Dorado, and of the Glasgow steamers, Burnley, Mornea, Belair, Cipero, Arecuna.

There is a line called the Demerara and Berbice Steamship Line, the London agents being Messrs. William Smith & Co., 86 Leadenhall Street. The steamers are despatched every three weeks; their names are Eeta, Ituni, Godiva.

Under the name of the Clyde Line of steamers, four steamers are despatched at stated intervals to Trinidad and Demerara.

There is also a steamer, the Barracouta, which makes a trip between New York and Demerara every six weeks, calling at St. Croix, St. Kitts, Montserrat, Antigua, Martinique, St. Lucia, Barbados, and Trinidad.

For Trinidad there is the Royal Mail Service, the Compagnie Générale Transatlantique, Scrutton's direct line, and the West India and Pacific Steamship Company (offices, The Temple, Dale Street, Liverpool). This Company, in conjunction with Harrison's Line (Chapel Street, Liverpool), provide a weekly service from Liverpool every Saturday. The Atlantic and West India Line (Messrs. Leaycroft & Co., Pearl Street, New York) provides one steamer monthly between New York and Trinidad. A new line is being established by Messrs. Gregor Turnbull & Co., of Glasgow, to run at stated intervals between Trinidad and New York. The Orinoco Line provides a steamer, the Bolivar, twice a month from Trinidad up the Orinoco to Ciudad Bolivar, the dates being arranged so as to be convenient to the Royal Mail passengers to make this trip. The Quebec Steamship Company issues through tickets between London, Liverpool, New York, and Trinidad, or between Bremen or Havre and Trinidad, viâ New York. Trinidad has also the Dutch Royal Mail Service and a Ciudad Bolivar Line, a monthly steamer from Trinidad to Carúpano, Ciudad Bolivar, Cumaná, La Guayra, and other places.

Barbados has the fortnightly Royal Mail Service, the weekly West India and Pacific or Harrison Line from Liverpool, a direct steamer from London, the Quebec Line, and the fortnightly arrival of a steamer from New York to Brazil, going and returning.

Jamaica is well favoured with steam communication. Since April 1842, when the Royal Mail Company began their contract with the Government, which contract has been regularly renewed, at stated intervals, ever since—the principal alterations being the increase of speed and the reduction of subsidy—the island has had the benefit of the Royal Mail Service. The voyage from Southampton, after calling at Barbados and Haïti, takes sixteen days; for instance, the steamer starts on every alternate Wednesday at 5 o'clock in the afternoon from Southampton, and arrives at Jamaica on the following Friday fortnight at 7 a.m. (local time). Jamaica has had an opportunity of witnessing the improvement in the boats of this service for nearly fifty years. The old Atrato and the new Atrato are in evidence, and the progress of steam navigation is very striking. In 1860 Holt's Line connected Jamaica with Liverpool. This is now the West India and Pacific Steamship Company. In 1872 the Atlas Company, owned by Messrs. Forwood, a well-known firm in Liverpool, started running steamers between Jamaica and New York. In 1880 the White Line and the London Line opened communication with Jamaica, and these were followed by the Anderson Line in 1881. They have been amalgamated into the Caribbean Line, now running frequently, but at irregular dates, between London and Jamaica. These steamers of the Caribbean Line not only go to Kingston, but call for produce at other ports of the island. The Clyde Line despatches a steamer monthly from Glasgow, bringing back produce to Glasgow or London as desired. The above are irrespective of the coasting service, which is frequent and efficient. A large number of vessels, in addition to the regular lines, are engaged in carrying large quantities of fruit to the United States from Jamaica.

The other colonies partake more or less in the advantages of the varied steam communication detailed above. They are all, except British Honduras, connected with Great Britain by the Royal Mail Steamers.

With regard to the Atlas steamers mentioned above the Company furnish the following summary of their service:—'We despatch steamers each alternate Saturday from New York to Jamaica, and further, that once a month we despatch a boat (sailing on a Friday intermediate with the regular Jamaica sailings) calling at Jeremie (Hayti), and thence proceeding to Kingston. We thus provide Jamaica with three calls, at even intervals, per month.'

To illustrate the above, an Atlas steamer leaves New York on January 23rd, and arrives at Jeremie (Hayti) on Thursday, 29th. It leaves

Jeremie on Friday, 30th, and arrives at Kingston at Saturday, 31st. It leaves Kingston on Monday, February 2nd, and arrives at Port Limon on Thursday, February 5th; leaves Port Limon on Saturday, February 7th, and arrives at New York on Monday, February 16th. The above is the monthly route. The fortnightly steamer leaves New York, say on Saturday, January 17th, and arrives at Kingston, Jamaica, on Friday, January 23rd.

Among the foreign lines trading between Europe and the West Indies, the following are the most important.

The vessels of the Compagnie Générale Transatlantique leave St. Nazaire on the 10th of each month, serving the French and several of the English Colonies, notably Trinidad and Demerara, and the Dutch colony of Surinam.

The Koninklijke West-Indische Mail Dienst, or Royal Dutch West India Mail Service, under contract with the Netherlands Government for the conveyance of mails, has its offices at 22 Gelderschekade, Amsterdam.

The steamers of this Line—Orange Nassau, Prins Willem I., Prins Maurits, and Prins Frederick Hendrik—sail on the 12th of each month from Amsterdam.

NOTE.—The above may not be a complete account of the steam communication, and any incompleteness will be remedied on receipt of further information.

PRINTED BY
SPOTTISWOODE AND CO., NEW-STREET SQUARE
LONDON

www.ingramcontent.com/pod-product-compliance
Lightning Source LLC
Chambersburg PA
CBHW051851300426
44117CB00006B/346